Science and the Sp

EDITED BY JAMES K. A. SMITH
AND AMOS YONG

# Science and the Spirit

## *A Pentecostal Engagement with the Sciences*

INDIANA UNIVERSITY PRESS
*Bloomington and Indianapolis*

This book is a publication of

Indiana University Press
601 North Morton Street
Bloomington, Indiana 47404-3797 USA

www.iupress.indiana.edu

*Telephone orders*   800-842-6796
*Fax orders*   812-855-7931
*Orders by e-mail*   iuporder@indiana.edu

∞ The paper used in this publication meets the minimum requirements of the American National Standard for Information Sciences—Permanence of Paper for Printed Library Materials, ANSI Z39.48-1992.

Manufactured in the United States of America

**Library of Congress Cataloging-in-Publication Data**

Science and the spirit : a Pentecostal engagement with the sciences / edited by James K.A. Smith and Amos Yong.
   p. cm.
   Includes bibliographical references and index.
   ISBN 978-0-253-35516-4 (cloth : alk. paper) — ISBN 978-0-253-22227-5 (pbk. : alk. paper) 1. Religion and science. 2. Pentecostalism. I. Smith, James K. A., [date]– II. Yong, Amos.
   BL240.3.S3495 2010
   261.5′5—dc22

                                                                            2010001685

1  2  3  4  5  15  14  13  12  11  10

# Contents

Preface    vii

Introduction: Science and the Spirit—Questions and Possibilities in the Pentecostal Engagement with Science    1
*James K. A. Smith and Amos Yong*

PART ONE · WHAT HATH AZUSA STREET TO DO WITH MIT?
THE BIG QUESTIONS

1. What Have the Galapagos to Do with Jerusalem? Scientific Knowledge in Theological Context    15
*Telford Work*

2. Is There Room for Surprise in the Natural World? Naturalism, the Supernatural, and Pentecostal Spirituality    34
*James K. A. Smith*

3. How Does God Do What God Does? Pentecostal-Charismatic Perspectives on Divine Action in Dialogue with Modern Science    50
*Amos Yong*

PART TWO · THE SPIRIT OF MATTER: QUESTIONS AND
POSSIBILITIES IN THE NATURAL SCIENCES

4. Does God Have a Place in the Physical Universe? Physics and the Quest for the Holy Spirit    75
*Wolfgang Vondey*

5. Does the Spirit Create through Evolutionary Processes? Pentecostals and Biological Evolution    92
*Steve Badger and Mike Tenneson*

6. Can Religious Experience Be Reduced to Brain Activity? The Place and Significance of Pentecostal Narrative    117
*Frederick L. Ware*

7. Serotonin and Spirit: Can There Be a Holistic Pentecostal Approach to Mental Illness?    133
*Donald F. Calbreath*

PART THREE · THE HUMAN SPIRIT: QUESTIONS AND
POSSIBILITIES IN THE SOCIAL AND TECHNOLOGICAL
SCIENCES

8. Can Social Scientists Dance? Participating in Science,
   Spirit, and Social Reconstruction as an Anthropologist and
   Afropentecostal   155
   *Craig Scandrett-Leatherman*

9. Is Integrating Spirit and Sociology Possible? A Postmodern
   Research Odyssey   174
   *Margaret M. Poloma*

10. Is There Room for the Spirit in a World Dominated by
    Technology? Pentecostals and the Technological World   192
    *Dennis W. Cheek*

List of Contributors   209

Index   213

# Preface

This book grows out of a multiyear, multifaceted research initiative, "Science and the Spirit: Pentecostal Perspectives on the Science/Religion Dialogue," funded by the John Templeton Foundation from 2005 to 2009. Given that Pentecostal engagements with science, and even the science/religion dialogue, were nascent at best, the first task of the initiative was to find and assemble a team of scholars from across the disciplines who were also familiar with and/or working from within the Pentecostal and charismatic streams of Christianity. We thus launched our project by announcing a competitive request for proposals in the fall of 2005 and gathered a team of experts to help us vet the proposals.

In the spring of 2006, we selected a team of ten scholars who represented a range of sciences and disciplines: Donald Calbreath (chemistry), Heather Curtis (history of religion), Paul Elbert (physics and biblical studies), Robert Moore (psychology), Margaret Poloma (sociology), Craig Scandrett-Leatherman (anthropology), Jeffrey Schloss (biology), Wolfgang Vondey (theology), Frederick Ware (theology), and Telford Work (biblical theology). While not all of their work appears in this volume—due to the vagaries of theoretical surprises and other obstacles—we are grateful for the contributions all of them have made to this research initiative, launching a conversation that we hope will mature and develop over the coming decade. Their contributions constitute the vanguard of this emerging dialogue between Pentecostalism and science.

Each of these scholars engaged in independent research on a project at the intersection of pentecostalism and science (broadly construed) during the 2006–2007 academic year. We then gathered together for a two-week, closed-door colloquium at Regent University School of Divinity in the June 2007, enjoying a period of intentional community as we lived, ate, worked, and played together on the shores of the Chesapeake Bay. Our colloquium was devoted to discussion of a common set of readings on science and the Spirit, including new work on emergence as well as other tradition-specific models of theological dialogue with the sciences. During this time we also enjoyed conversations with two guest lecturers who spent the day with us in conversation: Philip Clayton, a philosopher of religion at Claremont Graduate University (then Visiting Professor at Harvard Divinity School), and Darrell Falk, a biologist from Point Loma Nazarene University. Both engaged us at length and were willing to help us grapple with some of the specifics of a distinctly Pentecostal encounter with the sciences. The bulk of our efforts over the course of the two weeks were spent reading and discussing drafts of our individual research projects with a view to further developing and refining them for submission to peer-reviewed journals (see the introduction for further discussion). This give-and-take of mutual critique and encouragement was an important incubator for the work that has emerged from this research team. An important element of this discussion included the contributions from several graduate students who enrolled in Amos Yong's Ph.D. seminar on Renewal and Science: David Bradnick (who served as our note-taker for the colloquium), Malcolm Brubaker, Bradford McCall, and Stephen Mills.

In the fall of 2007, as we were further honing our research articles, we set to work on a second aspect of the project: the creation of a book that would address issues, tensions, and opportunities at the intersection of Pentecostalism and science in a way that would be accessible to undergraduate students in the sciences. Each of the scholars was commissioned to write a chapter that would address a "big question" in their field. While there was inevitable overlap between our advanced research and this task of writing for students, the ideal of accessibility meant that many of the chapters here look quite different from related research published in professional journals. Once again, collaboration and mutual feedback, including a one-day discussion after the annual meeting of the Society for Pentecostal Studies in March 2008, was an important element of this aspect of the overall project. In addition to detailed feedback from the editors, authors received feedback from colleagues which helped to hone and refine the chapters that follow.

\* \* \*

A project of this scope incurs many of the sorts of debts that we happily acknowledge. We are first and foremost grateful to the John Templeton Foundation for their tangible support of the "Science and the Spirit" research initiative (Grant #11876). We appreciate their willingness to take a risk on an emerging conversation because of their foresight regarding its global importance. We are also especially grateful to Paul Wason at the Foundation for his help with our initial proposal for funding. Alan Padgett (Luther Seminary), Donald G. York (University of Chicago), and Ralph W. Hood, Jr. (University of Tennessee at Chattanooga), made recommendations regarding the responses to the Request for Proposals we received and have served as consultants at various stages of the project.

The administration of the grant and its early logistics were capably and cheerfully managed by the staff of the Seminars in Christian Scholarship office at Calvin College. We are grateful to Joel Carpenter, current director of the Seminars program, as well as to Alysha Chadderdon (former office coordinator), Marilyn Rottman (former office assistant), and Mary Bennett (current office coordinator) for their cordial assistance with logistics and reporting. Steve Barkema and other staff members in the Communications and Marketing department helped us with the website, and a team from Westmont College, volunteered by Telford Work, provided and maintained the project listserv.

We are also grateful to the administration and staff at Regent University School of Divinity for their assistance. Dean Michael Palmer and administrative dean Joy Brathwaite have been supportive in various ways. Pidge Bannin and Lelia Fry (administrative assistants); Eric Newberg, Chris Emerick, Doc Hughes, and Renea Brathwaite (doctoral students); Elizabeth Keen (Regent University Library circulation supervisor); and Mark Stevenson (media services coordinator) were all helpful, especially in ensuring that our two-week colloquium went smoothly. Finally, thanks to Timothy Lim Teck Ngern, Amos Yong's graduate assistant, who helped to finalize the manuscript and to prepare the subject index.

Science and the Spirit

# Introduction: Science and the Spirit—Questions and Possibilities in the Pentecostal Engagement with Science

*James K. A. Smith and Amos Yong*

## Two Globalizations: Pentecostalism and Science

Pentecostal and charismatic Christianity has become one of the most significant religious movements in the twenty-first century, with a distinct emphasis on the role of the Holy Spirit.[1] The "outpouring" of the Spirit in the United States (at Azusa Street, Los Angeles, in 1906), anticipated and accompanied by similar revivals around the world, quickly spread around the globe such that today some of the most important movements in what Philip Jenkins (2002) describes as "the next Christianity" are pentecostal movements in Latin America, Africa, and Asia (Anderson 2007). As the heart of Christianity moves to the global south, we are finding that pneumatology is more important than the Western theological tradition might have led us to believe. And increasingly, pentecostal movements are focusing religious thought and practice on the role of the Spirit. In short, world Christianity *is* pentecostal and even pneumatic Christianity.

But when scholars or journalists think of pentecostals, visions of laboratories or particle accelerators don't usually come to mind. Pentecostalism is more likely to evoke images of Appalachian "pew jumping" or chaotic religious services that border on shamanism. This would seem to be the very antithesis of the world constructed by cool scientific rationality—prodded by innumerable instruments, explained by appeals to empirical data, and harnessed for progress. One of the signs of science's alleged triumph has been its claim to eliminate the ghost in the machine, not least the Holy Ghost. If science and technology is marching boldly into the future, pentecostal Christianity seems to be clinging to an outmoded premodern worldview.

And yet there are curious instances that suggest strange and unexpected concatenations of the two. Driving by a pentecostal megachurch, whether in suburban Dallas or sprawling Lagos, one will notice a tangled multitude of satellite dishes that harness microwaves and utilize the latest communicative technologies in order to broadcast and receive television programs devoted to divine healing (Hackett 1998). Or consider that in 1981 healing evangelist Oral Roberts founded the (rather short-lived) City of Faith Medical and Research Center at Oral Roberts University. Or we might simply note that an increasing number of pentecostal colleges and universities offer majors in premed biology. These sorts of developments suggest that the commonly accepted picture of pentecostal backwardness in the face of scientific progress is not true to the facts on the ground.

Pentecostal spirituality, and what might be described as a "pentecostal worldview" (Smith 2003a, 2003b), is a powerful cultural phenomenon, a unique form of "globalization" (Poewe 1994; Dempster, Klaus, and Petersen 1999). But given that it is such a "fantastic" form of Christianity—a kind of spirituality that harks back to what will seem a premodern view of the world as "enchanted"—globalized pentecostalism runs up against another powerful cultural force: the growth and expansion of modern science and technology, even a creeping "scientism" (à la Richard Dawkins [2006] and Sam Harris [2005]) that is experiencing its own globalization. Given that pentecostalism is distinctly modern in some respects and yet also pre- or even postmodern in other respects, this raises questions regarding how pentecostals will negotiate life in a late modern world, particularly as regions such as Africa and Asia emerge into modernity with the advent of globalization:

- Can a pentecostal worldview—which is focused on the miraculous and fantastic— inhabit the same world and the same cultural space as naturalistic science? Or are the two doomed to remain sequestered in parallel universes? Should we expect yet another "clash of civilizations" on this score?
- Must pentecostalism entail what most would expect—a head-in-the-sand ignoring of science, or worse, an anti-intellectual rejection of science? Doesn't the pentecostal appropriation of communications and media technology indicate otherwise? Or does this signal an internal contradiction between belief and practice?
- Does the utilization of modern medicine by pentecostals represent a kind of "backsliding" and the waning of a commitment to a distinctly pentecostal worldview? Or does this signal a more holistic pentecostal understanding of health and healing that is able to appreciate and absorb medical science?
- How can pentecostals so aggressively adopt the fruits of science in modern technology (e.g., media technology) without taking seriously the science that informs such technology?
- Does science necessarily entail the disenchantment of the world? In other words, does a serious involvement with science demand an aggressive naturalism that would rule pentecostal phenomena benighted and impossible?
- Can or should science ignore pentecostalism, or is science committed only to

providing a reductionistic assessment of pentecostal phenomena? Can science enjoy and gain from a mutual dialogue with pentecostalism?

- What would be unique about a distinctively pentecostal foray into the science/theology dialogue? Do pentecostals have something unique to contribute to existing conversations, drawing on the resources of pentecostal spirituality and practice?

## Pentecostalism and Science: An Emerging Conversation

The goal of this book is to address just these sorts of pressing questions. It represents one of the first projects, and certainly the most sustained initiative to date, that considers issues at the intersection of a pentecostal worldview and contemporary science.[2] In this respect, we hope it makes a timely contribution to current discussions as these two globalizing forces—pentecostal Christianity and modern science—continue to bump into one another around the globe. But we also hope it provides a glimpse into an emerging conversation. As such, the book is one of the initial reports from the front, so to speak.

We also believe the book is timely, not only because of the very visible nature of both pentecostalism and science, but also because of the shape of pentecostal theology and scholarship as pentecostalism enters its second century. Over the past century, pentecostals both in North America and beyond have retained a vital Spirit-centered spirituality but have also matured in their relation to culture. This is perhaps best seen in the emergence of pentecostal scholarship across the disciplines. One can see this illustrated in several related phenomena. For instance, the founding and growth of the Society for Pentecostal Studies (SPS), launched in 1970, has been a catalyst for pentecostal scholarship across the disciplines. Gathering together an ecumenical group of pentecostal and charismatic scholars from traditions ranging from the Assemblies of God to the Roman Catholic Church, the SPS provides a forum for the advancement of pentecostal scholarship. Though its initial focus was on history, biblical studies, and theology, the SPS now includes tracks in philosophy, ethics, and the social sciences. The society's journal, *Pneuma* (first launched in 1979 and now published by E. J. Brill), is widely respected (included in the ATLA's database) and is complimented by another journal, the *Journal of Pentecostal Theology*. There are also several book series devoted to pentecostal studies, including *Studies in Pentecostal and Charismatic Issues*, edited by Mark Cartledge, Neil Hudson, Keith Warrington, Max Turner, and Andrew Walker (Paternoster); *Global Pentecostal and Charismatic Studies*, edited by Andrew Davies and William Kay (E. J. Brill); and *Pentecostal Manifestos*, edited by James K. A. Smith and Amos Yong (Eerdmans), which seeks to provide a platform for pentecostal scholars to speak beyond "internal" conversations in a pentecostal ghetto and join more mainstream conversations.

One can note parallel developments in pentecostal higher education. The early pentecostal movement spawned a number of Bible schools, mission institutes, and other training centers focused on ministry and mission. Over the course of the twentieth century, some of these institutions were transformed into Bible colleges and then liberal arts colleges and universities; in addition, new colleges and seminaries were founded (Hittenberger 2007). By the end of the twentieth century, the United States boasted a wide network of accredited pentecostal and charismatic universities (including graduate and professional programs), and globally we have seen the emergence of pentecostal centers of higher education in Africa, South America, and the Pacific Islands (Wilson 2002). With this shift to liberal arts education and professional programs, pentecostals have had to move beyond a narrow concern with Bible, theology, and missions in order to engage the panoply of academic disciplines, including the social and natural sciences, with core curricula at colleges and universities including requirements in the sciences. However, there has been little reflection on what this engagement with science means for pentecostal spirituality, and even less reflection on what might be a uniquely pentecostal perspective on science.

We see this unique juncture as an instance of both challenge and opportunity. On the one hand, there is a clearly a need for pentecostal and charismatic traditions to take science seriously (see Yong 2005a). We live in a modern (or postmodern) world that reaps incredible benefits from science, and pentecostal communities have been quick to avail themselves of electronic and technological sciences. On the other hand, a naturalistic worldview—which tends to dominate science, or at least cultural perceptions of science—poses a serious challenge to the distinct sense of transcendence in charismatic spirituality. But naturalism in science is not the end of the story. Indeed, some of the most important discussions in science—particularly in dialogue with theology— have emphasized a new role for "spirit" as a *scientific* category (Clayton 2004; Clayton and Peacocke 2004; Welker 2006). It is increasingly being realized that "spirit" is a sufficiently fluid notion that not only raises challenges for but also potentially holds forth promise to advance research across the spectrum of both the human and the natural sciences (Yong 2005b). These developments represent a portal for pentecostal participation in the science/theology dialogue as well as an avenue for pentecostal engagement with and in the sciences.

This book is animated by the conviction that pentecostals need to seriously engage the sciences *as pentecostals* and need to be involved in the science and religion dialogue.[3] But we also believe that the "need" here is reciprocal: pentecostal spirituality, with its distinct emphasis on the Spirit and pneumatology, can yield unique insights for the broader science and religion dialogue. Indeed, we believe that pentecostal spirituality remains a largely "untapped resource" in current discussions. This book speaks to issues on both fronts: on the one hand, it addresses the sorts of questions that pentecostals bring to their first engagement with the sciences; on the other hand, it also addresses the sorts of concerns and worries that scientists would have about pentecostal spirituality. Finally, the book also articulates a distinctly pentecostal contribution to the growing science/theology dialogue.

The book is constrained, however—or better, it is organized—by an overarching concern: to produce a text that could be profitably read by undergraduate students.[4] Specifically, our hope is that the chapters that follow will provide a helpful systematic account of the issues at the intersection of pentecostalism and science for two sorts of students: on the one side, we have in mind students at pentecostal colleges and universities who are either majoring in science or studying science as part of a liberal arts core education requirement; on the other, we hope this book makes its way into the hands of pentecostal students studying science at "secular" or state universities, who bring many of the same questions to their studies though they will likely not find any helpful guides amongst the science faculty with whom they are studying. With this primary goal in mind, the book exhibits several features:

- The book is written by an interdisciplinary team of scholars and seeks to cover the range of the sciences, including the natural and social sciences. Part 1 offers what might be described as "meta" reflections on the big questions that are raised when pentecostals encounter the sciences, including issues related to the biblical narrative of creation and what sometimes appears to be the competing narrative of science, the challenges of thinking about divine action in a world explained by science, and the prospects for supernaturalism in a world that is explained by naturalistic science. After tackling these larger questions, the next two parts of the book proceed up the ladder of what is often referred to as the "hierarchy of the sciences," beginning in part 2 with the natural sciences (physics, biology, neuroscience, and biochemistry), and moving to the human and technological sciences (of anthropology, sociology, and technology) in part 3.[5]
- Each chapter poses a *question* that pentecostals will face when engaging the various sciences. For instance: "How does God do what God does?" "Does God have a place in the physical universe?" "Can there be a holistic pentecostal approach to mental illness?" We hope students will identify with these questions, will in some sense be able to own them as their own questions, and will read the chapters as attempts to provide some answers and responses to those questions.
- With the student in mind, each chapter tries to identify the particular challenges, even (perceived) threats, that pentecostals might sense when engaging, say, physics or biology or sociology. What aspects of these sciences might make them seem hostile to pentecostal belief and practice? How do the dominant paradigms in the sciences perhaps threaten pentecostal spirituality? Or how have they perhaps tried to "explain away" pentecostal religious experience? But the chapters are not just fixated on threats or challenges; they also locate opportunities and invitations within the sciences for uniquely pentecostal participation and contributions. In both ways, the book seeks to move beyond generic

accounts of the science/theology interface in order to name and identify issues that are specific to pentecostal belief and practice. Many of the chapters do this by also appealing to short case studies, anecdotes, or examples that are meant to concretize the issues in a way that makes them both accessible and tangible.

- Each chapter is a two-way street. On the one hand, our goal is to help pentecostals appreciate why it is important for pentecostals to not only "engage" the sciences but also contribute to and participate in the project of encouraging those called to do the work of science.[6] There is, one might say, a kind of inverse apologetic at work here, trying to "defend" the sciences against common pentecostal suspicion and antipathy. But on the other hand, many of the chapters also articulate a distinctly pentecostal account of the sciences that sometimes requires "defending" pentecostal spirituality in the face of its cultured, scientistic despisers. So if the chapters are meant to encourage pentecostals to see the sciences as a legitimate expression of the Spirit's work—what Yong (2005c) has called "academic glossolalia"—they are also offered as an unapologetic articulation of the viability of pentecostal spirituality in the face of a rampant naturalism, materialism, and reductionism that is often confronted in association with the sciences.[7]

In a textbook for undergraduate students, however, we acknowledge at least one lacuna in the following pages: a substantive discussion of the issue of biblical hermeneutics (the art of scriptural interpretation) in relationship to modern science. Many undergraduates, especially those from conservative religious backgrounds who attend evangelical and pentecostal institutions of higher education, begin their studies assuming the inerrancy (even if they have never heard the word) of the Bible read and understood literally. This presumption usually drives the quest to correlate biblical truths with modern science and results sometimes either in creationism (modern science reinterpreted to fit an anti-evolutionist and young earth interpretation of the biblical narrative, especially the Genesis account) or the rejection of faith (because the Bible is thought to be incompatible with evolutionary science). This is an unfortunate hermeneutical presupposition that none of the chapters address at length (although it is touched upon in Mike Tenneson and Steve Badger's discussion of their teaching of the biological sciences).

Yet our readers should take heart, since this is not an issue otherwise neglected in the wider theological academy. There are now excellent books on Genesis that show how to read the creation accounts, not in terms of modern science but in terms of the literary conventions of ancient Near Eastern literature.[8] Such an approach alleviates the need to find agreement between what the Bible says and what modern science says (an approach called concordism in some circles). In the wider scheme of things, there are also many accessible works that reveal the coherence of biblical and religious faith with that of contemporary evolutionary science so that students do not have to choose either one or the other.[9] Once students realize that the "plain sense" of the Genesis text in its original context does not equate with a literalist modern reading, then the need to develop a one-to-one correlation between the biblical witness and modern scientific data is alleviated.[10] At this point, then, conceptual space emerges both for creative theological reflection that is informed by the sciences and for rigorous scientific work that does not ignore theological perspectives and contributions.[11]

These achievements in wider evangelical and Christian scholarship will no doubt inform pentecostal biblical and theological reflection going forward. Thus far, pentecostals have in general neglected in-depth engagement with the Hebrew Bible, much less with the Genesis narrative. However, there are signs that pentecostals are gradually turning their attention to the Old Testament and revisiting even the creation accounts from a distinctively pentecostal perspective (e.g., see Abraham 2003, and Elbert 2006). We predict that the maturation among pentecostal biblical scholarship in general and pentecostal Hebrew Bible scholarship in particular will parallel and complement developments among pentecostal theologians and scientists who are laboring at the interface between the two fields of inquiry.

It is unlikely—and probably not even desirable—that pentecostals would one day devote their resources and energy to constructing particle accelerators. And it is unlikely that the legacy of pentecostal preachers and missionaries will be displaced by Nobel-winning pentecostal scientists, at least not any time soon. But we are already seeing pentecostals working in cancer laboratories, developing and utilizing media technologies, engaged in the health-giving work of psychology, and studying human behavior through the social sciences. The goal of this book is to encourage thoughtful, intentional reflection on the intersection of faith and scientific vocations with the hope of overcoming the "silo" effect that has tended to insulate these conversations from one another. In sum, they are offered as an affirmation that the Holy Spirit is living and active in the spirit of science.

## Notes

1.  Historically, the term *Pentecostal* refers to what are called "classical" Pentecostal denominations that grew out of the Azusa Street revival in 1906. In addition to exhibiting the features associated with charismatic Christianity, the "classical" Pentecostal (with a capital P) denominations are usually marked by the doctrine of "initial physical evidence," which stipulates that speaking in tongues (glossolalia) is the initial physical evidence of baptism in the Holy Spirit. "Charismatic" Christianity—whether in mainline denominations or independent churches—shares much in common with Pentecostalism but usually does not affirm the doctrine of initial evidence. Thus charismatic Christianity is sometimes referred to as "neo-pentecostal." In the remainder of this chapter, we will employ the term *pentecostal* (lower case p) to refer to both classical Pentecostal and charismatic

streams of the Christian tradition. For further discussion of these matters, see Yong 2005d: 18–21.

2. For earlier examples of pentecostal engagements with science, see Walker 1976, Elbert 1996, McHargue 1998, and Yong 2009b; see also Numbers 1992, and Yong and Elbert 2003.

3. Thus we hope that this book moves beyond generically "Christian" or "evangelical" engagements with science. For other examples of tradition-specific engagements with the sciences, see Oord 2009 (from the Wesleyan tradition), and Nesteruk 2003 and Knight 2007 (from the Orthodox tradition).

4. The "Science and Spirit" research initiative that gave birth to this book (see the preface) also produced advanced research at the intersection of science and religion, working from explicitly pentecostal perspectives. This more specialized scholarship, which would generally be too technical for students, will appear in peer-reviewed journals in the field. Some of the research that has already been published includes Bradnick 2008; Scandrett-Leatherman 2008; Smith 2008; Vondey 2009; Work 2008; Yong 2008 and 2009a.

5. In some respects, parts 2 and 3 of this book concern what Frederick Grinnell (2009, esp. part 1), calls the "everyday practice of science"; while the essays in part 1 concern what Grinnell identifies in chapter 6 as being concerned with the wider presuppositional issues that raise comparisons between science and religion, especially religious faith.

6. If pentecostals fail to engage the natural sciences, this will "allow others working in these disciplines to establish the plausibility structures for thinking in general and for worldview construction in particular" (Yong 2005c: 63).

7. This aspect is sometimes more amplified in the research cited in note 4 above.

8. In fact, it is evangelicals—e.g., Bailey 1993; Lamoureux 2008; Sailhamer 1996—who are leading the way to rethinking the nature of the creation accounts as ancient documents that should neither be measured by or against science nor vice versa. The emerging consensus is that "the Genesis creation account cannot be delineated as a scientific text" (Waltke and Fredricks 2001: 75), and that therefore should not be pitted against modern science (Waltke with Yu 2007, chap. 7).

9. Evangelicals who have written about the compatibility of evolution and Christian faith include Falk 2004; Giberson 2008; McGrath 1999: 192–93; and Wilcox 2004. Another accessible and winsome approach is by Lutheran scholars Peters (a theologian) and Hewlett (a scientist) 2006. Ayala 2006 also shows why Christian faith has nothing to fear from the evolutionary sciences.

10. Christians have always found resources from within their own faith to come to terms with the ongoing march of science and even to enable their work as scientists of the highest caliber. For a discussion of these developments in response to Darwin, see Livingstone 1987.

11. Examples of theological vitality informed by the sciences include Roman Catholic scholar John F. Haught (e.g., 1995, 2003, 2007) and evangelical

scholar Alister E. McGrath (2001–2003 and 2006). Part of our goal with this volume is to stimulate pentecostal theological reflection that engages rather than ignores or avoids the sciences.

## References

Abraham, Joseph. 2003. "Feminist Hermeneutics and Pentecostal Spirituality: The Creation Narrative of Genesis as a Paradigm." *Asian Journal of Pentecostal Studies* 6/1: 3–21.

Anderson, Allan. 2007. *Spreading Fires: The Missionary Nature of Early Pentecostalism.* New York: Orbis.

Ayala, Francisco J. 2006. *Darwin and Intelligent Design.* Minneapolis: Fortress.

Bailey, Lloyd R. 1993. *Genesis, Creation, and Creationism.* New York and Mahwah, N.J.: Paulist Press.

Bradnick, David. 2008. "A Pentecostal Perspective on Entropy, Emergent Systems, and Eschatology." *Zygon: The Journal of Religion and Science* 43: 925–42.

Clayton, Philip. 2004. *Mind and Emergence: From Quantum to Consciousness.* Oxford: Oxford University Press.

Clayton, Philip, and Arthur Peacocke, eds. 2004. *In Whom We Live and Move and Have Our Being: Panentheistic Reflections on God's Presence in a Scientific World.* Grand Rapids, Mich.: Eerdmans.

Dawkins, Richard. 2006. *The God Delusion.* New York: Houghton Mifflin.

Dempster, Murray W., Byron D. Klaus, and Douglas Petersen, eds. 1999. *The Globalization of Pentecostalism: A Religion Made to Travel.* Irvine, Calif., and Oxford: Regnum.

Elbert, Paul. 1996. "Biblical Creation and Science: A Review Article." *Journal of the Evangelical Theological Society* 39: 285–89.

———. 2006. "Genesis 1 and the Spirit: A Narrative-Rhetorical Ancient Near Eastern Reading in Light of Modern Science." *Journal of Pentecostal Theology* 15/1: 23–72.

Falk, Darrel R. 2004. *Coming to Peace with Science: Bridging the Worlds between Faith and Biology.* Downers Grove, Ill.: InterVarsity Press.

Giberson, Karl. 2008. *Saving Darwin: How to Be a Christian and Believe in Evolution.* San Francisco: HarperOne.

Grinnell, Frederick. 2009. *Everyday Practice of Science: Where Intuition and Passion Meet Objectivity and Logic.* Oxford: Oxford University Press.

Hackett, Rosalind I. J. 1998. "Charismatic/Pentecostal Appropriation of Media Technologies in Nigeria and Ghana." *Journal of Religion in Africa* 28: 258–77.

Harris, Sam. 2005. *The End of Faith: Religion, Terror, and the Future of Reason.* New York: W.W. Norton.

Haught, John F. 1995. *Science and Religion: From Conflict to Conversation.* New York and Mahwah, N.J.: Paulist Press.

———. 2003. *Deeper than Darwin: The Prospect for Religion in an Age of Evolution.* Boulder, Colo.: Westview Press.

———. 2007. *Christianity and Science: Toward a Theology of Nature.* Maryknoll, N.Y.: Orbis.

Hittenberger, Jeff. 2007. "The Future of Pentecostal Higher Education: The Ring, the Shire, or the Redemption of Middle Earth?" In Eric Patterson and Edmund Rybarczyk, eds., *The Future of Pentecostalism in the United States*. Lanham, Md.: Lexington Books, 83–103.

Jenkins, Philip. 2002. *The Next Christendom: The Coming of Global Christianity*. Oxford: Oxford University Press.

Knight, Christopher. 2007. *The God of Nature: Incarnation and Contemporary Science*. Minneapolis: Fortress Press.

Lamoureux, Denis O. 2008. *Evolutionary Creation: A Christian Approach to Evolution*. Eugene, Ore.: Wipf & Stock.

Livingstone, David N. 1987. *Darwin's Forgotten Defenders: The Encounter between Evangelical Theology and Evolutionary Thought*. Grand Rapids, Mich.: Eerdmans, and Edinburgh: Scottish Academic Press.

McGrath, Alister E. 1999. *Science and Religion: An Introduction*. Oxford and Malden, Mass.: Blackwell.

———. 2001–2003. *A Scientific Theology*. 3 vols. Grand Rapids, Mich.: Eerdmans.

———. 2006. *The Order of Things: Explorations in Scientific Theology*. Malden, Mass.: Blackwell.

McHargue, Lawrence T. 1998. "The Christian and Natural Science." In Michael D. Palmer, ed., *Elements of a Christian Worldview*. Springfield, Mo.: Logion Press, 147–77.

Nesteruk, Alexei. 2003. *Light from the East: Theology, Science, and the Eastern Orthodox Tradition*. Minneapolis: Fortress.

Numbers, Ronald L. 1992. "Creation, Evolution, and Holy Ghost Religion: Holiness and Pentecostal Responses to Darwinism." *Religion and American Culture* 2/2: 127–58.

Oord, Thomas Jay, ed. 2009. *Divine Grace and Emerging Creation: Wesleyan Forays in Science and Theology of Creation*. Eugene, Ore.: Pickwick Publications.

Peters, Ted, and Martinez Hewlett. 2006. *Can You Believe in God and Evolution? A Guide for the Perplexed*. Nashville, Tenn.: Abingdon.

Poewe, Karla, ed. 1994. *Charismatic Christianity as a Global Culture*. Columbia: University of South Carolina Press.

Sailhamer, John. 1996. *Genesis Unbound: A Provocative New Look at the Creation Account*. Sisters, Ore.: Multnomah Books.

Scandrett-Leatherman, Craig. 2008. "Anthropology, Polanyi, and Afropentecostal Ritual: Toward a Scientific and Theological Epistemology of Participation." *Zygon: The Journal of Religion and Science* 43: 909–23.

Smith, James K. A. 2003a. "Advice to Pentecostal Philosophers." *Journal of Pentecostal Theology* 11/2: 235–47.

———. 2003b. "What Hath Azusa Street to Do with Cambridge? Radical Orthodoxy and Pentecostal Theology in Conversation." *PNEUMA: Journal of the Society for Pentecostal Studies* 25: 97–114.

———. 2008. "Is the Universe Open for Surprise? Pentecostal Ontology and the Spirit of Naturalism." *Zygon: The Journal of Religion and Science* 43: 879–86.

Vondey, Wolfgang. 2009. "The Holy Spirit and the Physical Universe: The Impact of Scientific Paradigm Shifts on Contemporary Pneumatology." *Theological Studies* 70: 1–34.

Walker, Paul L. 1976. *Understanding the Bible and Science.* Cleveland, Tenn.: Pathway Press.

Waltke, Bruce, and Cathi J. Fredricks. 2001. *Genesis: A Commentary.* Grand Rapids, Mich.: Zondervan.

Waltke, Bruce K., with Charles Yu. 2007. *An Old Testament Theology: An Exegetical, Canonical, and Thematic Approach.* Grand Rapids, Mich.: Zondervan.

Welker, Michael, ed. 2006. *The Work of the Spirit: Pneumatology and Pentecostalism.* Grand Rapids, Mich.: Eerdmans.

Wilcox, David L. 2004. *God and Evolution: A Faith-Based Understanding.* Valley Forge, Pa.: Judson Press.

Wilson, L. F. 2002. "Bible Institutes, Colleges, Universities." In Stanley M. Burgess, ed., *The New International Dictionary of Pentecostal and Charismatic Movements.* Grand Rapids, Mich.: Zondervan, 372–80.

Work, Telford. 2008. "Pneumatological Relations and Christian Disunity in Theology-Science Dialogue." *Zygon: The Journal of Religion and Science* 43: 897–908.

Yong, Amos. 2005a. "The Spirit and Creation: Possibilities and Challenges for a Dialogue between Pentecostal Theology and the Sciences." *Journal of the European Pentecostal Theological Association* 25: 82–110.

———. 2005b. "Discerning the Spirit(s) in the Natural World: Toward a Typology of 'Spirit' in the Theology and Science Conversation." *Theology & Science* 3/3: 315–29.

———. 2005c. "Academic Glossolalia? Pentecostal Scholarship, Multi-disciplinarity, and the Science-Religion Conversation," *Journal of Pentecostal Theology* 14: 61–80.

———. 2005d. *The Spirit Poured Out on All Flesh: Pentecostalism and the Possibility of Global Theology.* Grand Rapids, Mich.: Baker Academic.

———. 2008. "Natural Laws and Divine Intervention: What Difference Does Being Pentecostal or Charismatic Make?" *Zygon: The Journal of Religion and Science* 43: 961–89.

———. 2009a. "The Spirit at Work in the World: A Pentecostal-Charismatic Perspective on the Divine Action Project." *Theology & Science* 7/2: 123–40.

Yong, Amos, ed. 2009b. *The Spirit Renews the Face of the Earth: Pentecostal Forays in Science and Theology of Creation.* Eugene, Ore.: Pickwick Press, 2009.

Yong, Amos, with Paul Elbert. 2003. "Christianity, Pentecostalism: Issues in Science and Religion." In J. Wentzel van Huysteen, gen. ed., *Encyclopedia of Science and Religion.* New York: Macmillan Reference Library, I: 132–35.

# PART ONE

# What Hath Azusa Street to Do with MIT?

*The Big Questions*

# 1   What Have the Galapagos to Do with Jerusalem? Scientific Knowledge in Theological Context

*Telford Work*

*How did everything happen and what does it mean? Famous scientists are lining up to tell us. But their scientifically inspired theories of everything almost never treat God as Christians do, so science seems to threaten the Christian master story. Christians respond to this situation in many ways, few of which really work. What do the things that science studies have to do with the things theology studies? Scientific knowledge and apocalyptic knowledge are related forms of wisdom. The "full gospel" of pentecostal and charismatic faith is an "obscure framework" that supports science and other kinds of ordinary learning. Its power to relate theology and the sciences fruitfully allows each discipline to strengthen the other—giving Christians, and especially pentecostals, a fuller understanding of salvation and embrace of science, and giving science a firmer hope, a greater framework, and a more appropriate focus.*

## What Have the Galapagos Islands to Do with Jerusalem?

Not long ago, I did some unusual Easter reading. Preparing for my next week's classes, I read two books I had assigned on evolution and religion: Daniel Dennett's *Breaking the Spell: Religion as a Natural Phenomenon* (2006) and Michael Shermer's *How We Believe: Science, Skepticism, and the Search for God* (2003).[1] Both develop the spiritual implications of the popular neo-Darwinian thesis that we are who we are because genes, traditions, species, groups, and ecosystems all interact in a "struggle" to replicate and thus "survive." Christians are not likely to find their arguments affirming. As Dennett (2006, 93) puts it: "Everything we value—from sugar and sex and money to music and love and religion—we value for reasons. Lying behind, and distinct from, *our* reasons are evolutionary reasons, free-floating rationales that have been endorsed by natural selection."

Dennett and Shermer are two ambitious examples of what Karl Giberson and Mariano Artigas call "oracles of science": "the 'public intellectuals' of this generation" who are "bringing science to the reading public in a way that engages them" (2007, 6–7).[2] Evolutionary master narratives like theirs are intriguing recent entries in more than a century of scientifically inspired theories of everything. These generally extrapolate from the findings of physical sciences, life sciences, and social sciences to draw out an overarching account of cosmic, terrestrial, biological, and human history.

Many theorists-of-everything take the fundamental logic of their field of expertise and use it (some would say force it) to tell the whole cosmic story. For instance, a physicist might search for the smallest and most basic units of matter and energy, time and space, catalog their behaviors, and understand the complex ways they interact so that it becomes theoretically possible to learn everything. A sociologist might do the same with sociology's basic unit, the human group, and determine that reality is socially constructed or politically determined. A biologist might take natural selection as the one dynamic that drives all life, the inanimate matter of which it is made, and even the thoughts (including the religious thoughts) of its species. Other theorists will develop more sophisticated accounts that respect the apparently irreducible complexity of different scientific disciplines. These scientifically inspired cosmologies are displacing the old metaphysical cosmologies of ancient, medieval, and modern philosophers (Witham 2005, 28–54), not only in intellectual circles but increasingly in popular imagination. They are also continuing the displacement of God that has been going on for several centuries among the learned of our culture.

Natural selection is not what we were celebrating at my church that Easter morning. Yet its paradigms surrounded us anyway, whispering dissents from inside my head as I sang in my Pentecostal church. And not only in mine. Evolutionary paradigms now inform basic convictions of American society— even the "fundamentalist" economics, political theory, marriage and family practices, medicine, and theology of some of their most vociferous "creationist" opponents.[3] In fact, I believe evolutionary paradigms comprise *the* most formidable intellectual challenge to Christian faith in our time. If the thirteenth century found university faculties torn between following Aristotle and following Jesus, "between Athens and Jerusalem" as the early church father Tertullian put it, in the twenty-first century our cars feature Darwin fish and Jesus fish. Whether we are picking educational curricula, bumper stickers,

Sunday reading, or gods and lords, we face this defining intellectual question: What have the Galapagos Islands to do with Jerusalem? *What do these scientific and theological worlds mean for one another?* Contemporary Christians have responded to the challenge of relating the two in a variety of ways. This chapter surveys the common answers to that question, then draws on Christian and scientific learning to offer its own.

First, a warning: Some readers will insist on reading the following list as a typology of ways of relating "God and creation" or "theology and science." I mean it more narrowly: as a specific catalog of common *Western Christian* responses to the rise of *scientifically inspired cosmologies*. The distinction is important. The task of science is very different from the more ambitious, and ultimately trans-scientific, task of recounting a story of everything. Likewise, Christian responses to that trans-scientific task are narrower projects than the general task of theology, which is to explore the wider implications of the good news of Jesus Christ; and both are of course distinct from the Christian faith in general, let alone God himself.

### Battle

Many American fundamentalists assert the primacy of the biblical story against all varieties of Darwinism. They are rarely anti-science; indeed, they usually make room in their cosmologies for a particularly narrow view of scientific method (usually science as practiced in experimental physics) and the findings they can assimilate. Yet, as if sensing the shift in the past century's intellectual winds, they have stopped worrying nearly as much about schools teaching subversive philosophies such as existentialism and socialism, and rallied instead to resist a worldview in which life might have come into being without the creative assistance of some intelligent agent. They are similarly defensive against astronomy with its old universe, geology with its old earth, anthropology with its prehistoric humanity and prehuman hominid behaviors, history with its biblical criticism, psychology with its materialistic view of the human "soul," and sociology with its paradoxical commitments to progressivism and cultural relativism. In this view, Daniel Dennett and his kind are theologically wrong and thus scientifically wrong too. Jerusalem and the Galapagos are kingdoms at war: divine light battling humanistic darkness.[4]

### Compartmentalization and Neglect

The constant ideological battles against these and other enemies of the faith are energizing for some, but others manage the tension by compartmentalizing their worlds into "Christian" and "secular" realms, each with its own rules. In biology, they read DNA; in church, Genesis. They regard the two as "non-overlapping magisteria" and relate them with vague and facile dichotomies such as the claim that science tells the "how," and religion, the "why" of things. They consider religion private, subjective, and transcendent, and science public, objective, and empirical. Many Christians agree with Stephen Jay Gould (2003) that "science tries to record and explain the factual character of the natural world, whereas religion struggles with spiritual and ethical questions about the meaning and proper conduct of our lives" (as cited in Giberson and Artigas 2007, 80). Dennett is thus not so much wrong as out of his depth, like preachers who appeal to quantum physics during their sermons and all who yield to the temptation to speak beyond their circles of competence.

Others compartmentalize by simply ignoring the unknown. Just as many scientific materialists are not interested in knowing what Christians think, many Christians do not care what scientists think. They are not necessarily hostile; it is just that their curiosity ends well short of the place where other disciplines seem to matter to what they do care about.

The trouble with these forms of segregation, of course, is that both sides still keep stepping on one another's territory *even while minding their own business.* There is not so much a natural boundary between theological and scientific cosmologies as a demilitarized zone, and an often-violated one at that.

### Imperialism and Domestication

Another common way to relate the Galapagos to Jerusalem is to take one to be the center of an empire in which the other is a mere client state. Christians have long drawn selectively on other traditions—whether scientific, theological, or otherwise—to strengthen their own. Augustine called classical rhetoric "Egyptian gold" to be plundered for the church's mission to preach. He reasoned that since (as some say today) "all truth is God's truth," it is only right to use all these resources to benefit God's people and serve the kingdom of God. Likewise, American pentecostals made use of Social Darwinian capitalism (an ideology of trade in which economic might makes right) and modern broadcasting technologies to get the word out (Wacker 2006, 135–43). These interlopers often treat the spiritual as more important than the material and thus the scientific. Why would anyone study religion scientifically instead of being a missionary? In concerning themselves with the things of this world, Dennett and company are preoccupied with the wrong things.

Other believers invert these priorities and submit the Christian tradition to the governance of the scientific tradition. Science seems firm enough, objective enough, and above all *familiar* enough, to be trustworthy. So if scientists learn, say, that "religious feeling" emanates from a certain part of the brain when it is stimulated, these Christians will accept those results and try to adjust their views of God to fit them. If physics trades Newton's mechanistic causes and effects for Einstein's deterministic space-time and then Bohr's probabilistic quanta, theology will recast God's relationship with the world obligingly.

In both of these last two responses, one story effectively occupies the other. Either theology's Jerusalem domesticates science's Galapagos, or else science reduces theology to "religion" and religion to "a natural phenomenon" that is really best studied through the sciences.

The real trouble with both is not just insurgents on each side who refuse to bow down to the other side's emperor, who *refuse* to be assimilated, but populations that simply *cannot* be assimilated. Literalistic creation science must disregard or distort the massive and accumulating credible evidence of humanity's evolutionary origins and character[5] as well as the signs that the Bible's creation accounts are not literal chronologies.[6] Intelligent Design theory, already unattractive to scientists as a "science stopper," cannot match its rivals' elegance and explanatory power. Likewise, naturalistic accounts of "religion" misrepresent traditions such as historic Christianity that do not fit their scientific paradigms. Dennett's and Shermer's learned speculations on the rise of religious ideas and experiences uncannily ignore two thousand years of insistent Christian testimony that the bedrock of our tradition is not some mystical experience, archetypical figure, or compelling idea, but simply the apostles' testimony to Jesus' death and resurrection and the powerful outpouring of his Holy Spirit (see, e.g., Wright 2003 and Bauckham 2006). In other words, neither side can really afford to take the other side's evidence seriously. Both of these camps of imperialists are fighting for what all empires treasure: its vision of reality, whose most stubborn enemy is not disbelievers but reality itself.

### Pragmatism

The most common Western stance toward Christianity and science is pragmatism, which claims the *fruits* of both of these traditions without their disciplinary baggage. We widely appreciate benefits of religion that we call "spirituality," and we even more widely appreciate benefits of scientific discoveries through what we call "technology." This attitude turns the Galapagos and Jerusalem into trade partners and vacation destinations. Pragmatism is the style of the consumer, the business, and the university: not really to respect the grand claims of the humanities, the arts, or the sciences, but to arrange them in ways that seem pleasing and useful for some other end. Pragmatists can read Dennett and Shermer (and the Bible too) to glean information to use in the marketplace, the cocktail circuit, at home, or in the study—but not to learn the Truth.

There are even more ways to relate the Galapagos and Jerusalem: merging them (syncretism), isolating them as mere opinions (pluralism and relativism), and condemning both as probing mysteries better left alone (skepticism). Scientific cosmologies jostle more and more with Christian convictions, and Christians do not agree on what to do about it. The casualties of our inadequate responses—lost faith, strained relationships, impoverished educations, and missed opportunities—all indicate an urgent need for further thinking.

Here the pentecostal tradition offers key resources for a cosmology in which both science and theology enjoy more hospitable and fruitful places.

That claim will surprise some who think of pentecostalism as a theological and intellectual backwater. Seeing the pentecostal and charismatic tradition (I will usually treat the two as interchangeable) as a contributor to understanding in a scientific age will mean setting aside some stereotypes. For instance, pentecostals are usually lumped with fundamentalists, despite our different histories and divergent instincts. Our outlook is called otherworldly, but pentecostals have been adept businesspeople and strategic missionaries and have become a powerful political force worldwide. We are often called anti-intellectual; and we certainly tend to distrust intellectual *culture,* but not intelligence or learning as such. Misunderstandings like these indicate that the movement's inner logic is not widely grasped.

## Theology's Obscure Framework

The Pentecostal movement's center is an experience of the powerful presence of the Holy Spirit in a way reminiscent of the young church in the book of Acts, yielding spiritual gifts for making disciples of all nations (Kay and Dyer 2004: xix).

Of course, pentecostals are not alone in appreciating the Spirit in this way. Eastern Orthodox Christians, Roman Catholics, and Protestants of all stripes agree. Our Christian *experience* or *knowledge* of God is interpersonal in a way that makes the most natural form of Christian confession a narrative. An account of how pentecostals can contribute to Christian understanding in a scientific age must begin on the ecumenical ground they share with others who trust in "God the Father Almighty, maker of heaven and earth . . . in the Holy Spirit, the holy catholic Church, the communion of saints, the forgiveness of sins, the resurrection of the body, and the life everlasting." The God we know is our beginning and our end, our creating Father and our indwelling Holy Spirit.

The center of the Scriptures and the creeds is the story of Jesus. His good news is not a subplot or another narrative alongside others; it is *the same story of the triune God.* He too is Alpha and Omega: only-begotten before all worlds, set to return at the end of the age. The Son's eternal Father receives at the end as well as sends at the beginning; Jesus' eternal Spirit broods and breathes life in the beginning as well as flows from Christ's body at the end; by the eternal Son all things were made, and his kingdom will have no end. There is nothing exclusively Pentecostal or charismatic about this story. It is the deep structure of Christian theology. It is also the framework in which all life and learning have their place.

Science is a way of learning, and it is a form of life. As a way of learning, science senses consistencies in the universe that can be *discovered:* isolated, identified, and even explained in terms of consistencies that are already known. As a form of life, science trains us *to think scientifically:* to become familiar with these consistencies, with consistency's wonder and beauty and the elegance of the simplicity that underlies it; to be trained to expect to learn and explain more; and to be equipped in the practices of intuition, experimentation, conclusion, and communication that generate and sustain scientific knowledge.

These activities suit God's orderly and purposeful creation in which human beings have unique relationships and responsibilities. Science is a form of *wisdom,* one variety of proverbial insight into the workings of everyday life: "God gave Solomon wisdom and understanding beyond measure, and largeness of mind like the sand on the seashore.... He spoke of trees, from the cedar that is in Lebanon to the hyssop that grows out of the wall; he spoke also of beasts, and of birds, and of reptiles, and of fish" (1 Kings 4:29–33).

However, when science is pursued apart from those covenantal relationships and responsibilities, its knowledge is radically incomplete and even distortive. An episode in Jesus' life demonstrates this: "To test him they asked him to show them a sign from heaven. He answered them, 'When it is evening, you say 'It will be fair weather; for the sky is red.' And in the morning, 'It will be stormy today, for the sky is red and threatening.' You know how to interpret the appearance of the sky, but you cannot interpret the signs of the times" (Matthew 16:1–3). This is a basic and consistently biblical assertion about how forms of learning properly relate. Jesus juxtaposes two ancient traditions of learning: not "science and religion" or "science and theology"—let alone sciences and humanities!—but *science* and *apocalypse.*

These two things are easily mischaracterized. To us, scientific knowledge seems to be natural reason, and apocalyptic knowledge, divine revelation. Protestants may add that the reasoning is an achievement and the revelation a gift. Modernists will construe the reasoning as objective, public knowledge and the revelation as subjective, private faith. But how then could Jesus treat meteorology and eschatology as analogous and shame his opponents by comparing them?

Relating science to apocalypse recalls the struggle to relate the Galapagos and Jerusalem. Is it a battle where Christian faith defeats secular book learning? Is it a hierarchy in which only the love of Christ is worth our whole attention? No, Jesus' apocalyptic framework is friendlier to science than either of those strategies. Because both traditions offer wisdom, Jesus sees the "worldly wise" as better positioned to appreciate him and to judge those who do not: "The queen of the South will arise at the judgment with this generation and condemn it, for she came from the ends of the earth to hear the wisdom of Solomon, and behold, something greater than Solomon is here" (Matthew 12:42). What qualifies the Queen of Sheba to judge is not anti-intellectualism but zeal for and openness to every kind of wisdom.

Yet intellectual snobs, materialists, and pragmatists will not find much support here for privileging Solomon's style of wisdom. The history of God in Jesus Christ supplies inside information that the world's learned do not even know to look for.

Not even the world's spiritually learned. Jesus is not comparing reason to faith, the secular to the sacred, or the physical to the spiritual. If he were, his surprising parallel contrast would not make sense: "The men of Nineveh will arise at the judgment with this generation and condemn it; for they repented at the preaching of Jonah, and behold, something greater than Jonah is here" (Matthew 12:41). Jesus' audiences do not dichotomize reason and faith, secular and sacred, or physical and spiritual as modern Westerners do. They simply want signs from above, within the conventional "scientific" and "religious" categories that already make sense to them. Instead of confining his revelation of the kingdom to either of these traditions, Jesus promises a perverse unveiling from below that transcends both: "An evil and adulterous generation seeks for a sign, but no sign will be given to it except the sign of Jonah" (Matthew 16:4). That apocalyptic sign, his death and resurrection, reveals "the plan [oikonomia] of the mystery hidden for ages in God who created all things, that through the church the manifold wisdom of God might now be made known" (Ephesians 3:9–10). The revelation of God in Christ does not set aside wisdom; it is wisdom. But not Solomon's or even Jonah's kind.

The apostolic faith juxtaposes scientific knowledge and apocalyptic knowledge, not as we usually do, as two independent realms of knowledge or styles of learning, but as two distinct and intrinsically related forms of discovery. The apocalyptic wisdom of God "is greater than" the scientific wisdom of Solomon. The sign of the Son of Man "is greater than" the repentance that Jonah preaches. The hidden oikonomia, or "economy" of God, meaning what God has done in Jesus Christ, is in some sense greater than the everyday economy of creation. The unveiling of God in Christ is greater than the unveiling of creation through all ordinary inquiry, including scientific and ethical inquiry.

Greater in what sense? Not in any of the ways Jerusalem jostles with the Galapagos as rival cosmologies! Rather, Solomon's and Jonah's "lesser" economy is old and inaugural (protological, pertaining to first things), and the Son of Man's greater one is new and climactic (eschatological, pertaining to last things). Science helps describe an age that is truly significant but is passing away. The lesser economy is continuous, and the greater is discontinuous; science pertains to the predictable, which was brought into being and is being remade in acts of sheer creation. God's presence is indirect in the lesser and direct in the greater ("something greater *is here*"). These qualities make the lesser order of knowledge familiar but the greater one strange (so it is "outsiders" who respond, as the Gentiles from Sheba and Nineveh had). The lesser economy is also subordinate—one of powers and principalities—so that its teachers mistake Jesus' power as demonic (Matthew 12:22–24), while the greater economy is of the Spirit of God (Matthew 12:28–32).

These analogies reveal the greater *oikonomia* to be *ultimate:* it frames the lesser economy. We know consistencies of natural and social creation only because there *is* a creation, and we know natural and social patterns of grace only because God redeemed it.

At the same time, the greater *oikonomia* is *obscure:* it is interpersonal, revolutionary, and unpredictable. Here it contrasts not only with Solomon's wisdom but even with Jonah's preaching. God's message disappointed Jonah because love of Israel's enemies was consistent with God's compassion (Jonah 4:1–2). But the gospel *keeps* shocking us, even after decades. Though frustrated students appeal too quickly to its mystery when struggling to understand something new, they are still right to use the term. The Lord's mercies are new every morning.

Both creation's lesser economy and God's greater *oikonomia* are fields for learned traditions. However, science is unlike theology in that it explores things that do not depend in the same way on the Spirit's disclosure. Its buried treasure is in principle open for anyone to uncover: "general revelation" if you will. What is special about "special revelation" is that the Spirit discloses the eschatological: the *telos* or end of all things that is hidden in the depths of the Father's thoughts and displayed in his Christ. This christological location of theological knowledge is what gives theological tradition its comprehensive scope that frames all other traditions, including scientific traditions.

These qualities set limits on how well training for one discipline will apply to the other. I sometimes jest that "theology is about everything," but it isn't really. Christian theology specializes in God's wisdom and is often painfully ignorant of Solomon's. Likewise, scientific training can be a poor tutor for the kingdom's scribes when it tempts them to capture the unfamiliar in the familiar. Particle-physicist-turned-Anglican-clergyman John Polkinghorne (2005) develops a marvelous account of divine interaction with the universe at the quantum level, but his proposals for reconciling contemporary science with Christian faith are less helpful as they move away from the field of expertise that informs his fundamental vision and toward the level of human moral agents with our miracles, prayer, and prophecy.[7] The *oikonomia's* obscure framework *remains* more obscure than its counterpart. So all properly interpreted experience must honor the ultimacy and the obscurity of the good news as well as the penultimacy and the blatancy of scientific and other ordinary knowledge.

## The Evolutionary Epic and the Pentecostal Cosmic Narrative

Christ's apocalyptic framework for common wisdom sheds new light on the usual stances of science and theology toward one another. It appreciates the strengths of our conventional ways of relating the Galapagos and Jerusalem, diagnoses their weaknesses, and suggests more fruitful approaches. Consider how it contrasts with my Easter reading from Daniel Dennett and Michael Shermer, along with some of their fellow cosmic storytellers.

E. O. Wilson regards what he calls "the evolutionary epic" as "probably the best myth we will ever have" (2004: 201). He sounds progressive, triumphalistic, even apocalyptic (a tone he may have picked up as a young Southern Baptist in Alabama) when he claims that humanity has evolved an unprecedented capacity to transcend ourselves and should act on it. For Shermer, the evolutionary paradigm is a more ambiguous cosmic myth: "We are a fluke of nature, a quirk of evolution, a *glorious contingency*" (2003: 231).[8] The cosmos thrills him because it has no point other than its own twists and turns. George Johnson considers both Wilson's progressivism and Shermer's anti-progressivism unwarranted inferences from inconclusive data, though his ending to *Fire in the Mind* shows that he wants Wilson to be right (1996: 328).

For all their differences, all three are empires of the Galapagos. They all strive to colonize or even defeat Jerusalem with an all-encompassing, scientifically inspired framework. Indeed, they suffer from the same logical flaw, one that is endemic in cosmologies grounded in the evolutionary epic: the genetic fallacy. They confuse a thing's origin with its meaning.[9] Dennett's elaborate speculations on the rise of belief in God are shot through with the same genetic fallacy. His "best current version of the story science can tell about how religions have become what they are" (2006: 103) is at best educated guesswork—an "evolutionary 'just so' story" that aims to inspire future research. Its assessment of the human condition, bleaker than Shermer's yet striving like Wilson's, reads rather like Ecclesiastes' wise observations on ordinary life. But Ecclesiastes makes for a poor canon-within-the-canon. Its weary insight into commonalities does not supply the energy of Israel's Scriptures or even its Wisdom Literature, let alone the explosive New Testament.

Easter is not a time for Ecclesiastes. On that Sunday morning on which I read Dennett and Shermer, our sermon centered elsewhere, on Romans 8:11: "If the Spirit of him who raised Jesus from the dead dwells in you, he who raised Christ Jesus from the dead will give life to your mortal bodies also, through his Spirit that dwells in you." This is clearly a different epic than

Shermer's, Wilson's, Johnson's, and Dennett's evolutionary ones, not least for its note of *hope.*

The resurrection—not a scientific event but a solid historical one—is the crowning of the Christian master narrative. It brings the joyful church's Spirit and grounds its hopeful life. Christian pneumatology supplies the decisive clue connecting "nature," mortal creation (which the Creator Spirit brings to life in Genesis 1–2), with "eternity," immortal creation (which the Savior Spirit inaugurates in raising Jesus from the dead), in our lives and imaginations (which the Perfector Spirit bequeaths as "the mind of Christ" that searches and shares his mysteries). Ordinary life and the cosmic *oikonomia*, current things and ultimate things, meet definitively in the life, anointing, death, and resurrection of the *homo sapiens* Jesus of Nazareth.

Peter Hocken, a charismatic Catholic priest, articulates the pneumatological and eschatological orientation of pentecostal experience:

> The basic link between the experience of spiritual renewal and the awakening of hope for the second coming of Jesus lies in the gift of the Holy Spirit. . . . As the Holy Spirit makes the Church more eschatological, the Spirit is restoring the fullness of the New Testament hope. This hope is of total salvation, the deliverance of all creation from its bondage to decay, the establishment of the new heavens and the new earth, our resurrection in glorified spiritual bodies, in which there will be total communion with all the saints and angels in the perfect harmony and eternal life of the Most Holy Trinity. (2004: 44–46)

My Foursquare Church would never speak in quite this way, but that Easter we were effectively agreeing with Hocken's rich description of the majestic unity of pentecostal eschatology. Its disposition orients all pentecostal worship (Kay and Dyer 2004: 27).

Because pentecostal sensibilities are especially tuned to the last things rather than the first things, pentecostals are well positioned to criticize the false progress of Wilson's evolutionary trajectory, the dysteleological features of cosmologies like Shermer's, and the latent deism in Johnson. What is *in* the universe is immensely significant for the doctrine of creation; but what is determinative is what the universe is *becoming* as the new creation approaches, led by the Spirit, and arrives in the midst of the old.

Pentecostalism has a distinctive respect for divine action. It sees the Holy Spirit's powerful indwelling in the church as the current center (though not the exclusive terrain) of God's eschatological work, focused in baptism in the Holy Spirit—an "empowerment for Christian service" (Macchia 2006: 110) that is more like the Catholic sacrament of holy orders than baptism or confirmation. This doctrine is integral to a distinctive Christology that confesses Jesus as Savior, Spirit Baptizer, Healer, and Coming King (see Dayton 1988, as cited in Welker 2006: 112n4). The specifically pentecostal vision of Christ as healer and Spirit baptizer funds more than the common Christian conviction that God acts supernaturally. It knows the Holy Spirit as realizing God's desire for new creation *through the apostolic fellowship's normal exercise of his transforming power in signs and wonders.*

Other Christian traditions acknowledge these as the Spirit's work but make them exceptional. Some relegate them to an apostolic age now past or to a subpopulation of saints. Some restrict them to a liturgy in which God's normal presence is now sacramental in the eucharistic host, kerygmatic in the Word of God preached, or communal in the gathering of two or three in Jesus' name. Even where pentecostals share these sensibilities, they still resist all exceptionalism because "Jesus Christ is the same yesterday, today, and forever" (Hebrews 13:8). Acts 2 makes it clear that every disciple, *all flesh,* should be Spirit-baptized for powerful and even miraculous service (cf. 1 Corinthians 14:5). So "signs and wonders analogous to those described in premodern biblical accounts are expected as normal occurrences in the lives of believers" (Poloma 2006: 156).

Doesn't this make pentecostalism a theology of anti-nature rather than nature? There are quite understandable reasons to think so—including the words of pentecostals themselves. Alexander Boddy, faith healer and founder of British Pentecostalism, wrote in 1910:

> Imagine now that a very bad cold is coming on. The old symptoms tell us that it will go through the inevitable stages unless something unusual happens. But you know now that *Christ is your life.* You know that you are a new creature in Christ Jesus. . . . You are sure that this cold is not the will of God. It can in no way bring glory to Him, whereas deliverance from it will be a help to others and may induce them to trust Him also. You recognize that this cold is from Satan. . . . You hold on to the truth that you are whole because you are in Jesus Christ, and you show your belief by *really* "praising God" for victory. As you do this unflinchingly you will find that Satan has to go. Perhaps instantaneously, perhaps gradually, the whole thing vanishes, and the unbelievers around will say, "It is really strange how such an one gets rid of a cold." Satan is beaten! (2004: 54–55)

Identifying Satan as the universal pathogen for humanity (and other species too?) is not going to produce first-rate epidemiology. It dichotomizes God and nature and forces dilemmas on disciples who want to serve God with their gifts. Consider Harold Horton's dichotomy between modern medicine and the church's mission, in 1934:

> We must most emphatically state that modern medicine is not the legitimate fulfillment of Jesus' command to "heal the sick." Rather is it the negation, the neglect, if not the positive denial of it. And this is equally true of genuinely born-again "Christian doctors." The only "Christian physicians" acknowledged in the Scrip-

tures are those ordinary believers who heal miraculously. . . . God's way, the only way revealed in the Word, is healing by supernatural divine power. (2004: 61)

Relegating Solomon's wisdom to "the world" denies the divinity of the Wisdom through whom creation came to be (Proverbs 8) and through whose flesh creation was renewed (John 1). Such an attitude drives an anti-empiricism that subordinates the senses to "faith," as articulated here by healing evangelist T. L. Osborn: "Your natural senses have nothing to do with faith, and true faith must ignore them. If you walk by faith, you cannot walk by sight. If you are to consider the Word of God as true, then you cannot always consider the evidences of your senses as true" (2004: 70). So much for laboratories and scientific observation! This pentecostal Jerusalem has little to offer the sciences but disdain, and little to offer those who suffer but a "prosperity gospel" that will soon disillusion the faithful.

Spiritualism and anti-naturalism *are* persistent pentecostal temptations. However, many pentecostals have learned to resist them—not by betraying the charismatic tradition but by appealing to it. Oral Roberts founded a pentecostal university with both a prayer center and a medical school because, he said,

> God teaches He alone is the Source of our total supply: "But my God shall supply all your need according to his riches in glory by Christ Jesus" (Phil. 4:19); and "I am the LORD that healeth thee" (Exod. 15:26). Our total supply most certainly includes our deliverance from sickness and disease. Therefore, both healing coming through supernatural intervention, through believing the gospel and the prayer of faith, and healing coming through medicine or surgery really come through God our Source. (Roberts 2004: 80)

The anti-naturalism of the first generations of pentecostals was in part a fundamentalistic reaction against the prevailing naturalism of modern secularism and liberal Christianity. Later generations of pentecostals moved away from it by appealing to the supernatural to restore respect for the natural as a means, not just an object, of grace.

Similarly, practitioners of spiritual warfare have nurtured the movement's appreciations for psychological health (see Kraft, Kearny, and White 2004) and social justice (see Wessels 1997). Tongues were originally understood as being a gift from God to empower cross-cultural mission to peoples of other languages (Kay and Dyer 2004: 211), and charismatic liturgy has led the worldwide enculturation of Christianity (Yong 2005: 31–32, 161–62, 266). Pentecostalism has addressed its tendency toward anti-naturalism with a more sophisticated respect for nature *in light of* the kingdom's normal signs and wonders. Rapid sociological transformations of pentecostals from the margins toward the center of their cultures demonstrates the same capacity to honor the normality of the Spirit's powerful presence in the natural order.

These pentecostal qualities have worked powerfully in my own life. I can testify to the difference that robust pentecostal pneumatology made to my own understanding of God's involvement in the world. As a college senior, someone introduced me to charismatic Christianity with a copy of Pat Robertson's *Shout It from the Housetops* (1986). Further (and higher quality) reading and visiting a charismatic Bible study on campus provided my first real appreciation of the Holy Spirit as both personal and eschatological. This was crucial in healing the breach that had opened up between the scientific, deistic, even neo-Darwinian world of my secular education and the religious world of my new mildly Reformed, premillennial faith. Pentecostal theology transformed my understanding of God in the world. It resolved discontinuities that had held my knowledge of science, history, and the like aloof from my emerging evangelical faith. In effect, it began the restoration of my intellectual wholeness and put me on a course that has led to a career professing theology and championing the sciences at an evangelical liberal arts college.

## A Scientific and Spiritual Gift Exchange

Pentecostal sensibility embraces the natural and the supernatural, the accessible wisdom of Solomon and the obscure wisdom of God. These realms of human knowledge are differently focused, relatively autonomous, and radically open to one another in ways that point to eschatological resolution. The wisdom of God creates, encloses, and judges ordinary wisdom as its wellspring and destination; the knowledge of ordinary things anticipates, entertains, and may receive the divine *oikonomia* as its salvation and healing. Their harmony is promising for pentecostal theology and contemporary science in several ways.

First, though pentecostals often suffer from their own Jerusalemite imperialism, which manifests itself in an overly narrow vision of salvation and an anti-intellectual attitude toward science, in fact our eschatology supports the opposite. The indwelling Spirit does not avoid, contradict, or negate nature, rendering our life in the Spirit dualistic or gnostic. The Spirit embraces human nature in ways that make Christian life holistic and even, in a peculiarly pentecostal way, sacramental.

Pentecostalism's truly Trinitarian grasp of God's *oikonomia* can underwrite an embrace of the natural sciences, the social sciences, and other traditions of human learning about nature that is freer and more theologically anticipatory than many Christian alternatives. It opens communications between the wisdom of God and human wisdom. It insists on the clarity that miracles bring to the overarching framework in which ordinary processes have their place. And its appreciation of the normativity of the Spirit's actions in the world through his indwelt church lends much-needed scientific qualities such as explanatory power, predictive power, and falsifiability to eschatological proposals.

The pentecostal quest for holiness can also benefit from scientific insights, including insights from evolutionary biology and evolutionary psychology. Christians have struggled forever against vices of "the flesh"—passions and habits that stubbornly resist the kingdom. Charismatics have often blamed the devil and sought supernatural remedies for what the New Testament tends to treat with practical asceticism and pastoral good sense. This reductive spiritualism leads to psychological damage, shattered faith, and disrespect. Without denying the reality of the demonic, pentecostals might draw on natural and social sciences for a robust *teleological* account of human qualities that may simply have outlived their usefulness in the last days. Unconditional family loyalty or human aggression might be, not the devil prowling for prey, but a good gift from God that sustained life until a community of hominids could be appointed *imago dei,* become theologically and biologically human, and begin a walk with God that would someday manifest his reign on earth. If "the flesh" is in part a throwback to fading or obsolete contexts from both bygone times of human origins and the old order that Christ's kingdom entered and conquered, then we should not revile it and thus impugn our Creator, nor try to cast it out as if it were a foreign object, but we should simply leave it behind as we press onward toward our goal in Christ Jesus (Philippians 3:13–14).

Science can also inform pentecostal supernaturalism.[10] When methodologically valid studies fail to identify statistically significant rates of miracles, the lesson may not be that such studies are flawed or sinful, but that miracles are rare. Indeed, they may always have been rare, even during the charismatic heyday of Acts 2–5. It takes many fewer signs and wonders for God to make an unforgettable point, for Luke to weave a decades-long narrative, and for the Galatians to recognize the Spirit among them (Galatians 3:5) than it takes to establish statistically significant rates of, say, supernatural healing at a 95 percent confidence interval. The Spirit's activity seems to be normal but occasional, falling between grandiose pentecostal claims that collapse under scrutiny and categorical denials that credible evidence contradicts. If so, pentecostalism's moderating over the last century could be a healthier respect for "charismatic normalcy."

If the Spirit sovereignly but rarely works miracles, then the methods best suited to studying them may not belong to the social or natural sciences but to historiography. History is methodologically open to apocalypse and to these two intersecting economies in ways that science is not: it is narrative in shape, accessible to both scientists and theologians, already prestigious and influential in both disciplines, and intuitive to outsiders.

Second, theological resources have a place in the sciences that bear upon humanity's future. The faith, hope, and love of Christ will not displace epidemiology in the biological sciences! But if Jesus' human life really is paradigmatic for our future, then they ought to *inform* anthropology, psychology, and the other social sciences.

A third promising avenue for future interaction between pentecostal theology and contemporary science is ecclesiological. Every interdisciplinary study of pneumatology and nature has to wrestle with the awkward fact that detailed theological information on the Spirit overwhelmingly speaks at the level of the personal and interpersonal, and specifically the level of *the church*. Yet this is as it should be. Recall the Apostles' Creed, which ends in the fellowship of saints, the forgiveness of sins, the resurrection of the body, and the life everlasting. By contrast, biblical testimony to the Spirit's role in and over natural creation is sparse, scattered, and vague. Any fully Christian doctrine of creation, any accurate catalog of the various God–world relationships, and thus any proper philosophy of science, must focus on Israel, Jesus Christ, and the eternal church. Otherwise, contemporary theories of divine action such as emergence, supervenience, and downward/upward causation (see Murphy 1997) do not themselves say enough about creation's goal to give a properly Christian description of the universe, though they could certainly contribute to one.[11] One day a better-trained Christian scientific corps might craft more *scientifically* appealing alternatives to the ambiguous (Shermer, Johnson), dysteleological (Dennett), and falsely optimistic (Wilson) analyses that dominate our imaginations.

These possibilities leave us, who are at the crossroads of these intersecting economies, somewhere else than the warring fiefdoms of Jerusalem and the Galapagos—at an unlikely place that is perhaps like that little mission in Los Angeles in which "the very atmosphere of heaven had descended" to restore a nearly forgotten reality that soon swept the world.

## Notes

1. Dennett is a philosopher at Tufts University who informs his work on the philosophy of mind from the conventions and insights of certain schools of evolutionary biology. An enthusiastic atheist, he treats religions of all kinds as the by-products of once-useful human evolutionary adaptations. Shermer is a columnist for *Scientific American* who is fascinated by human religious belief. An adolescent Christian whose faith in God ended in college, he subsequently founded *Skeptic* magazine and has turned his scientific training on the question of why human beings are religious.

2. Only some oracles of science are themselves practicing scientists. Among the figures prominent in this chapter, E. O. Wilson is, while Daniel Dennett, Michael Shermer, and George Johnson are not.

3. Consider, for example, the Christian bumper sticker in which an *ichthys,* or "Jesus fish," labeled "truth," devours a smaller "Darwin fish"—an unintentionally ironic embodiment of Darwin's principle of survival of the fittest (see Kallenberg 2002, 49).

4. These fundamentalists' secular counterparts are "the new atheists" such as Dennett, Richard Dawkins, and Christopher Hitchens, who show unbridled contempt for any belief in God.

5. See Falk 2004 for an accessible and informed argument for the compatibility of Christian faith and evolutionary biology.

6. Many Pentecostal and charismatic Christians, especially in the United States, read the Genesis creation narratives as literalistic historical and scientific reporting. I read Genesis 1 and Genesis 2–3 as historical in the sense that they portray a real past—the coming into being of Israel's context: its universe, its earth, its land, and its human race. However, the literary genre suggests that these chapters are not attempting to portray Israel's prehistory literally. From the lattice-like structure of Genesis 1's first six days to the figural details in Genesis 2–3, these accounts do not reproduce the more literal forms of historical reporting that one finds elsewhere in the Old Testament, the Torah, or even later in Genesis. Similar figural historical appeals include Daniel 7's apocalyptic portrayal of the rise and fall of empires and Isaiah 5's parabolic description of Israel's beginning (echoed by Jesus in the Synoptic Gospels). That neither the Genesis 1 sequence nor the Genesis 2–3 sequence is confirmed by scientific evidence (no scientific field finds plant life to predate the sun, moon, and stars, or finds humanity to have arisen before trees or animals) reinforces my conviction that we misread these stories when we either take them as literal scientific or historical chronologies or dismiss the reality of the past they figurally portray. Accordingly, we need not assume that the Bible's creation accounts in Genesis, the Psalms, or elsewhere are incompatible with evolutionary origins for life, including human life. The primary concern of Genesis is the origin of Israel, not the origin of species.

7. A possible reason for this kind of deficiency, which is not Polkinghorne's but Christianity's in general, is developed in Work 2008.

8. This is the kind of leap from expertise to cosmological speculation that Giberson and Artigas (2007) complain about among "oracles of science."

9. This is a particularly ironic failure in light of the neo-Darwinian insight into biological "cooption" and "exaptation," evolutionary phenomena in which a trait originally useful in one way ends up serving a different purpose. A more consistent application of the principle would be more open to ways in which the biological origins of forces involved in Christian faith could differ radically from their eschatological roles in the kingdom of God. Just as tail feathers on male peacocks are no longer for flying but are for demonstrating reproductive fitness, so the singing voices of human beings may no longer be primarily for demonstrating reproductive fitness but for praising our triune Redeemer.

10. See James K. A. Smith's chapter 2 in this volume.

11. I am not qualified to write such a narrative, but I have sketched the very beginning of one in Work 2007, 33–45.

## References

Bauckham, Richard. 2006. *Jesus and the Eyewitnesses: The Gospels as Eyewitness Testimony.* Grand Rapids, Mich.: Eerdmans.

Boddy, A. A. 2004. "Health in Christ." In William K. Kay and Anne E. Dyer, eds., *Pentecostal and Charismatic Studies: A Reader*. London: SCM, 52–56.

Dayton, Donald. 1988. *Theological Roots of Pentecostalism*. Metuchen, N.J.: Scarecrow.

Dennett, Daniel. 2006. *Breaking the Spell: Religion as a Natural Phenomenon*. New York: Viking.

Falk, Darrel R. 2004. *Coming to Peace with Science: Bridging the Worlds Between Faith and Biology*. Downers Grove, Ill.: InterVarsity.

Giberson, Karl, and Mariano Artigas. 2007. *Oracles of Science: Celebrity Scientists versus God and Religion*. New York: Oxford.

Gould, Stephen Jay. 2003. *The Hedgehog, the Fox, and the Magister's Pox: Mending the Gap between Science and the Humanities*. New York: Harmony.

Hocken, Peter. 2004. "The Holy Spirit Makes the Church More Eschatological." In William K. Kay and Anne E. Dyer, eds., *Pentecostal and Charismatic Studies: A Reader*. London: SCM, 43–46.

Horton, Harold. 2004. "The Gifts of the Spirit." In William K. Kay and Anne E. Dyer, eds., *Pentecostal and Charismatic Studies: A Reader*. London: SCM, 60–64.

Johnson, George. 1996. *Fire in the Mind: Science, Faith, and the Search for Order*. New York: Vintage.

Kallenberg, Brad J. 2002. *Live to Tell: Evangelism in a Postmodern Age*. Grand Rapids, Mich.: Brazos.

Kay, William K., and Anne E. Dyer, eds. 2004. *Pentecostal and Charismatic Studies: A Reader*. London: SCM.

Kraft, Charles H., Ellen Kearney, and Mark H. White. 2004. *Deep Wounds, Deep Healing: Discovering the Vital Link between Spiritual Warfare and Inner Healing*. Ann Arbor, Mich.: Vine.

Macchia, Frank D. 2006. "The Kingdom and the Power: Spirit Baptism in Pentecostal and Ecumenical Perspective." In Michael Welker, ed., *The Work of the Spirit: Pneumatology and Pentecostalism*. Grand Rapids, Mich.: Eerdmans, 110–13.

Murphy, Nancy. 1997. *Anglo-American Postmodernity: Philosophical Perspectives on Science, Religion, and Ethics*. Boulder, Colo.: Westview.

Osborn, T. L. 2004. "Healing the Sick." In William K. Kay and Anne E. Dyer, eds., *Pentecostal and Charismatic Studies: A Reader*. London: SCM, 70–73.

Polkinghorne, John C. 2005. *Science and Providence: God's Interaction with the World*. West Conshohocken, Pa.: Templeton.

Poloma, Margaret. 2006. "The Future of American Pentecostal Identity: The Assemblies of God at a Crossroad." In Michael Welker, ed., *The Work of the Spirit: Pneumatology and Pentecostalism*. Grand Rapids, Mich.: Eerdmans, 147–65.

Roberts, Oral. 2004. "Expect a Miracle: My Life and Ministry." In William K. Kay and Anne E. Dyer, eds., *Pentecostal and Charismatic Studies: A Reader*. London: SCM, 77–83.

Robertson, Pat. 1986. *Shout It from the Housetops*. Virginia Beach: CBN.

Shermer, Michael. 2003. *How We Believe: Science, Skepticism, and the Search for God*, 2nd ed. New York: Holt.

Wacker, Grant. 2006. "Early Pentecostals and the Study of Popular Religious Movements in Modern America." In Michael Welker, ed., *The Work of the Spirit: Pneumatology and Pentecostalism*. Grand Rapids, Mich.: Eerdmans, 126–46.

Welker, Michael, ed. 2006. *The Work of the Spirit: Pneumatology and Pentecostalism.* Grand Rapids, Mich.: Eerdmans.

Wessels, G. Francois. 1997. "Charismatic Christian Congregations and Social Justice— A South African Perspective." *Missionalia* 25/3: 360–74 [www.geocities.com/missionalia/wessels.htm].

Wilson, Edward O. 2004. *On Human Nature.* Cambridge, Mass.: Harvard University Press.

Witham, Larry. 2005. *The Measure of God: History's Greatest Minds Wrestle with Reconciling Science and Religion.* San Francisco: HarperCollins.

Work, Telford. 2007. *Ain't Too Proud to Beg: Living through the Lord's Prayer.* Grand Rapids, Mich.: Eerdmans.

———. 2008. "Pneumatological Relations and Christian Disunity in Theology-Science Dialogue." *Zygon: The Journal of Religion and Science* 43: 897–908.

Wright, N. T. 2003. *The Resurrection of the Son of God.* Minneapolis: Fortress.

Yong, Amos. 2005. *The Spirit Poured Out on All Flesh: Pentecostalism and the Possibility of Global Theology.* Grand Rapids, Mich.: Baker Academic.

## Recommended Reading

Barbour, Ian G. 2000. *When Science Meets Religion.* New York: HarperCollins.

Falk, Darrel R. 2004. *Coming to Peace with Science: Bridging the Worlds Between Faith and Biology.* Downers Grove, Ill.: InterVarsity.

Giberson, Karl. 2008. *Saving Darwin: How to Be a Christian and Believe in Evolution.* San Francisco: Harper.

Giberson, Karl, and Mariano Artigas. 2007. *Oracles of Science: Celebrity Scientists versus God and Religion.* New York: Oxford.

McDonnell, Kilian. 2003. *The Other Hand of God: The Holy Spirit as the Universal Touch and Goal.* Collegeville: Michael Glazer.

Newbigin, Lesslie. 1989. *The Gospel in a Pluralist Society.* Grand Rapids, Mich.: Eerdmans.

Pinnock, Clark. 1996. *Flame of Love: A Theology of the Holy Spirit.* Downers Grove, Ill.: InterVarsity Press.

Polkinghorne, John C. 1998. *Science and Theology: An Introduction.* Minneapolis: Fortress.

Stenmark, Mikael. 2004. *How to Relate Science and Religion: A Multidimensional Model.* Grand Rapids, Mich.: Eerdmans.

Witham, Larry. 2005. *The Measure of God: History's Greatest Minds Wrestle with Reconciling Science and Religion.* San Francisco: HarperCollins.

## 2    Is There Room for Surprise in the Natural World? Naturalism, the Supernatural, and Pentecostal Spirituality

*James K. A. Smith*

> *It would seem like the world of science—governed by laws, prediction, and uniformity—leaves little room for the "signs and wonders" of the Spirit who would surprise us. This is particularly true if science requires a commitment to "naturalism"—a worldview which affirms that "nature is all there is." In other words, it would seem like science and pentecostalism are mutually exclusive, exhibiting two different and conflicting worldviews. In this chapter we will grapple with this tension, first by clarifying just where the tension lies through a survey of various naturalisms and their relationship to the project of science. We'll conclude by considering the unique ontology (philosophy of reality) that is embedded in pentecostal spirituality and explain why this is not in conflict with science, though it is in conflict with naturalism.*

### Miracles in the Laboratory? Physics at the Altar?

As a way to open up our question, consider a sort of case study. Picture a student, let's call her Allison, who has recently enrolled in the premed program at the state university. Ever since she was a young girl she has dreamed of being a medical missionary—showing the love of God to the poor and oppressed in forgotten corners of the world precisely by bringing the healing and restoration that is possible through medical treatment and preventative health care. Since a deeply transformative youth retreat in her sophomore year of high school, Allison has clung to Jesus' announcement of the "good news" in Nazareth as her own vocational motto:

> The Spirit of the Lord is on me,
> because he has anointed me
> to preach good news to the poor.
> He has sent me to proclaim freedom for the prisoners
> and recovery of sight for the blind,
> to release the oppressed,
> to proclaim the year of the Lord's favor. (Luke 4:18–19)

As a "Spirit-filled" Christian, Allison believes—yea, knows—that sometimes God brings about such healing in miraculous, surprising ways. But she understands that God also brings healing through the wisdom of medical care and therapeutic practice. Even as a pentecostal, she doesn't experience any tension between these: no sense of either/or. Rather, she is convinced that God works both "naturally" and "supernaturally"—that the Spirit's healing power can be channeled through the hands of both the surgeon and the evangelist. And so, motivated by a desire to embody the Good News, Allison is pursuing a medical education as a way to continue Jesus' mission of bringing the gospel to the nations through the work of healing and restoration.

But now, halfway through her first semester of biology, she has found that her professors don't exactly feel the same way. For them it *is* an either/or scenario: either the rigorous "knowledge" of science or the superstition and "magic" of pentecostal spirituality. Her professor seems fixated on the issue, perhaps because as a Yankee professor at a southern state university he thinks it his special vocation to debunk his "hillbilly" students of their quaint Christian superstitions. So he repeatedly emphasizes that modern medicine is based on the cold, hard reality of modern science, which has no room for any sort of transcendent God, let alone a Holy Spirit who would "mess around with" the natural order—the "way things are," as he so often puts it. Rather, he persistently hammers the claim that the material (or "natural") world is "all there is"—that all biological and physical realities must be explained in terms of natural mechanisms. In short, if medicine is to be rooted in science, then it must also accept the first article of scientific orthodoxy: naturalism. "Before any doctor takes the Hippocratic oath," the professor once proclaimed, "he must first subscribe to the creed of naturalism."

So it would seem that Allison is faced with a choice between what appear to be mutually exclusive options: the price of admission to medicine is to subscribe to the religion of naturalism—the very antithesis of her charismatic sense that the Spirit is living and active in bodies and minds today. Science, she's been told, requires the assumption that nature is "all there is"; in short, the one thing that science can't tolerate is *super*naturalism. In short, it would seem like the notion of a pentecostal scientist is a contradiction in terms.

Is it possible to be a pentecostal and a scientist? Many people from both sides would be quick to answer no—and a pentecostal student embarking on study in biology or physics or chemistry likely feels this tension and hears admonitions from both sides. On the one hand, naturalistic scientists who assume that the material world is the sum total of reality would see pente-costal talk of the Spirit and supernatural miracles as gobbledygook, a super-stitious hangover from pre-Enlightenment days gone by. On the other hand, many pentecostal and charismatic Christians might be equally suspicious of "secular" science, which denies the existence of God and assumes that ma-terial reality is all there is. Indeed, Allison probably had more than one char-ismatic pastor or friend discourage her from stepping into the tainted (and tainting) halls of science at a state university. Indeed, even students at pente-costal or charismatic universities might experience the same tension.

Pentecostalism and science seem like two radically different, even bitterly opposed, worldviews. Both purport to tell very different stories about the world and the nature of reality. On the one hand, the steady progress of the natural sciences has explained all sorts of phenomena that were previously "explained" by appeals to demons and spirits, even sprites and fairies. While we might now appreciate the fiction of a fantastic, magical world like *Lord of the Rings,* our forebears imagined that such was the *real* world. But the irrup-tion of various Enlightenments (French, German, English, Scottish) in the sixteenth to eighteenth centuries, along with the exponential growth of sci-ence since then, led to what is often described as the "disenchantment of the world." The fantastic, animated world of the premodern imagination was re-duced to the cold, mechanical, mathematical, and predictable world of Bacon, Descartes, and Newton. Empirical observation of consistent regularities gave rise to science's abilities to disclose the "laws" of nature. And this natural le-gal code, as it were, constitutes a kind of tyranny that would tolerate no excep-tions or breaches. The implications of this were quickly made explicit: if there were no exceptions to the stern regularity of natural "laws," then that meant there could be no such thing as miracles, which—pretty much by definition—constituted violations of the laws of nature (Hume 1975). The universe was taken to be a closed system, immune to any interventions or interruptions by any meddling deity.[1] Sealed off as an autonomous and independent machine, the material universe was understood to be a self-sufficient system that ran on its own steam, according to its own rules, without any interference from something (or Someone) outside of or beyond it. In other words, there was no room for any supernatural events—no room for God to intervene and act within the world. The world-picture bequeathed to us by modernity and science was a world inhospitable to a pentecostal worldview that sees the Spirit of the living God continually present and active in the world.

And yet, right in the heart of modernity's triumph, in the heady days of confidence and progress at the turn of the century and before the ghastly horrors of the coming world wars (which harnessed scientific power for ghoulish ends), pentecostal revivals began to break out around the world. As the modern scientific world-picture became increasingly dominant and began to make itself felt in an explosion of technology, there was at the same time a revival of a Christianity that was open to and expected the miraculous and the supernatural. But pentecostals weren't flocking to the labs, and scientists weren't exactly making the pilgrimage to Azusa Street. Rather, the two functioned as parallel universes. The proximity and growth of both generated a growing tension that Allison experienced at a sort of microcosmic level in her biology classroom.

In this chapter I want to first *clarify* this tension. In particular, I will argue that the tension and apparent conflict is not between pentecostalism and science per se, but rather between pentecostalism and *naturalism*. In other words, "science" is not a worldview. Rather, science is a set of practices for empirically investigating and explaining natural phenomena. As such, it is not itself a worldview, but most often it is allied with the worldview of naturalism. My goal is to distinguish between science and naturalism in order to clarify just where the tension lies for pentecostalism. I will then argue that the practice of the natural sciences does not require the adoption of naturalism; in other words, there is nothing about the nature of scientific practice which requires the metaphysical assumption that nature is "all there is."[2] Thus, there is no inherent conflict between pentecostalism and science, though there is an essential tension between pentecostalism and naturalism. In order to get there, we first need to understand what is meant by "science" and "naturalism."

## Defining Science, Defining the Tension

Allison's professor has suggested that it is *science* that is antithetical to Christian faith, and even more so to charismatic and pentecostal spirituality, which claims that the Spirit continues to regularly surprise by speaking, healing, and revealing. Science, he has told her, has no room for "signs and wonders."

But what is the professor assuming about "science" when he makes such a claim? What is it about science that should rule out the miraculous? Just what is "science?" And is it science that is the problem here? Or is the professor smuggling some other assumptions *into* science? If so, what are those assumptions? Are they really "scientific?" Is he confusing "science" with something else? In other words, is he collapsing two different things into one amalgamated thing called "science?" To sort through these questions, we need to get some working definitions on the table.

First, how should we define "science?" Too often the term is left as a sort of black box into which all sorts of ideas and assumptions are poured without really defining and clarifying the term. So the term "science" is invoked in such a way that everyone thinks they know what it means, and yet rarely is it carefully defined. It's easy enough to think of examples of science or sciences: we know that physics and chemistry and biology are "sciences," but we also assume that philosophy, history, and literature are not. (Psychology, sociology, and political science are on the boundary for many.) We can also recognize "science" when we see it: when we walk through a laboratory with beakers and microscopes, or when we are in an observatory with a mammoth telescope. But what is it that makes us identify these examples and environments with "science?" Two features can be identified.

First, science is a *cultural* institution. "Science"[3] is not a naturally occurring entity like igneous rocks or sea horses; that is, science is not something that either emerges from the swamp or falls from the sky apart from human making. Rather, science is a network of material practices, constructed environments (including laboratories, instrumentation, etc.), traditions of apprenticeship, learned rituals, and so forth. While it is concerned with the study of "nature," science is not itself "natural"; it is a product of culture. It has a *history,* including the social history of experimentation, the politics of the Royal Society, the material dynamics of apprenticeship, the economics of instrumentation and technological developments, and the cultural embeddedness of medicine. Robert Brandom articulates the nature/culture distinction as the distinction between things that have *natures* and things that have *histories.* While the stuff of physics has a "nature," physics as a discipline of scientific study has a history. And in fact, "even concepts such as *electron* and *aromatic compound* are the sort of thing that has a history" (2000: 26–27). So the sciences are cultural products; indeed, the very distinction between nature and culture is itself a cultural formation. The encounter between theology and science is not equivalent to an encounter between theology and *nature.* As Joseph Rouse comments,

> Scientific practices are often construed as apart from any surrounding culture, and even free from culture, but such construals are not adequate to the richness and complexity of scientific work. Recognizing the intimate entanglement of the sciences with other practices does not diminish or blur their significance but instead acknowledges their pervasiveness throughout the world. (2002: 166)

This is not a debunking project; that is, I'm not out to point out that science is a cultural institution in order to dismiss it, nor do I think that this is license to ignore it. Rather, the point is to *situate* science *as* a cultural institution in order to clarify and understand what could be at stake in the professor's claim.

Second, as a cultural institution, science is a set of practices (and related instruments) nurtured by traditions and communities of enquiry in order to foster the *empirical* study of nature through observation and experimentation. It is concerned with understanding, explaining, and predicting the operations of nature—from volcanic activity to heart murmurs—often (but not always) with a view to improving the human situation vis-à-vis nature. "Science," then, is a constellation of practices and institutions that is especially attentive to nature, that is interested in describing and perhaps even explaining nature, and that exposes itself to nature's push-back through the rigor and discipline of experimentation and observation. These practices often yield the fruit of predictive capacity because nature exhibits a kind of regularity and consistency that is law-like. To pick a cliché example, science can "predict" that the sun will rise tomorrow precisely because it has observed the constant regularity of the earth's rotation and has even "explained" it in such a way that we can confidently predict the breaking of a new dawn tomorrow. We can create pharmaceuticals to combat depression on the basis of observations, over time, of how certain chemical processes exhibit certain patterns even when malfunctioning.

So science is a cultural institution constituted by practices of empirical observation that are attentive to the regularities of nature, with a view to understanding, explaining, and predicting the operations of "nature" (where "nature" might include the macro-operations of climate or the microscopic operations of a cell). The question, then, is whether such an institution and set of practices is somehow inherently in conflict with a pentecostal worldview, which affirms not only that a transcendent God created the world, but that the Spirit of God remains living and active within the "natural" world.

Why should we think science and pentecostalism are in conflict? Two reasons are commonly given. One argument—let's call it the "regularity thesis"—argues that pentecostal claims to miracles would constitute exceptions to the "regularity" that we observe in the so-called laws of nature. In other words, science's careful, attentive observation of the world has unveiled the law-like regularity of nature with such vivacity, and has harnessed this regularity with such successful predictions, that we must conclude that there can be no exceptions to the rules. That is, there can't be any miracles. And if there are no miracles, then there is no healing, no divine revelation, no tongues of fire, no resurrections from the dead. In short, no "signs and wonders." This was basically the argument of David Hume already in the eighteenth century, though he was targeting "historical" miracles like Jesus' resurrection, not contemporary miracles such as those claimed by charismatic Christians.[4]

A second argument—we'll call it the "naturalist thesis"—argues that insofar as science necessarily assumes naturalism as its basis, pentecostal supernaturalism is ruled out of court. In other words, according to the naturalist thesis, science both assumes and shows us that the natural world is "all there is"; therefore, there can be no supernatural Spirit that is operative in the world.

I'm going to address these concerns in reverse order. First, we'll consider just what traffics under the banner of "naturalism" in order to evaluate the cogency of the naturalist thesis's claim that pentecostalism and science are antithetical. Then, in the final section, I will evaluate the regularity thesis regarding the "laws" of nature from a pentecostal perspective.

## Naturalism, Science, and Religion

The second claim—which is the sort of claim made by Allison's biology professor—is based on the assumption that science necessarily assumes naturalism. But what is meant by "naturalism"? Despite wide agreement by scientists and philosophers that "we are all naturalists now," it is surprisingly difficult to find a clear articulation of just what defines naturalism. It might be better to instead speak of naturalism*s* in the plural. As a baseline, Goetz and Taliaferro define naturalism as "the philosophy that *everything that exists is a part of nature and that there is no reality beyond or outside of nature*" (2008: 6, emphasis original). However, such a definition is only helpful if one defines "nature." For instance, it could be the case that immaterial spirits such as angels are taken to be "natural"—as a normal, given part of the created universe. Or one might have a picture of nature that includes various levels or layers of phenomena. So this definition is only helpful if we further consider the "nature of nature" (Goetz and Taliaferro 2008: 6). A survey of the options would note various shades or kinds of naturalism.

- *Reductionistic* naturalism asserts that all that exists is material or physical; or, conversely, nothing that is immaterial exists. This is sometimes described as "nothing buttery" naturalism because it asserts the existence of *nothing but* the material physical universe. There is no nonphysical something-other in the universe. As such, reductionistic naturalism amounts to a *materialism* or a *physicalism* and claims that all phenomena—including human behavior and culture—can ultimately be explained by physical or chemical properties and systems. Complex human behavior, including cultural phenomena like religion, are attributed to biological processes, which are themselves reduced to chemical and physical processes (e.g., Dennett 2006). Thus such physicalism is also a *reductionism*. This is the most radical form of disenchantment of the world: the physicalist not only has no room for a transcendent God, but s/he also has no room for a "soul" or even a "mind." The "self"—as a free, rational, decision-making agent—is a sort of fiction conjured by systems of neurons and chemical processes. Thus Goetz and Taliaferro (2008: 7) describe reductionistic naturalism as "strict" naturalism; whereas others, like Plantinga, describe it as "metaphysical" naturalism because it involves a metaphysical or ontological claim that the physical universe is "all there is."

- *Nonreductionistic* naturalism is a modified version that is not quite as "strict"; thus, Goetz and Taliaferro (2008: 8) describe it as "broad" naturalism. This view shares strict naturalism's rejection of any transcendent or supernatural phenomena, but within the natural world it makes room for more complex phenomena that cannot be simply reduced to physical and chemical processes. In other words, nonreductionistic, or "broad" naturalism is still very much a naturalism, but it claims that included in the furniture of the natural universe, as it were, are things that cannot be adequately explained by mere physical processes. For instance, the nonreductionistic naturalist would suggest that "mind" or "the self" is a unique, distinct reality that *emerges from* physical and chemical processes but cannot be adequately explained by them. So the "natural" world, for the broad naturalist, has more layers or complexity than it does for the strict naturalist. However, it remains a *metaphysical* naturalism because it still asserts that "there aren't any supernatural beings" (Plantinga 2002: 1).

Despite some differences, what unites both "strict" and "broad" naturalism (or reductionistic and nonreductionistic naturalism) is a common rejection of "supernaturalism," by which is meant both the metaphysical claim that there are nonphysical entities and the claim that any supernatural natural entity could intervene or interrupt the material, physical universe. Thus both strict and broad naturalism share in common an *anti-supernaturalism*. In this respect, they should be distinguished from a third kind of naturalism:

- *Methodological* naturalism is sometimes distinguished from the two metaphysical naturalisms just considered. Methodological naturalism is agnostic with respect to metaphysical claims about what constitutes the furniture of the universe; instead, methodological naturalism is a pragmatic, working assumption in scientific practice that acts *as if* the universe were a closed, autonomous system. In other words, methodological naturalism works with the expectation that things will basically continue to operate in the future as they have in the past, *as if* the world were "merely" natural, governed only by natural laws that dictate uniformity and regularity. So metaphysically speaking I might be a *super*-naturalist— that is, I might assert that beings exist which are *not* physical or "natural"—and yet as a scientist working in the lab I might approach the material universe *as if* it were merely natural. If I am trying to reproduce experiments and make predictions about natural processes, my experiments are not going to get very far if I keep expecting miraculous interruptions of the "normal" order of things—even if I might think such exceptions and interruptions are *possible*. Or if I'm looking for the causes of an illness or disease, as a methodological naturalist I will confine my exploration to processes and effects that can be empirically observed; I will abstain from attributing such illnesses to supernatural or demonic factors. So though I am a *metaphysical* supernaturalist, I operate as a *methodological* naturalist for the sake of experimentation and observation. If metaphysical naturalism represents a radical disenchantment of the world, we might say that methodological naturalism represents a minimal disenchantment of the world.

Now, Allison's biology professor argued that pentecostalism is antithetical to science because science operates on the basis of naturalism. From what he said, we can see that he meant some form of *metaphysical* naturalism, and likely *strict* naturalism. So we need to ask: Is pentecostalism antithetical to naturalism? It seems clear to me that insofar as a pentecostal worldview assumes a trinitarian God, and particularly the continued active presence of the (nonphysical!) Spirit of God in the natural world, that pentecostalism is antithetical to metaphysical naturalism, whether strict or broad.[5]

However, we need to keep in mind that this was not Allison's opening concern. Her question was not whether pentecostalism was antithetical to naturalism, but whether it was in conflict with *science*. This is a crucial distinction, and making the distinction allows us to assert that, although pentecostalism is in conflict with metaphysical naturalism, this does not entail that pentecostalism is in conflict with science. The question is whether science *necessarily* assumes *metaphysical* naturalism. The biology professor's claim that science is inherently naturalistic is not in itself a scientific claim. That is, the metaphysical claim that nature is "all there is" is not required by science, nor does it issue from scientific findings. That it is not required by science is clear from the history of science, in which many of the most important pioneers in empirical research simply did not hold to metaphysical naturalism. On the contrary, their experimental interest in the natural order was underwritten by their belief in a Creator and sustainer of the universe (see, e.g., Hunter 2007: 13–34). They believed that a nonmaterial, supernatural being existed, and far from compromising their investigations of the natural world, it spurred them on. So metaphysical affirmation of nonmaterial beings is not necessarily antithetical to science.

Furthermore, metaphysical naturalism—despite how it is often presented—is not itself a scientific finding or conclusion. It is a *pre*-scientific claim. In fact, one could argue that it is a *quasi*-theological claim—a fundamental commitment to a particular story about reality made on the basis of faith. Thus naturalism is not a scientific finding or theory but is more on the order of a worldview—a faith-story about the world.[6] Thus naturalism—despite the professor's claim—is not itself scientific; it is more akin to *religion*.

This is a point conceded by naturalists themselves. For instance, John Searle remarks, "There is a sense in which materialism is the religion of our time, at least among most of the professional experts in the fields of philosophy, psychology, cognitive science, and other disciplines that study the mind. Like more traditional religions, it is accepted without question and it provides the framework within which other questions can be posed, addressed, and answered" (2004: 48). In a similar way, Jerry Fodor is happy to describe his naturalist stance as a kind of "scientism" (cited in Goetz and Taliaferro 2008: 14), and Douglas Hofstadter (1980: 434) owns up to the fact that "others, like me, find in reductionism the ultimate religion."

So the professor's dogmatism regarding naturalism is actually religious and theological in character—albeit it is a naturalistic religion and theology. This means that the status of his claims for naturalism is not underwritten by empirical data but is rather rooted in faith—just like Allison's commitment to a pentecostal worldview. So in fact, Allison and the professor are on level ground; they just adhere to two different faiths. Despite the professor's claims about pentecostal "superstition" and "hocus-pocus," in fact, his own naturalism remains a kind of faith. Pentecostalism cannot be ruled as inherently antithetical to science just because it is religion; if that were the case, naturalism would also be antithetical to science! The upshot of this is that the practice of science as careful empirical observation of the material world does not require that one subscribe to the *religion* of naturalism. Therefore, there is no inherent conflict between pentecostalism and science.[7]

## Regularity and Law: The Spirit's Faithfulness and the Spirit's Surprises

Let's turn, then, to the regularity thesis—the claim that science precludes the "signs and wonders" claimed by pentecostal experience because such miraculous events would violate the regularity of natural law, which is the backbone of scientific prediction and success. If we can't count on the regularity and uniformity of natural processes, the "regularist" contends, then everything is up for grabs: what might have been a cause or factor in one experiment can't be counted on or replicated in another experiment. If the universe were open to surprise—to interventions by the Spirit into the regular order—then we could never make successful empirical predictions on the basis of repeated observation. While apples usually fall to the earth when released time and time again, if the universe were open to irregularities, then we could never really count on the apple falling. There might be instances of intervention where such regular occurrences are interrupted. If effects could be caused by all kinds of different, arbitrary actions by God or other spirits, then we could never scientifically come to any conclusions about regular causes. For instance, if on the basis of observation it seems that certain kinds of depression are regularly caused by disordered neural receptors, then we can begin to draw conclusions from the data and begin to work on pharmaceuticals that will address this problem. But if we think that the universe is "open" to other (supernatural) influences, then we could never know how or when those supernatural causes would be the cause in any particular instance. The success of science is predicated on the regularity of natural law, which in turn requires a "closed" universe that exhibits law-like regularity. No regularity, no science. But from a pentecostal perspective that means no *ir*regularities, no miracles—and thus no meaningful charismatic experience. Or to put it otherwise, it would seem that the price of admission to science for the pentecostal would be relinquishing any claims to the miraculous—to irregular surprises of the Spirit.

To do justice to this thesis, let me point out two issues related to the regularist thesis. First, we can now appreciate just what is at stake in the notion of methodological naturalism. The Christian or pentecostal scientist who is a methodological naturalist, practically speaking, may be open to the notion of supernatural agents functioning as causes within the natural world. However, as a scientist, the methodological naturalist has taken a kind of Nazirite vow and has voluntarily sworn off any appeal to supernatural causation for *scientific* explanations of natural phenomena.[8] She has not ruled out such causation or declared it impossible (contra Hume) but has merely suspended judgment and, in the laboratory, has decided to act *as if* the universe were a closed system of law-like regularity. This is because such abstinence from appealing to divine causation has a strong track record of yielding incredibly helpful and productive results. When metaphysical supernaturalists adopt a *methodological* naturalism, they are seeking to honor some of the force of the regularity thesis.

Second, while I would certainly argue that affirmation of miraculous "surprises" of the Spirit is an absolutely central and nonnegotiable aspect of a pentecostal worldview, I also think it is not only permissible but necessary for pentecostals to appreciate that the Spirit is at work not only in the fantastic and miraculous but also in the mundane and regular. That is, I think that pentecostals would do well to appreciate the force of the "minimal" or low-grade disenchantment that is associated with methodological naturalism. When I go to the doctor, I'd much rather see one using a scientific approach that has a reliable sense of how arteries function and how the lungs operate than a shaman using whale's teeth to summon healthy spirits to move my blood. And when I board the plane, I count on engineers who have made their calculations based on evidence-based approaches to air pressure and lift, rather than a group of seers counting on invisible magical beings to hold up the plane. So too, if Allison is going to become a pentecostal physician, often and for the most part, she will do well to make diagnoses and prognoses on the basis of what she knows of biological systems and pathological patterns. This need not be to the exclusion of prayer for "surprises," but neither is hope and faith in divine healing antithetical to the pursuit of healing by scientific means.

Such a conclusion is not a "watering down" of pentecostal commitments. In fact, this too can be explained in terms of a pentecostal pneumatology, or doctrine of the Holy Spirit. Methodological naturalism works with the expectation that things will basically continue to operate in the future as they have in the past—that the physical, chemical, and biological systems of the cosmos have a kind of regularity and uniformity. And in daily practice, we are all methodological naturalists of a sort. While it is true that the rotation of the earth depends upon the unique activity of God at all times (Colossians 1:17), we all generally expect the sun to rise tomorrow like clockwork, as if it weren't even a question. Even if we confess a radical sense of the Spirit's presence in creation, this presence manifests itself for the most part in fairly predictable ways that are themselves indications of God's character and faithfulness (Lamentations 3:22–24). So the affirmation of the Spirit's dynamic presence in creation is not opposed to recognizing that for the most part, this presence is manifested by God's steady, sustaining care of the universe along the lines of what seem like "laws." And it would really be spurning God's faithful, steady presence not to recognize this. A pentecostal worldview does not require rejecting a sense of a steady, faithful presence of the Spirit in creation—even if it does remain open to the ways in which God might surprise us (ontological surprises!).

There is nothing inconsistent about working from a pentecostal worldview and affirming a minimal disenchantment or a kind of methodological naturalism. This is important to emphasize precisely because some pentecostals have thought that the confession of God's dynamic, fantastic, and miraculous work in creation required ignoring this steady, law-like manifestation of the Spirit's presence in the world. While a pentecostal worldview affirms both the dynamic presence of the Spirit in creation and a non-dualistic emphasis on bodily healing, some pentecostal traditions try to be more spiritual than the Spirit by rejecting the Spirit's more mundane operations that are discerned by medical science. It is precisely this hyper-supernaturalism that makes me think that a healthy dose of minimal disenchantment and methodological naturalism might actually be a *better* way to recognize *all* the ways that the Spirit is dynamically present in creation.

That said, let me close by nuancing these matters just a bit and suggesting that the genius of a pentecostal ontology (or understanding of reality) might push us to reject the dominant metaphor of methodological naturalism, namely, the metaphor of "closure," along with the attendant notion of "intervention." What defines methodological naturalism is a commitment to working *as if* the universe is closed to outside, or supernatural, influences or causes. In other words, the methodological naturalist acts *as if* the universe is not open to surprise. This yields a picture of the cosmos as a kind of autonomous, enclosed, self-sufficient system. Even metaphysical supernaturalists buy into this picture and its metaphor by arguing that the universe is open to divine "intervention" and interruption. But in such a picture, God and the world are discrete entities, leaving the world "naturally" devoid of God's action and presence: God only "acts" when he intervenes in this system, which otherwise hums along just fine without him. The resulting picture is an implicit deism.

I want to suggest that a refined pentecostal understanding of science might also eschew even the language of a universe "open" to divine action because such language communicates a sense that apart from divine *intervention,* the universe is not animated by the Spirit of God. It assumes a picture of the world, and of the God/world relation, that actually cedes an *autonomy* to the natural order that is akin to deism. I call this the "discretion" model because it carves out "the world" as a discrete, autonomous realm that God then has to "enter"—a functionally closed system that God comes to "interrupt" or in which God "intervenes." This "discretion" model—the sense that God and the world are "discrete"—is shared by both the naturalists who reject such interventions and the supernaturalists who claim such interventions. Both basically see "nature" as an autonomous system; what they disagree about is whether God can/does intervene into this discrete, closed system.

But should we think of the cosmos ("nature") as a discrete, closed, autonomous system, as both naturalists and supernaturalists assume? I think such an assumption rests on a problematic theology of creation. In particular, it rests on a theology of creation that is devoid of any sense of the essential, constitutive, dynamic presence of God the Spirit *in* creation (Yong 2006). I suggest that embedded in a pentecostal social imaginary is an understanding of the God/world relation that eschews the "discretion" model and refuses to grant "nature" the autonomy of a closed system. Rather, the Spirit is always already present at and in creation. The Spirit's presence is not a postlapsarian or soteriological[9] "visiting" of a creation that is otherwise without God; rather, the Spirit is always already dynamically active in the cosmos/world/nature. God doesn't have to "enter" nature as a visitor and an alien; God is always already present in the world. Thus creation is *primed* for the Spirit's action.

This pentecostal ontology can allow us to account both for regularity and for the miraculous. The law-like uniformity of the cosmos that the methodological naturalist seeks to honor is better described as the Spirit's faithful regularity. The constancy of physical, chemical, and biological systems need not be ascribed to any kind of "closure," but rather it can be described as the mundane, faithful presence of the Spirit by which the Son holds together the universe (Colossians 1:17). But this picture also allows us to recognize the possibility of the "miraculous," not as interruptions of the "natural" order or as "interventions" into an otherwise closed universe, but rather as especially intense ways in which the Spirit is active and present within nature. Because nature is always already inhabited by the Spirit, it is also primed for (not merely "open to") special or unique singularities; these will not be "anti-nature," because nature is not a discrete, autonomous entity. Rather, we can think of these "special" miraculous manifestations of the Spirit's presence in creation as more *intense* instances of the Spirit in creation—or as "sped-up" modes of the Spirit's more "regular" presences (C. S. Lewis 1947). Augustine describes them as "extraordinary" actions that are meant to refocus our attention on the "miraculous" nature of the ordinary. A "miracle" is not an event that breaks any so-called laws of nature, since nature does not have such a reified character. A miracle is a manifestation of the Spirit's presence that is "out of the ordinary," but even the ordinary is a manifestation of the Spirit's presence. Augustine enjoins us to see nature *as* miracle and thereby to adopt a more robust theology of creation that yields a more elastic concept of "nature" (Gousmett 1988).

In summary, Allison need not experience any inherent conflict between her pentecostal worldview and the task and vocation of science. Granted, because of a dominance of the worldview of naturalism in the sciences, she will at times experience tensions—but these are tensions between two worldviews, not between science and religion per se. Her belief in the steady, faithful presence of the Spirit's operation in nature will prompt her to be attentive to the regularities that are so often exhibited and that, when carefully observed and explored, can yield important scientific fruit. But she can also remain open to the Spirit's extraordinary manifestations of his presence. The same Spirit is found in the lab and at the altar.

## Notes

1.  In a way, deism persisted for a time as a sort of hangover: God didn't have any role to play in the "day-to-day operations," so to speak, but was kept around as the one who provided the "venture capital" for the whole project of "nature." In a way, the Intelligent Design movement represents a certain revival of deism, it seems to me.

2.  I am extending Alvin Plantinga's Reformed critique of naturalism (first broached in Plantinga 1993 and 2002, and more fully developed in his Stanton Lectures) to more specifically pentecostal concerns.

3.  It's even tendentious to keep talking about "science" as if it were some monolithic reality. Just what makes neuroscience, physics, and ecology part of the same thing, "science?" We ought, instead, to get into the habit of talking about the sciences.

4.  While all Christians have something at stake in defending miracles (insofar as Christian faith stands or falls with the bodily resurrection of Jesus), for pentecostal and charismatic Christians the issue of miracles is not merely historical. Pentecostal/charismatic spirituality is defined by an expectancy that the Spirit continues to do signs and wonders. Thus pentecostals have even more at stake in the miraculous—which also means that they experience even more tension with modern "science."

5.  Whether pentecostalism is antithetical to *methodological* naturalism is a more complicated issue, to which we will turn in the next section. Suffice it to say here that insofar as methodological naturalism is metaphysically agnostic, it does not seem to be essentially in conflict with a pentecostal worldview.

6. It might be helpful to also distinguish naturalism from evolution. I take (metaphysical) naturalism to be, in essence, a worldview; whereas evolution is a scientific theory rooted in scientific findings and data. Just as I'm arguing that pentecostalism is antithetical to naturalism but not science, so I would argue that there is no inherent conflict between pentecostalism and evolution. In other words, it is important to distinguish naturalism and evolution just as it is important to distinguish naturalism from "science" per se.

7. This doesn't mean, of course, that there will not be conflicts and skirmishes. These will result from at least two things. First, some conflicts arise because what parades itself as neutral, objective science is actually loaded with naturalistic assumptions that are not themselves scientifically warranted. But second, there will sometimes be conflicts because pentecostals may cling to beliefs that are unsustainable in the face of careful attention to "nature"—to the shape of creation. However, this is not the same as saying that pentecostalism must accommodate itself to "what science tells us."

8. I suggest that this is like a Nazirite vow because the Nazirite abstains not from things that are inherently bad but rather from several specific things for a time (see Numbers 6:1–21).

9. That is, a "visitation" of the Spirit after the fall and for the purposes of salvation.

## References

Brandom, Robert. 2000. *Articulating Reasons: An Introduction to Inferentialism*. Cambridge, Mass.: Harvard University Press.

Dennett, Daniel. 2006. *Breaking the Spell: Religion as a Natural Phenomenon*. New York: Viking.

Goetz, Stewart, and Charles Taliaferro. 2008. *Naturalism*. Grand Rapids, Mich.: Eerdmans.

Gousmett, Chris. 1988. "Creation Order and Miracle According to Augustine." *Evangelical Quarterly* 60: 217–40.

Hofstadter, Douglas. 1980. "Reductionism and Religion." *Behavioral and Brain Sciences* 3: 433–34.

Hume, David. 1975. "Of Miracles," Section X. *Enquiries Concerning Human Understanding and Concerning the Principles of Morals*, ed. L. A. Selby-Bigge, 3rd ed., rev. P. H. Nidditch. Oxford: Oxford University Press.

Hunter, Cornelius G. 2007. *Science's Blind Spot: The Unseen Religion of Scientific Naturalism*. Grand Rapids, Mich.: Brazos.

Lewis, C. S. 1947. *Miracles*. New York: Macmillan.

Plantinga, Alvin. 1993. *Warrant and Proper Function*. Oxford: Oxford University Press.

———. 2002. "The Evolutionary Argument against Naturalism: An Initial Statement of the Argument." In James Beilby, ed., *Naturalism Defeated? Essays on Plantinga's Evolutionary Argument Against Naturalism*. Ithaca, N.Y.: Cornell University Press, 1–14.

Rouse, Joseph. 2002. *How Scientific Practices Matter: Reclaiming Philosophical Naturalism.* Chicago: University of Chicago Press.

Searle, John. 2004. *Mind: A Brief Introduction.* Oxford: Oxford University Press.

Yong, Amos. 2006. "*Ruach,* the Primordial Waters, and the Breath of Life: Emergence Theory and the Creation Narratives in Pneumatological Perspective." In Michael Welker, ed., *The Work of the Spirit: Pneumatology and Pentecostalism.* Grand Rapids, Mich.: Eerdmans, 183–204.

## Recommended Reading

Alexander, Denis. 2001. *Rebuilding the Matrix: Science and Faith in the 21st Century.* Grand Rapids, Mich.: Zondervan.

Brown, Colin. 1984. *Miracles and the Critical Mind.* Grand Rapids, Mich.: Eerdmans, and Exeter, UK: Paternoster Press.

Cartledge, Mark J. 2006. *Encountering the Spirit: The Charismatic Tradition.* Maryknoll, N.Y.: Orbis.

Cox, Harvey Gallagher. 1995. *Fire from Heaven: The Rise of Pentecostal Spirituality and the Reshaping of Religion in the Twenty-first Century.* Reading, Mass.: Addison-Wesley.

Diemer, Johann H. 1977. *Nature and Miracle.* Toronto: Wedge Publishing Foundation.

Geisler, Norman L. 1992. *Miracles and the Modern Mind: A Defense of Biblical Miracles.* Grand Rapids, Mich.: Baker.

Geivett, R. Douglas, and Gary R. Habermas, eds. 1997. *In Defense of Miracles: A Comprehensive Case for God's Action in History.* Downers Grove, Ill.: InterVarsity Press.

Hummel, Charles E. 1986. *The Galileo Connection: Resolving Conflicts between Science and the Bible.* Downers Grove, Ill.: InterVarsity Press.

Lewis, C. S. 1970. *God in the Dock: Essays on Theology and Ethics.* Grand Rapids, Mich.: Eerdmans.

Morris, Tim, and Donald N. Petcher. 2006. *Science and Grace: God's Reign in the Natural Sciences.* Wheaton, Ill.: Crossway Books.

Nichols, Terence L. 2003. *The Sacred Cosmos: Christian Faith and the Challenge of Naturalism.* Grand Rapids, Mich.: Brazos Press.

Schaaffs, Werner. 1974. *Theology, Physics, and Miracles.* Washington, D.C.: Canon Press.

# 3 How Does God Do What God Does? Pentecostal-Charismatic Perspectives on Divine Action in Dialogue with Modern Science

*Amos Yong*

*Pentecostal spirituality and piety rests on the conviction that God is present and active in the world through the Holy Spirit. Yet pentecostal claims about divine action through the Spirit are increasingly problematic in the world of modern science. Developments in modern medicine, expansion of communications technologies, and the arrival of the digital age—all combine to "disenchant" the twenty-first-century world pentecostals inhabit. This essay attempts to articulate a pentecostal theology of God's activity against the backdrop of a brief survey of Christian theologies of divine action since the scientific revolution. The author proposes a new reading of the many tongues of the day of Pentecost as anticipating the many discourses of the various scientific disciplines. Simultaneously, pentecostal views regarding the eschatological Spirit (related to the "last days") are presented as a language of faith that may parallel and even contribute to the renaissance of teleological perspectives (related to final causes) in contemporary science.*

## Introduction: Divine Action in a Postmodern World?

At the heart of the modern pentecostal experience is the second half of Luke's narrative, which some English translations have titled "The Acts of the Holy Spirit." This account tells of the Holy Spirit's empowering the disciples to take the gospel to the ends of the earth and enabling them to speak in unknown tongues, heal the sick, and accomplish other signs and wonders. The early modern pentecostal revival at Azusa Street was understood by its participants as restoring to the church these mighty acts of the Spirit. The manifestation of tongues, healings, miracles, and the other spiritual gifts distinguished pentecostal practices from those of other Christian churches and traditions. For many pentecostal believers, this palpable presence and activity of the Spirit was felt not only during congregational worship but in their daily lives. The most distinctive pentecostal testimonies rejoiced over the fact that while the devil and his minions had intended harm to their lives, the Holy Spirit had instead preserved them from the works of the evil one, provided for their material needs, healed their bodies, and saved and sanctified their souls.

Over the course of the last century, however, more and more pentecostals, especially in the Euro-American West, have entered into and embraced the world of modern science and medicine, the telecommunications age, and the digital era. Whereas Azusa Street pentecostals reveled in charismatic and other related manifestations, contemporary pentecostals who have climbed the social ladder and have gained a certain measure of cultural respectability are almost indistinguishable from other Christians in their worship and spiritual piety. Whereas early pentecostals fasted and prayed, laid hands on the sick, and rebuked and exorcised the devil who oppressed human bodies, minds, and souls, contemporary pentecostals oftentimes look first toward medicine for relief (e.g., Tylenol), rely on medical expertise (e.g., the surgeon), or seek a "naturalistic" diagnosis (e.g., one has epilepsy rather than is possessed by an evil spirit). And while pentecostals have always availed themselves of the latest developments in media technology to spread the good news, many are now also calculating that certain communicative strategies will bring in so many visitors and have thereby been accused of "marketing" the gospel. In each of these cases, premodern sensibilities seem to be gradually if not inexorably replaced by modern and postmodern habits shaped by the advances of science and technology.[1]

The common question amidst these developments is, Where is the hand of God and the power of the Holy Spirit? Is the Holy Spirit less and less in the charismata, the wondrous, and the marvelous, and more in the "still small voice" and in the mundane things of this world? Is the Holy Spirit now healing through doctors and pharmaceutical devices instead of through miraculous interventions? Is the Spirit's presence and activity manifest through "glitzy" communicative media that may or may not include sound preaching and teaching? If any or all of this is true, is there not a risk of "naturalizing" the acts of God and, in the long run, eliminating the need to talk about divine action altogether? To put the question bluntly, might scientific explanations remove any need to appeal, as pentecostals often do, to the Holy Spirit?

*How Does God Do What God Does?*　51

This essay explores these questions in two parts. First, I briefly lay out various models of divine action that have been proposed in the history of Christian thought. This will help us see that there have been questions raised by the broader Christian tradition about how God acts in the world that can help pentecostals think through the issues. Second, building on this discussion, I sketch one possible pentecostal theology of divine action in dialogue with modern science. My hypothesis is that the many tongues of Pentecost can be analogously understood to include, in our time, the many disciplinary languages across the spectrum of modern science, and that these all bear witness in their own way to the work of the Spirit, who is heralding and ushering the kingdom of God "in the last days."[2]

## Divine Action: Models Ancient and Modern

Pentecostals have not been the only Christians who have been challenged to think about how God acts in the world. In what follows, I present a number of models of divine action that have been emerged in three specific periods across the history of Christian thought. In each case, I will comment briefly on the scientific developments underlying these proposals, describe the theological theories of divine action, and identify the unresolved challenges confronting these responses.

### Classical Theology: Medieval and Reformation Views of God as "First Cause"

The rediscovery of Aristotle in the medieval period precipitated new approaches to investigating the natural world (see Lindberg 1992: chaps. 10–11, and Ferngren 2002: part 2). In contrast to the Platonic view that all changing phenomena are but manifestations of the unchanging and ultimate realm of ideal forms accessible primarily through reason,[3] the Aristotelian conviction was that the forms of things were internal to things themselves and that experiential engagement with the physical world and all its parts was the surest way to determine the way things were. It was the scholastic embrace of Aristotle that led to the emergence of the empirical method of early modern science.[4]

The Aristotelian impact on theology can be seen in Thomas Aquinas's (1224–74) "five ways" of argument for the existence of God. Each argument began with observations about the natural world and reasoned from there—drawing explicitly from Aristotelian physics and cosmology—toward the Aristotelian notion of a necessary being. For example, most pertinent for our purposes, is Thomas's argument from motion: (a) there is no movement that is purely self-caused; (b) an infinite regress of movers is self-contradictory; thus, (c) there must be a first Unmoved Mover, which is identifiable as God.[5]

Thomas insisted that even if Aristotle was right in his hypothesis about the eternity of the world, an infinite regress of cosmological causes would require an ontological first cause to explain why there was the unending sequence of causation at all (see Trundle 1999: 87–93). Hence, for Thomas, the Aristotelian notion of causation—including not only material, formal, and efficient causation but also teleological (or final) causation, which for Aristotle resides within living organisms[6]—required a First Cause.

But how does this First Cause interact with other or secondary causes? Thomas and other medieval theologians had no problem saying that God as First Cause provides the ontological grounding for (in the sense of makes possible) and/or concurs with (in the sense of allows) secondary creaturely causes. In the Aristotelian scheme of things, even inanimate objects have inherent features that constitute their secondary causal powers. Hence, divine primary causality functioned ontologically in concordance—simultaneously—with creaturely secondary causality that functioned cosmologically.[7] Things become more complex, however, when dealing with secondary causes involving sentient (living and conscious) beings, and especially free agents. At this level, the Thomistic solution was a theory of "double agency" in which every event features the full agency of both God and free creatures.[8] God's creation and sustenance of free agents allows them to act independently; paradoxically, God also acts in and through such agents in each event without violating the integrity of creaturely freedom. The result is a compatibilist (the freedom to do what one wants, which is compatible with various determining constraints) rather than libertarian (the freedom to do otherwise) notion of creaturely freedom in much of classical Christian theology.

The medieval notions of *concordance* and *double agency* have become central features of the classical theological tradition, especially once Reformation theologies adapted the idea of God as First Cause providing for, sustaining, and concurring with secondary causes.[9] A contemporary restatement of this theological vision has been provided by Vernon White (1985). Given divine concurrence with every event, White defends a robust theology of providential action such that there are no accidents in the universe. Within this overarching theological framework, evil events are those permitted by God in order to bring about a greater good that is currently incomprehensible to human minds except through the eyes of faith. But can there be "special" divine actions or interventions in this theological scheme? White suggests that such would be events that are related to God's eschatological and soteriological purposes; hence, these are special because of their place in God's ultimate purposes, not because they are a product of a different kind of divine action.

Many theologians remain unconvinced that this classical theological account of God's action in the world suffices with regard to the problem of evil or the paradox of creaturely freedom. Furthermore, there are additional questions about God's interaction with free agents, such as if and how we can talk about God's answering prayer or of God's intervening into creaturely affairs. The theology of concurrence or divine agency seems to either require that God "builds in" ahead of time God's involvement both in the prayers themselves and in God's responses to them, or leads to the conclusion that God's ontological action is a superfluous level of explanation once cosmological causes are identified and Occam's razor is applied.[10] Finally, at a more technical level, the theory of double agency seems to result in the following dilemma: either there are two sufficient causes for any event, which is contradictory or threatens the unity of any event; or, if the unity of action in any event is insisted upon, this threatens the duality of causes or of agency (see Thomas 1990).

## Modern Theology: Deism and Other Alternatives

The medieval conviction of God as First Cause underlying all cosmological or secondary causes fed into the early modern theory of God's acting uniformly in all things. Underneath this specifically theological notion were developments in the sciences regarding the uniformity of nature. The scientific revolution during the early modern period nurtured a growing awareness in the Western world that there were universal natural laws at work that ordered the movements of the world and its parts. In astronomy, the Copernican revolution regarding the heliocentrism of the solar system, Johannes Kepler's (1571–1630) three laws of planetary motion, and Isaac Newton's (1643–1727) law of universal gravitation—laws of gravitation and of motion, and notions of absolute space and time—all combined to establish the regularities of heavenly and earthly bodies.[11] Parallel to this, the mechanical philosophers, led by René Descartes (1596–1650), rejected the existence of final causes—understood in terms of goods, purposes, or ends—in nature, and argued instead that all material entities, including the bodies of sentient beings, were extensions in space and time that were subject to the laws of physics and governed by efficient causes.[12] By the nineteenth century the principle of uniformitarianism—the idea that all processes in the world occur now as they have in the past—had come to be widely accepted in such emerging disciplines as paleontology, geology, and biology (Hooykaas 1963). In the latter, Charles Darwin's theory of evolution via natural selection provided an explanatory framework for understanding species variation in a mechanical universe.

Against this backdrop, the deists suggested the watchmaker analogy: just as watches are set in motion by watchmakers, after which they operate according to their pre-established mechanisms, so also was the world begun by the God as creator, after which it and all its parts have operated according to their pre-established natural laws. With these laws in perfectly in place, events have unfolded according to the prescribed plan, with no need for God to intervene. But deism resulted in an absentee God, or at least one who was present only as an spectator rather than as interactive with the world. Contemporary developments of the deistic idea have gone in at least two directions: either a radicalizing of deism toward an impersonalistic, naturalistic, and historicist ground-of-being or source-of-creativity (Kaufman 2004), or an attempt to re-engage such an absentee deity through a theory of God as uniformly active in all things (Wiles 1986). At its best, the result is a subjectivizing of divine action: special acts of God are those events that human beings *perceive* to be indicative of ultimate meaning, value, and hope in their lives (Wiles 1997).

Unsurprisingly, many theists have resisted these notions of God that reduce divine action at best only to the singularity of the creation of the world. In response, process theists, informed by the philosophy of Alfred North White-head (1861–1947), have articulated an alternative view called process theology in which God is uniformly active in luring the world as a whole and all of its parts toward the divinely intended goal. In line with deism's resistance to any kind of interventionist deity (because of its convictions regarding the mechanical nature of the world and its view of God's creative perfection not requiring God to "fix" the world's broken parts), process theology is also wary about understanding God as acting upon the world from the "outside." Rather, God acts "within" the world as an internal lure, persuasively (rather than coercively) drawing the world forward (Barbour 2001). Whereas deism attempts to avoid the problem of evil altogether (either because an impersonal deity does not raise the theodicy question or because a mechanical universe does not define events within it in moral categories of either good or evil), process theology acknowledges the possibility and actuality of gratuitous or need-less evils, given the genuine spontaneity of all dynamic processes as well as the real freedom of all sentient creatures to ignore rather than embrace the divine lure. The potentially fatal weakness of process theology's view of divine action is that a God who is only able to act persuasively may not be able to actually bring about God's intentions for the world.

In part as a response to the (perceived) impotence of the process deity, open theists reintroduce into the equation what they consider to be neglected aspects of biblical theism (Pinnock et al. 1994). Chief among these is the notion of God as intervening in or interacting with human affairs. Open theists do not deny that God works primarily according to the natural laws that God once established and now upholds. They also agree with process theology both that there is real evil in the world and that such is related to the risk of God's creation of agents with libertarian freedom. Finally, also in line with process theism, there is a genuine openness to the future that is settled in time by the decisions of free creature; thus, God's knowledge of the future is continuously shifting as possibilities turn into actualities. The difference is that open theists generally insist that God can intervene into the causal fabric of the world at any time (even if such incursions may be rare), even to the point of suspending the laws of nature or of overriding creaturely freedom.[13] In response to the charge that such an interventionist view renders God as just one agent in the world alongside others, open theists insist that they are taking seriously the portrayal of divine action in the biblical narrative (e.g., Griffin 1997).

## Contemporary Science: God's Action in a "Gappy" World

The current discussions regarding divine action have also been complicated by the arrival of a post-Einsteinian view of the physical universe. Whereas Einstein's general and special theories of relativity have replaced Newtonian views of absolute space and time with a space-time continuum and matter-energy equivalence (see Wolfgang Vondey's essay in this volume), these formulations have been understood to apply primarily to the macro-rather than microscopic world. In the atomic and subatomic domains, however, quantum mechanical theories have been developed to account for phenomena that evade classical (Newtonian) mechanical as well as relativity (Einsteinian) theoretical explanations. For one, quantum objects display both wave (non-local) and particle (quantized) features simultaneously (the wave-particle duality), an impossibility in the Newtonian world of larger objects whereby things are either waves or particles, but not both at the same time. Furthermore, quantum systems are both probabilistic and indeterministic (the uncertainty principle), whereas Newtonian objects are deterministic. Last but not least, quantum objects separated from one another nevertheless seem to be instantaneously influential on each other—the impossibility known as the quantum entanglement—while classical mechanics prohibits such "spooky" action-at-a-distance of one object on another. In sum, in the realm of quantum mechanics, basic human perceptions about how the world works no longer seem to hold.

Nevertheless, it has been precisely the onset of quantum cosmological theories that has buoyed the scientific quest for identifying God's action in the world. A recent extended dialogue between theologians and scientists called the Divine Action Project (DAP) has attempted to articulate a model of non-interventionistic objective special divine action (NIOSDA).[14] Each of the three qualifiers is important. "Non-interventionistic" refers to the conviction that the God who created the laws of nature will not violate (intervene upon) them; "objective" means that such divine activity is a factual event, not just an epistemological interpretation of events that attributes them to God; and "special" means that there must be some events that have happened that would not have happened if God had not acted.

If deism proffered divine action as subjective and non-interventionistic, and open theism countered with divine action as objective but interventionistic, DAP participants hope to defend a view of God's action as objective and special on the one hand, yet non-interventionistic on the other. What is needed are "open spaces" in the world through which God could act without having to circumvent natural processes. Such ontological openness in the causal nexus of the world—if they existed and could be identified—would serve as venues for NIOSDA that in principle would not be overturned (as would epistemological gaps in our knowledge) through the ongoing discoveries of science. DAP participants have suggested two domains that might secure NIOSDA: quantum indeterminacy and chaos dynamical systems.

The possibility of God's action at the quantum mechanical level—quantum divine action (QDA)—is attractive since the indeterminacy postulated at this level derives essentially from the probabilistic nature of reality itself. This intrinsic unpredictability is suggestive of ontological "gaps" in the world that allow for non-interventionist divine action. In theory, God's activity at the quantum level could consist either of collapsing the wave function or influencing one of its many probabilities. Various proposals have ensued: that God acts in all quantum events; that God acts only in some; or that God has acted in all quantum events prior to the emergence of human consciousness, and only in some since then. For QDA models, then, God is the "hidden variable" at the quantum level, at least a necessary, albeit insufficient, cause of quantum events.

For physicist-theologian John Polkinghorne (1995), the unpredictability of chaotic or nonlinear dynamic systems provides a more viable model for God's activity in the world than QDA models.[15] Given the sensitivity of chaotic systems to initial conditions, and given especially the vulnerability, openness, and interrelatedness of such dissipative systems with their environments, divine action can proceed through the input of what Polkinghorne calls "active information" that either adjusts the system's initial conditions and hence shifts (sometimes dramatically) its trajectory, or constrains or tweaks the evolution of the system through interaction with other environmental systems. And because chaotic systems are drawn toward their futures by infinitely variable "strange attractors" unassociated with energy states, divine action can causally nudge them without either "intervention" (since chaotic systems are ontologically gappy) or cost (since there is no added energy required to take systems in any direction). While acknowledging that classical chaos theory is governed by deterministic equations, Polkinghorne replies that these might be "interpreted as downward emergent approximations to a more subtle and supple physical reality. They are valid only in the limiting and special cases where bits and pieces are effectively insulated from the effects of their environment" (1995: 153).

Responses to the DAP have not been optimistic.[16] If Polkinghorne's attempt to turn chaos theory from a deterministic to an indeterministic science is less than persuasive to most researchers, QDA proposals are problematic because of various theological issues related to the measurement problem: even if God were to collapse the wave function, either God would then be dependent on the probabilistic outcome of the measurement (in which case, di-

vine sovereignty would be threatened) or God would have to unilaterally determine the outcome by overriding the probability calculus (in which case,
the non-interventionist character of QDA seems undermined). But assuming
that these difficulties can be overcome does not help since it takes too long to
get the desired macroscopic effects from divine agency enacted at the level of
quantum events.

The preceding discussions reveal why some theologians have suggested
that any search for a scientifically identifiable causal nexus for divine action
is mistaken (Smedes 2004). On the one hand, identifying a causal joint might
compromise divine transcendence or creaturely autonomy, or it might compromise both. On the other hand, insisting on the observability and measur-
ability of divine action may undermine the integrity of scientific explanation
focused on empirical phenomena as well as raise challenging theological questions, since theology has generally not understood God as just one more agent
in the world alongside other actors. How then might pentecostals engage the
dialogue between science and theology on divine action?

## How Does God Act in the World? A Contemporary
## Pentecostal-Charismatic Perspective

In the remainder of this essay, I will sketch a pentecostal contribution
to a theology of divine action in dialogue with modern science. In brief, my
thesis is that the pentecostal experience of the Holy Spirit opens up to what
might be called a pneumatological theology of divine action that (a) invites
the multiple perspectives offered by the many scientific disciplines, and (b)
provides a theological viewpoint that potentially contributes to the renaissance of teleological explanation in contemporary science.

### Many Tongues, Many Sciences: Divine Action in
### Multidisciplinary Perspective

In previous work I have proposed a contemporary reading of the Pentecost narrative in Acts 2 that sees the many tongues declaring the glory of
God as a metaphor for understanding how many different linguistic and cultural perspectives can also be vehicles for declaring all truth as God's truth
(Yong 2005a: chap. 4). By extension, I have suggested (Yong 2005c) that the
many scientific disciplines present a multiplicity of discourses that also reveal
how nature declares the glory of God (Psalm 19:1). In what follows, I want to
develop this argument that is usually applied to the natural world by looking
at the pentecostal phenomenon of speaking in tongues (glossolalia). I wish to
show not only that our understanding of glossolalia can be fruitfully illuminated by the various scientific perspectives but also that our understanding of
God's action in the world need not be threatened by scientific explanations.[17]

From the standpoint of the sciences, note that tongues speaking can be analyzed at many different levels.[18] We could begin at the level of the cognitive sciences, where recent developments now allow us to observe brain functions of those engaged in glossolalic prayer (e.g., Newberg et al., 2006). Unsurprisingly, we note distinctive brain patterns as well as the activation of certain brain sites that can be compared and contrasted with what happens with people engaged in non-glossolalic but nevertheless prayerful activity (e.g., Newberg et al., 2003). From here, there are short steps from the neurosciences to the neurophysiological sciences, next to the neuropsychological sciences, and then to the psychological and psychosocial sciences. At the latter levels, research suggests that tongues speaking may be learned behavior (Samarin 1972: chap. 4), or that tongues-speakers may fit certain psychological profiles.[19] In contrast to earlier researchers that sought to identify glossolalia as pathological (and that have largely been discredited), more recent assessments indicate that tongues-speakers are no more or less abnormal than non-tongues-speakers. Rather, the former are less likely to experience depression and exhibit a less hostile personality type; there may even be therapeutic benefits to consistent glossolalic practice (Castelein 1984; Gritzmacher, Bolton, and Dana 1988).

More strictly sociological approaches to glossolalia may emphasize its functionality as a means of religious socialization (Hine 1973; Holm 1978) or draw attention to its prevalence among more socially marginalized people groups (e.g., Anderson 1979: Bradfield 1979). Parallel to this, cultural-anthropological perspectives have called attention to how glossolalia serves as a semiotic marker among communities experiencing social upheaval in the transition from a premodern to a modern world (Goodman 1972). On the other hand, recent collaborative and multidisciplinary approaches have shown that glossolalia flourishes among well-adjusted and upwardly mobile people groups as well (Cartledge 2002, 2006).

Predictably, polemicists have attempted to draw from selected scientific data to attack pentecostals personally—for example, as being typically hysterical (Gonsalvez 1982)—or to undermine pentecostal spirituality and piety as a whole (Preus 1982). Such polemics are, however, inevitably reductionistic. Explanation provided at any one level—neurobiology, psychology, or sociology, for example—is thought to completely account for the phenomenon in question. But this is an extra-scientific conclusion that is smuggled in rather than one derivable from any individual data set. It assumes either that a lower-level explanation exhaustively captures all there is to be known about what is under discussion or that the world itself is a closed system of causes and effects that excludes a religious or theological dimension.

It is questionable, however, whether science can produce such a conclusion by itself. It seems instead that any adequate explanation of religious phenomenon, including glossolalia, should pay attention also to the religious and theological explications of its practitioners. When this is factored in, a genuine encounter between science and religion would proceed in two directions. On the one hand, scientific viewpoints would complement and even enrich our religious and theological descriptions rather than threaten them; on the other hand, religious and theological perspectives would also add depth to scientific accounts by providing "thick descriptions" of the phenomenon under investigation (Yong 1997). So whereas a psychological or sociological deprivation theory would reduce tongues speaking to a single or lower-level variable, a "transcendency deprivation" (Malony and Lovekin 1985: 259) perspective would recognize each level of explanation as valid in its own way, yet seek a holistic viewpoint that includes the religious and theological dimensions involved in practitioner self-understandings (cf. Yong 1998). After all, even according to the biblical narrative, "All of them were filled with the Holy Spirit and began to speak in other languages, as the Spirit gave them ability" (Acts 2:4). So if the activity of the Holy Spirit does not preclude the role of human beings, why should a theological rendition preclude scientific explanations and vice versa?

Note, however, that we are here not arbitrarily making room for pentecostal interpretations. Rather, there is an increasing recognition that phenomena at each level up the hierarchy of sciences—physics, chemistry, biology, psychology, sociology—is in some way causally constituted by the lower level but is, once having emerged, irreducible to that lower level. So while lower-level explanations can illuminate observations at the next level to some degree, only a blatantly reductionist approach will think itself able to provide an exhaustive account. At the same time, the emergentist hypothesis also recognizes the validity of the various scientific discourses each at their own levels, without negating the need for higher-level perspectives (Clayton 2004; Clayton and Davies 2006; Yong 2006).[20] How then might a pentecostal religious and theological outlook enrich our understanding of glossolalia?

### Heralding the Kingdom: Pneumatological Eschatology and Teleology in Science

I now want to suggest that a specifically pentecostal account of glossolalia not only further illuminates the phenomenon of tongues speaking but also potentially contributes to the current re-emergence of teleological thinking regarding final causation across the spectrum of the sciences. To make this argument, I invite the reader to think about divine action, not in terms of the efficient and material causality that is studied by the sciences, but in specifically theological and, especially, eschatological terms. By this I mean that a pentecostal perspective sees the gifts of the Spirit, including glossolalia, as being made available "in the last days" (Acts 2:17) and understands the workings of the Holy Spirit as directed toward the ushering in of the coming kingdom of God.

What does it mean to say that God acts in the world teleologically or eschatologically?[21] Let me unpack this pentecostal theological claim at four levels. First, at the level of pentecostal glossolalia, I suggest that Spirit-inspired tongues speech is the language that yearns for, anticipates, and heralds the coming reign of God. With the apostle Paul, we might say that tongues is the language of the Spirit given to establish human solidarity with the creation as we await the final redemption to be accomplished in the coming kingdom (Romans 8:22–27; cf. Macchia 1992). Second, if glossolalia might be said to be the language of the kingdom, then the gifts of the Holy Spirit may be said to be signs and harbingers of the kingdom. More specifically, the charisms—tongues and interpretations, miracles, healings, etc. (1 Corinthians 12:7–10)—signify the "future" of God in the present and provide us with a foretaste of the kingdom to come (Ervin 2002). This is because, third, the charisms represent the gift of God's Spirit to the world. The day of Pentecost itself birthed the church as the body of Christ and the fellowship of the Spirit, and it is this en-spirited body of believers that signals, ushers in, and embodies the reign of God in the present. Finally, of course, the works of the Spirit are directed toward the kingdom because it is the task of the Spirit to bear witness to the work of the Son, whose incarnational life, sacrificial death, and unexpected resurrection were Spirit-inspired announcements of the impending reign of God. The "acts of the Holy Spirit" in the church are in this case simply an extension of the workings of the Spirit in the Son of God. These incarnational and pentecostal missions are God's acting in the world, not as an efficient cause (from the past), but rather eschatologically and even teleologically (according to the designs of the kingdom from the "future"). Yet this is not any kind of mysterious backward causation; rather, since God's "future" has already intersected with our "present" in Christ and the Holy Spirit, this is a specifically theological form of divine action and, hence, of explanation.

Now I need to add that nothing about this theological account detracts from scientific insights provided at their appropriate levels of explanation. With regard to glossolalia, for example, such an eschatological interpretation does not undermine the neurobiological, physiological, psychological, or social-scientific perspectives mentioned earlier. Each level of explanation is appropriate as far as it goes, so long as reductionistic and totalizing views are resisted. In fact, scientific analyses provide what might be called "views from below"—or observational perspectives—that necessarily complement more strictly theological accounts that might proceed "from above."

But acceptance of the scientific accounts means that pentecostal Christians can only identify divine action retrospectively, in faith, according to the normative measures provided in the life of the Spirit-inspired Christ and the lives of the earliest Spirit-empowered Christian communities. Yet such retrospective explications that are overlaid on scientific descriptions are not thereby merely subjective, eliminating the objectivity of divine action sought for by the NIOSDA principle described above. Precisely because the theological interpretation is also understood, in faith, as normative descriptions of the coming kingdom, the pentecostal wager is that there will be an eschatological form of verification whereby the reality of God's action in the world will be established.

I now want to suggest that such a specifically pentecostal account of God's eschatological action may be said to provide a theological parallel to what in the scientific disciplines is called teleological explanation. Teleology, the study of design or purpose, was central to the Aristotelian metaphysic. As we saw earlier, Aristotle included final causality—explanation of something according to its purposes, such as bird wings evolved to achieve flight—alongside efficient, formal, and material causality. Marginalized from mainstream science during the early modern period when explanation was limited to efficient and material causation, final causes have nevertheless never been fully exorcized from the scientific enterprise. In recent times, teleology has re-emerged, especially in the biological sciences, where they were dominant through the medieval period, and have since been more dormant, albeit never completely absent (e.g., Denton 1998; Grene and Depew 2004: chap. 10). At the same time, teleological thinking has also become increasingly prominent in the cosmological sciences, especially in speculations regarding the anthropic principle— the idea that the physical constants of the universe have been finely tuned from the beginning to not only allow for the emergence of human forms of life (the weak anthropic principle) but perhaps also to lead inexorably to such life forms (the strong anthropic principle) (Barrow and Tipler 1986; Bertola and Curi 1988; E. Harris 1992). There is a growing awareness that scientific explanations are impoverished apart from perspectives informed by final causality, that anti-reductionist science in some ways invites teleological reflection, and that even the predictability of scientific explanation seems to assume a teleological mode of reasoning (Nagel 1979; Rescher 1986).

I suggest that the pentecostal account of eschatological divine action functions for theology similarly to the ways in which teleological accounts function for science. A pentecostal pneumatological theology of divine action would understand the work of the Holy Spirit as bringing about the coming reign of God in the present age. It would hence be a language of faith that need not displace scientific explanations, even while such a discourse may potentially inform the presuppositions of scientific research, contribute to the formulation of scientific hypotheses, and shape scientific interpretations (see Russell 2002: 12–17).

## Transitional Conclusions

The preceding comments are general in the extreme and beg for further theological elucidation as well as scientific corroboration. Yet I am confident that such a sketch of a pneumatological theology of divine action, informed by pentecostal experiences and perspectives, opens up new vistas for both theological and scientific work.[22] By way of conclusion, let me briefly summarize the foregoing by presenting seven theses that invite further reflection and research.

Thesis 1: Pentecostal Christians do not have to embrace classical Christian construals of the God-world relationship insofar as these have attempted to define divine action according to the terms of Aristotelian efficient and material causality. Rather, from the pentecostal perspective, God's action is eschatological—ahead of us, yet dynamically embracing our histories—and thus can be seen as a theological rendition of final causality.

Thesis 2: In response to the mechanistic cosmology of deism, pentecostals posit instead the dynamic eschatology informed by a pneumatological theology. Hence, pentecostal understandings of the "laws of nature" will be more loose than rigid: nature is generally reliable, regular, and orderly, although capable also of surprising us—such being the essence of the coming kingdom.

Thesis 3: Process theology may correctly articulate divine action as persuasive rather than noncoercive (because God is not embodied); however, this is not because God is the chief exemplification of any metaphysical principle (pace Whitehead), but because the trinitarian God is the source and, more importantly, the goal of all things.

Thesis 4: Pentecostals will continue to insist on a more robust notion of God's action in the world; however, divine action must be understood eschatologically and teleologically with reference to God's purposes in bringing about the coming kingdom and hence is beyond the analytical framework of science.[23]

Thesis 5: Pentecostals therefore may be inclined to agree with critics of the Divine Action Project that the quest for a causal joint between God and the world (or between God as primary cause and the world's creatures as secondary causes) may be futile. Instead, the workings of the Spirit of God are identifiable or discernible only through the eyes of faith, hermeneutically informed by the biblical narrative, in anticipation of the kingdom to come.[24]

Thesis 6: Scientific discourses would also be recognized as hermeneutical enterprises without invalidating scientific explanations from any number of disciplinary perspectives. So long as they remain at or within their appropriate levels of analysis, the entire range of scientific findings will not threaten pentecostal claims about divine action but instead can (and should) be drawn upon to enrich and inform pentecostal theological self-understanding.

Thesis 7: Pentecostals are rightly reluctant to abandon interventionist language, even as they must be cautioned against the seduction to imagine God in this framework as one agent in the world among others. However, divine interventionist action is explicitly theological (not scientific) discourse that is sustained by specifically religious practices such as testimony (with regard to past events), doxology (with regard to human beings as worshippers), and prayer (with regard to future anticipations).

The preceding discussion probably raises more questions than it answers for students beginning the study of science and wondering how that might be compatible with pentecostal beliefs and practices. However, we have identified many if not most of the important issues and suggested how pentecostals might begin to think about these matters in ways that avoid compromising either their faith or the work of science. At the very least, the road forward does not at this time require that we choose one over the other. Since the Holy Spirit will lead us into all truth and that truth must lie ahead of us anyway (eschatologically), that kind of progress is worth more than any definitive answers we might have thought we had found. Hence, welcome to the journey in which we attempt to track the winds of the Spirit, whose comings and goings will continue to keep us looking.[25]

## Notes

1. For an anthropological and cultural account of this shift in pentecostal circles overlapping West Africa and Britain from the 1960s through 1990s, see H. Harris 2006.
2. My "many tongues includes many disciplinary languages" is an analogy that extends our understanding of the metaphor. If pentecostal scholars have already argued (convincingly in my opinion) that the many tongues of the day of Pentecost are inclusive of the many peoples, cultures, and languages of the world (see, e.g., Solivan 1998: 112–18; Macchia 1998), then may not the Spirit also speak through new "languages"—e.g., of Deaf culture (see Yong 2007: esp. 87–89) or of the emerging sciences (Yong 2005c)—as human conventions evolve?
3. For Plato, reality essentially consists of ideas or forms; the things of this world are but variable replicas of these eternal ideas—so any particular table is what it is because it participates in, embodies, and instantiates the ideal form of table.
4. In brief, the empirical method is a means of gaining knowledge via the collection of data; included in the empirical method is experimentation, the pursuit of data via the manipulation of one or more variables in an experiment.
5. The Aristotelian framework of Thomas's argument from motion is discussed in Kenny 1969, chapter 2.

6. Aristotle's four causes are really four types of explanation (see Sorabji 1980: 40). Take a table, for instance. Its material cause consists of its parts and their interaction (e.g., legs or top consisting of wood); its formal cause is its pattern or essence (Plato's ideal forms); its efficient cause is the activity (in the case of a table-manufacturing factory) or agency (in the case of a carpenter) that puts it together; and its final cause is the end it serves (e.g., those intended for the dining room are made one way, while those holding up computers are made differently). There remains a debate within and outside of Aristotelian studies about whether or not final causes can be attributed to nonhuman and, especially, non-intelligent things. For our purposes, however, this question does not need to be resolved. Suffice to note that for Aquinas, the entire causal nexus of a thing is set within a sequence of events that requires an initial cause, which Aquinas called God.

7. A much more radical theological theory that rejects secondary creaturely causation is *occasionalism:* all events are occasions through which God brings about their perceived effects. For occasionalists like Malebranche and Berkeley, it was precisely the theological idea of God as the only real cause—the creator, sustainer, and conserver—of all phenomena that guarded against the notion of created things as having their own autonomous causal powers (see Freddoso 1988: 112–15).

8. A more recent proponent of Thomas's "double agency" theory is the Anglican philosophical theologian Austin Farrar; see Hebblethwaite and Henderson (1990) for essays engaging Farrar's proposal from a full range of perspectives.

9. Protestant Reformation theologians like Luther and especially Calvin emphasized divine causality as preceding rather than concurring with secondary causes (see Työrinoja 2002: 55–59), while counter-Reformation theologians like Francisco Suarez leaned toward emphasizing the concurrence of divine and creaturely causation (see Freddoso 1991).

10. William of Ockham was a fourteenth-century logician whose "law of parsimony" (also known as "Occam's razor") insisted that needless assumptions be jettisoned when otherwise sufficient explanations existed. To return to our table, there is no need to posit God's activity in the making of tables when there are table-manufacturing factories or carpenters identifiable.

11. For an overview of how Newton understood God's relationship to the world, see Cohen 1969.

12. For Descartes, human minds were nonmaterial substances that interfaced with material human bodies through the pineal gland; this dualism has plagued the Cartesian philosophy, especially after the pineal gland hypothesis was thoroughly discredited.

13. Elsewhere, I have discussed the various ways in which divine foreknowledge is related to divine providence in classical, deistic, process, and open theologies; see Yong 2003.

14. For a summary, see Wildman 2004; a wider discussion of divine action in dialogue with science is Tracy 2006.

15. I provide a more extensive analysis of Polkinghorne's theological method in Yong 2005f.

16. See Koperski 2000, Saunders 2000, and Sansbury 2007 for a sampling of critical responses.

17. We are shifting our focus just a bit from the earlier part of this paper, moving from asking about *how* and *whether* God could/does *act* in the world to focusing now on *naming* or *recognizing* events *as* divine action. Yet this is an important and even needed shift, since to affirm the possibility of divine action in general without being able to identify divine action in particular would be vacuous.

18. For a wide-ranging set of research articles through the mid-1980s, see Mills 1986.

19. For example, Kildahl (1972) suggests that glossolalics have more submissive personalities, are more suggestible, and are more dependent on authority figures. For further discussion, see Frederick Ware's chapter later in this volume.

20. It might be countered that I picked the "easy case" of glossolalia, which involves a high degree of human participation anyway. I think, however, that my supervenience account can also illuminate pentecostals' claims about miraculous healings; see the articles referred to in the next note.

21. In the following, I summarize the proposals presented in Yong (2008 and 2009), even as I consider these statements as seed-thought for further reflections to come.

22. I have elsewhere argued for the fruitfulness of developing a pentecostal theology of science (Yong 2005a: chap. 7; 2005d), as well as of introducing pneumatological categories into the theology and science conversation (Yong 2005b; 2005e). This essay represents an extension of these previous ideas but at the same time invites others to engage the work opened up at the interface of pentecostal Christianity and the sciences.

23. In other words, I would say that miracles or divine activity in the conventional pentecostal understanding do happen today, although they are empirically inexplicable and thereby only eschatologically comprehensible. Given the empirical language of science, the language of faith is not fully translatable—hence my attempts to correlate "eschatological" with "teleological" language.

24. Hence at one level, I am not sure I am very much further down the road than where Pannenberg brought us with his *Jesus—God and Man* (1977) in terms of what he called "eschatological verification." I would add, however, that my proposal allows pentecostals to weigh in on this matter on pentecostal terms, rather than solely on the terms established by other discourses.

25. Thanks to my graduate assistants, Bradford McCall and Sophronia Vachon, for helping me keep an undergraduate reading audience in mind; any obscurity in the preceding, however, remains my responsibility, not theirs.

## References

Anderson, Robert Mapes. 1979. *Vision of the Disinherited: The Making of American Pentecostalism.* Oxford: Oxford University Press.

Barbour, Ian G. 2001. "God's Power: A Process View." In John Polkinghorne, ed., *The Work of Love: Creation as Kenosis*. Grand Rapids, Mich.: Eerdmans, 1–20.

Barrow, John D., and Frank J. Tipler. 1986. *The Anthropic Cosmological Principle*. Oxford: Oxford University Press.

Bertola, F., and Umberto Curi, eds. 1988. *The Anthropic Principle: Proceedings of the Second Venice Conference on Cosmology and Philosophy*. Cambridge: Cambridge University Press.

Bradfield, Cecil David. 1979. *Neo-Pentecostalism: A Sociological Assessment*. Washington, D.C.: University Press of America.

Cartledge, Mark J. 2002. *Charismatic Glossolalia: An Empirical-Theological Study*. Aldershot, UK, and Burlington, Vt.: Ashgate.

——, ed. 2006. *Speaking in Tongues: Multi-Disciplinary Perspectives*. Milton Keynes, UK, and Waynesboro, Ga.: Paternoster.

Castelein, John Donald. 1984. "Glossolalia and the Psychology of the Self and Narcissism." *Journal of Religion and Health* 23/1: 47–62.

Clayton, Philip. 2004. *Mind and Emergence: From Quantum to Consciousness*. Oxford: Oxford University Press.

Clayton, Philip, and Paul Davies, eds. 2006. *The Re-Emergence of Emergence: The Emergentist Hypothesis from Science to Religion*. Oxford: Oxford University Press.

Cohen, I. Bernard. 1969. "Isaac Newton's Principia, the Scriptures, and the Divine Providence." In Sidney Morgenbesser, Patrick Suppes, and Morton White, eds., *Philosophy, Science, and Method: Essays in Honor of Ernest Nagel*. New York: St. Martin's Press, 523–48.

Denton, Michael. 1998. *Nature's Destiny: How the Laws of Biology Reveal Purpose in the Universe*. New York: Free Press.

Ervin, Howard. 2002. *Healing: A Sign of the Kingdom*. Peabody, Mass.: Hendrickson.

Ferngren, Gary B., ed. 2002. *Science and Religion: A Historical Introduction*. Baltimore: Johns Hopkins University Press.

Freddoso, Alfred J. 1988. "Medieval Aristotelianism and the Case against Secondary Causation in Nature." In Thomas V. Morris, ed., *Divine and Human Action: Essays in the Metaphysics of Theism*. Ithaca, N.Y.: Cornell University Press, 74–118.

——. 1991. "God's General Concurrence with Secondary Causes: Why Conservation Is Not Enough." In James E. Tomberlin, ed., *Philosophical Perspectives,* vol. 5: *Philosophy of Religion*. Atascadero, Calif.: Ridgeview Publishing Co., 551–85.

Gonsalvez, Emma. 1982. "A Psychological Interpretation of Religious Behaviour of Pentecostals and Charismatics." *Journal of Dharma* 7: 408–29.

Goodman, Felicitas D. 1972. *Speaking in Tongues: A Cross-Cultural Study of Glossolalia*. Chicago: University of Chicago Press.

Grene, Marjorie, and David Depew. 2004. *The Philosophy of Biology: An Episodic History*. Cambridge: Cambridge University Press.

Griffin, William Paul. 1997. *The God of the Prophets: An Analysis of Divine Action*. JSOTSup 249. Sheffield: Sheffield Academic Press.

Gritzmacher, Steven A., Brian Bolton, and Richard H. Dana. 1988. "Psychological Characteristics of Pentecostals: A Literature Review and Psychodynamic Synthesis." *Journal of Psychology and Theology* 16/3: 233–45.

Harris, Errol E. 1992. *Cosmos and Theos: Ethical and Theological Implications of the Anthropic Cosmological Principle*. Atlantic Highlands, N.J.: Humanities Press.

Harris, Hermione. 2006. *Yoruba in Diaspora: An African Church in London*. New York: Palgrave Macmillan.

Hebblethwaite, Brian, and Edward Henderson, eds. 1990. *Divine Action: Studies Inspired by the Philosophical Theology of Austin Farrer*. Edinburgh: T & T Clark.

Hine, Virginia H. 1973. "Pentecostal Glossolalia—Toward a Functional Interpretation." In Benjamin Beit-Hallahmi, ed., *Research in Religious Behavior: Selected Readings*. Monterey, Calif.: Brooks/Cole, 276–307.

Holm, Nils G. 1978. "Functions of Glossolalia in the Pentecostal Movement." In Thorvald Källstad, ed., *Psychological Studies on Religious Man*. Acta Universitatis Upsaliensis: Psychologia Religionum 7. Uppsala and Stockholm: Almqvist & Wiksell, 141–58.

Hooykaas, R. 1963. *The Principle of Uniformity in Geology, Biology and Theology: Natural Law and Divine Miracle*. Leiden: E. J. Brill.

Kaufman, Gordon D. 2004. *In the Beginning—Creativity*. Minneapolis: Fortress.

Kenny, Anthony. 1969. *The Five Ways: St. Thomas Aquinas' Proofs of God's Existence*. New York: Schocken Books.

Kildahl, John P. 1972. *The Psychology of Speaking in Tongues*. New York: Harper and Row.

Koperski, Jeffrey. 2000. "God, Chaos, and the Quantum Dice." *Zygon* 35/3: 545–59.

Lindberg, David C. 1992. *The Beginnings of Western Science: The European Scientific Tradition in Philosophical, Religious, and Institutional Context, 600 B.C. to A.D. 1450*. Chicago: University of Chicago Press.

Macchia, Frank D. 1992. "Sighs Too Deep for Words: Toward a Theology of Glossolalia." *Journal of Pentecostal Theology* 1: 47–73.

———. 1998. "The Tongues of Pentecost: A Pentecostal Perspective on the Promise and Challenge of Pentecostal/Roman Catholic Dialogue." *Journal of Ecumenical Studies* 35/1: 1–18.

Malony, H. Newton, and A. Adams Lovekin. 1985. *Glossolalia: Behavioral Science Perspectives on Speaking in Tongues*. New York and Oxford: Oxford University Press.

Mills, Watson E., ed. 1986. *Speaking in Tongues: A Guide to Research on Glossolalia*. Grand Rapids, Mich.: Eerdmans.

Nagel, Ernest. 1979. *Teleology Revisited and Other Essays in the Philosophy and History of Science*. New York: Columbia University Press.

Newberg, Andrew, Michael Pourdehnad, Abass Alavi, and Eugene G. D'Aquili. 2003. "Cerebral Blood Flow during Meditative Prayer: Preliminary Findings and Methodological Issues." *Perceptual and Motor Skills* 97/2: 625–30.

Newberg, Andrew B., Nancy A. Wintering, Donna Morgan, and Mark R. Waldman. 2006. "The Measurement of Regional Cerebral Blood Flow during Glossolalia: A Preliminary SPECT Study." *Psychiatry Research: Neuroimaging* 148: 67–71.

Pannenberg, Wolfhart. 1977. *Jesus—God and Man*. Trans. Lewis L. Wilkins and Duane A. Priebe. Philadelphia: Westminster.

Pinnock, Clark H., et al. 1994. *The Openness of God: A Biblical Challenge to the Traditional Understanding of God*. Downers Grove, Ill.: InterVarsity.

Polkinghorne, John. 1995. "The Metaphysics of Divine Action." In Robert John Russell, Nancey Murphy, and Arthur R. Peacocke, eds., *Chaos and Complexity: Scientific Perspectives on Divine Action*. Vatican City State: Vatican Observatory, and Berkeley, Calif.: Center for Theology and the Natural Sciences, 147–56.

Preus, Klemet. 1982. "Tongues: An Evaluation from a Scientific Perspective." *Concordia Theological Quarterly* 46/4: 277–93.

Rescher, Nicholas, ed. 1986. *Current Issues in Teleology*. Lanham, Md.: University Press of America.

Russell, Robert John. 2002. "Bodily Resurrection, Eschatology, and Scientific Cosmology." In Ted Peters, Robert John Russell, and Michael Welker, eds., *Resurrection: Theological and Scientific Assessments*. Grand Rapids, Mich.: Eerdmans, 3–30.

Samarin, William J. 1972. *Tongues of Men and Angels: The Religious Language of Pentecostalism*. New York: Macmillan.

Sansbury, Timothy. 2007. "The False Promise of Quantum Mechanics." *Zygon* 42/1: 111–21.

Saunders, Nicholas T. 2000. "Does God Cheat at Dice? Divine Action and Quantum Possibilities." *Zygon* 35/3: 517–44.

Smedes, T. A. 2004. *Chaos, Complexity, and God: Divine Action and Scientism*. Leuven: Peeters.

Solivan, Samuel. 1998. *The Spirit, Pathos, and Liberation: Toward an Hispanic Pentecostal Theology*. Sheffield: Sheffield Academic Press.

Sorabji, Richard. 1980. *Necessity, Cause, and Blame: Perspectives on Aristotle's Theory*. Ithaca, N.Y.: Cornell University Press.

Thomas, Owen. 1990. "Recent Thoughts on Double Agency." In Brian Hebblethwaite and Edward Henderson, eds., *Divine Action: Studies Inspired by the Philosophical Theology of Austin Farrer*. Edinburgh: T & T Clark, 35–50.

Tracy, Thomas F. 2006. "Theologies of Divine Action." In Philip Clayton and Zachary Simpson, eds., *The Oxford Handbook of Religion and Science*. Oxford: Oxford University Press, 596–611.

Trundle, Robert C. 1999. *Medieval Modal Logic and Science: Augustine on Necessary Truth and Thomas on Its Impossibility without a First Cause*. Lanham, Md.: University Press of America.

Työrinoja, Reijo. 2002. "God, Causality, and Nature: Some Problems of Causality in Medieval Theology." In Eeva Martikainen, ed., *Infinity, Causality and Determinism: Cosmological Enterprises and Their Preconditions*. Contributions to Philosophical Theology 6. Frankfurt: Peter Lang, 45–60.

White, Vernon. 1985. *The Fall of a Sparrow: A Concept of Special Divine Action*. Exeter, UK: Paternoster.

Wildman, Wesley J. 2004. "The Divine Action Project, 1988–2003." *Theology and Science* 2/1: 31–75.

Wiles, Maurice F. 1986. *God's Action in the World: The Bampton Lectures for 1986*. London: SCM.

———. 1997. "Revelation and Divine Action." In Paul Avis, ed., *Divine Revelation*. Grand Rapids, Mich.: Eerdmans, 100–111.

Yong, Amos. 1997. "'Tongues,' Theology, and the Social Sciences: A Pentecostal-

Theological Reading of Geertz's Interpretive Theory of Religion." *Cyber-journal for Pentecostal/ Charismatic Research* 1 [http://pctii.org/cyberj/cyber1.html].

———. 1998. "Tongues of Fire in the Pentecostal Imagination: The Truth of Glossolalia in Light of R. C. Neville's Theory of Religious Symbolism." *Journal of Pentecostal Theology* 12: 39–65.

———. 2003. "Divine Knowledge and Relation to Time." In Thomas Jay Oord, ed., *Philosophy of Religion: Introductory Essays*. Kansas City, Mo.: Beacon Hill Press/Nazarene Publishing House, 136–52.

———. 2005a. *The Spirit Poured Out on All Flesh: Pentecostalism and the Possibility of Global Theology*. Grand Rapids, Mich.: Baker Academic.

———. 2005b. "Discerning the Spirit(s) in the Natural World: Toward a Typology of 'Spirit' in the Theology and Science Conversation." *Theology and Science* 3/3: 315–29.

———. 2005c. "Academic Glossolalia? Pentecostal Scholarship, Multi-disciplinarity, and the Science-Religion Conversation." *Journal of Pentecostal Theology* 14/1: 63–82.

———. 2005d. "The Spirit and Creation: Possibilities and Challenges for a Dialogue between Pentecostal Theology and the Sciences." *Journal of the European Pentecostal Theological Association* 25: 82–110.

———. 2005e. "Christian and Buddhist Perspectives on Neuropsychology and the Human Person: *Pneuma* and *Pratityasamutpada*." *Zygon: Journal of Religion and Science* 40/1: 143–65.

———. 2005f. "From Quantum Mechanics to the Eucharistic Meal: John Polkinghorne's Vision of Science and Theology." *The Global Spiral: A Publication of the Metanexus Institute* 5/5 [www.metanexus.net/magazine/ArticleDetail/tabid/68/id/9285/Default.aspx].

———. 2006. "*Ruach,* the Primordial Waters, and the Breath of Life: Emergence Theory and the Creation Narratives in Pneumatological Perspective." In Michael Welker, ed., *The Work of the Spirit: Pneumatology and Pentecostalism*. Grand Rapids, Mich.: Eerdmans, 183–204.

———. 2007. *Theology and Down Syndrome: Reimagining Disability in Late Modernity*. Waco, Tex.: Baylor University Press.

———. 2008. "Natural Laws and Divine Intervention in Theology and Science: What Difference Does Being Pentecostal or Charismatic Make?" *Zygon: The Journal of Religion and Science* 43/4: 961–89.

———. 2009. "The Spirit at Work in the World: A Pentecostal-Charismatic Perspective on the Divine Action Project." *Theology and Science* 7/2: 123–40.

## Recommended Reading

Collins, C. John. 2000. *The God of Miracles: An Exegetical Examination of God's Action in the World*. Wheaton, Ill.: Crossway.

Gwynne, Paul. 1996. *Special Divine Action: Key Issues in the Contemporary Debate (1965–1995)*. Rome: Editrice Pontificia Universita Gregoriana.

Hansson, Mats J. 1991. *Understanding an Act of God: An Essay in Philosophical The-*

*ology.* Studia Doctrinae Christianae Upsaliensia 33. Uppsala, Sweden: Acta Universitatis Upsaliensis.

Lameter, Christoph. 2006. *Divine Action in the Framework of Scientific Thinking: From Quantum Theory to Divine Action.* Newark, Calif.: Christianity in the 21st Century.

Peters, Ted, and Nathan Hallanger, eds. 2006. *God's Action in Nature's World: Essays in Honour of Robert John Russell.* Aldershot, UK: Ashgate.

Saunders, Nicholas. 2002. *Divine Action and Modern Science.* Cambridge: Cambridge University Press.

Schwöbel, Christoph. 1992. *God: Action and Revelation.* Studies in Philosophical Theology 4. Kampen, The Netherlands: Kok Pharos, 1992.

Thomas, Owen C., ed. 1983. *God's Activity in the World: The Contemporary Problem.* American Academy of Religion Studies in Religion 31. Chico, Calif.: Scholars Press.

Tracy, Thomas F., ed. 1994. *The God Who Acts: Philosophical and Theological Explorations.* University Park: Pennsylvania State University Press.

Ward, Keith. 1991. *Divine Action.* London: Collins.

# PART TWO

## The Spirit of Matter

*Questions and Possibilities
in the Natural Sciences*

# 4 Does God Have a Place in the Physical Universe? Physics and the Quest for the Holy Spirit

*Wolfgang Vondey*

*This chapter considers the challenges of the pentecostal-charismatic Christian who wishes to engage the physical sciences. The separation of physics and theology is characterized as primarily a separation of method rather than a difference of content. The author suggests that a spirit-oriented approach to the physical universe has significant implications for the observation and explanation of natural phenomena from both a scientific and a theological perspective. This pneumatological method is illustrated in the work of Isaac Newton and Albert Einstein and in the integration of the notion of "spirit" in their understanding of the physical universe. Both epistemologically and experimentally, the concept of "spirit" opens the doors for pentecostals to engage physics explicitly as pentecostals. From a pentecostal-charismatic perspective, the Spirit-filled physicist is perhaps the image that best represents the unity of physics and theology.*

## Introduction: Locating God in the Universe

The student of modern physics is confronted with a wide range of challenges. Classical wave theory, relativistic dynamics, quantum mechanics and its applications to atomic physics, nuclear physics, particle physics, solid state physics, or statistical physics may comprise just a small part of a given course. The classic challenge between theory and praxis is stretched out in the classroom among readings, lectures, discussions, problem assignments, exams, computer simulations, and laboratory work. All of these tools expose the student to the fascinating phenomena of the natural world. As in most sciences, the tools of the physicist are specific to the discipline. Theological questions are not in the immediate purview of physics. To put it differently, scientific inquiry is not intended to pursue questions of faith. But what about those who do not wish to leave their faith outside of the laboratory?

The online dictionary *Wikipedia*, a widely used resource of popular definitions among college students, describes physics as "an experimental science," "the general analysis of nature, conducted to understand how the world around us behaves." Theology, on the other hand, is described as reasoned discourse about God, with particular application to Christianity. The words "science" and "nature" play no role in the definition of theology, while the term "God" does not appear in the description of physics. Both the scientist and the theologian will caution that the tools of learning physics are not intended as instruments to address the concerns of faith. Theology and physics are not opposites—they simply seem to have nothing to do with each other!

One particular reason for this separation is the "experimental" aspect of physics. Theology, after all, may include the *experience* of a divine manifestation, but one can certainly not speak of an *experiment* with God. Algebra, geometry, calculator syntax, motion graphs, vectors, and other tools cannot "measure" the existence of God. Nor are they intended to do so. The main difference between physics and theology therefore seems to lie in the respective methods of each discipline, the former based on the empirical observation of nature, the latter on the revelation of that which is *not* directly discernable from the physical universe. In other words, one might argue that the study of physics is an intentional pursuit of human beings for the purpose of understanding nature. The study called theology, on the other hand, although it is also a deliberate human and cultural pursuit, is more intimately connected with the revelation or self-manifestation of God's presence in the world. This distinction may not immediately raise concerns about the compatibility of each view. However, it does raise the question of whether theology has anything to say about nature and whether physics has anything to say about God. From this perspective one might ask, Does God have a place in the physical universe?

The difficulty of asking the question of God's place in nature lies in the fact that it is often read exclusively from either a scientific or a theological perspective. A negative answer to the question naturally thwarts any further inquiry: If God has no place in the cosmos, then physics and faith hold no common ground. A positive answer, on the other hand, seems to suggest that God's place can be verified *both* experimentally and theologically. From a scientific perspective, one might say that God is present either "nowhere," "everywhere," or "somewhere." From a theological perspective, on the other hand, each of these possibilities carries significant implications.

The proposal that God is "nowhere" might initially be confused with atheism, the notion that God does not exist at all. However, more accurately, this idea emphasizes the *absence* of God from creation, a concept that stands at the root of deism and generally argues that God does not intervene in the laws of nature. A strong reliance on the power of scientific reason further suggests that in a deistic universe the supernatural and miraculous have no place (Barr 2006: 19–21), since they revert essentially to an explanation of God's presence that is not scientifically verifiable (see Smith, chapter 2 in this volume). In this view, God's place is outside the physical universe. Physics and theology share no common ground.

The concept that God is "everywhere," on the other hand, informs two very different theological proposals: pantheism and panentheism. The first concept suggests that God and the material universe are equivalent: everything (*pan*) is God (*theos*). Here, physics and theology are different only in methodology— not in content. The second concept, panentheism, proposes that the cosmos is contained *in* God but does not exhaust God. The content and method of theology therefore exceed that of physics; the physicist is able to approach the presence of God in but not beyond the physical universe.

So, what about the idea that God is "somewhere"? Two immediate challenges arise when we consider a particular "place" for God in the cosmos. First, the traditional notion of the ubiquity of God seems to suggest that God is everywhere rather than somewhere. If we locate God in *some* place, we seem to suggest that God is not in *another* place. Second, and as a result of the former, if we wish to locate God in *some* place in the cosmos, just *what kind* of place is able to contain God's presence? The Christian response to these concerns has traditionally pointed to the human being as the place for God's presence. Jesus Christ is, after all, the unique instance of the unity of the human and divine. Furthermore, the New Testament teaches that human beings are the temple of the Holy Spirit (see 1 Corinthians 3:16, 6:19). Pentecostals have given particular significance to this idea of the "presence" of God's Spirit in the human being. However, the human being is not a primary concern of physics. It seems that the student of biology or psychology may obtain some illumination of the intimate connection between humankind and God; physics, however, offers no such insights. In other words, one can be both a pentecostal and a physicist, since one seems to have little to do with the other.

In this chapter, I want to investigate the connection between questions of faith and the scientific pursuit of physics. The focus is on addressing the question how a pentecostal-charismatic physicist, who is interested in the study of physics for the sake of scientific inquiry and the fascination wrought by the thoughts and practices of the discipline, can pursue this task without separating it from the rest of the Christian life and its theological concerns. Examining the relationship of theology and physics in general, and the significance of pentecostal faith and practice in particular, I argue that a separation of theology and physics is the result of a neglect of *method* rather than *content*. In other words, the student of physics does not need to engage the entire field of knowledge of the theologian in order to be a Christian and a physicist. Rather, an awareness of the methodologies of contemporary physics allows us to engage the study of nature without separating that task as "scientific" from its "theological" counterpart.

Moreover, I suggest that the pentecostal-charismatic community is particularly suited for a reconciliation of faith and science due to the expectation that an encounter with God who is spirit can occur in any place and at any time. To this end, I will outline the methodological basis of two significant physicists, Isaac Newton (1642–1727) and Albert Einstein (1879–1955) and their understanding of the physical universe in terms of "spirit."[1] In so doing, I do not propose that either scientist instrumentalized physics for the sake of his theological viewpoint. On the contrary, both pursued the understanding of the physical universe strictly on the basis of scientific parameters. Nonetheless, neither did they separate questions of faith from their lives as scientists, even if their views are not always considered orthodox. In a sense, this essay is primarily interested in the story of physics rather than in the laboratory. At the same time, the stories of Einstein and Newton carry implications for the experimental side of physics that should be of particular interest to the pentecostal-charismatic community and all who are interested in a spirit-oriented perspective of the physical universe.

### Einstein and Newton: Tracing the Trajectories of Modern Physics

No other scientists have had a greater influence on the shape of modern physics than Isaac Newton and Albert Einstein. Not surprisingly, a look at their respective work, separated by two centuries, reveals quickly that each provides a different trajectory for a methodological approach to the physical universe. The issue of concern is not so much the obvious change in subject matter from force, gravitation, and motion to field, electromagnetism, or thermodynamics, but the procedure underlying each scientific endeavor. More precisely, the term "method" does not primarily refer to the use of mathematics but to what Newton called the "rules for the study of natural philosophy" (1999: 794–96), the techniques for observing and explaining natural phenomena. A closer examination of the methodology of Newton's work reveals that Newton chose to express the results of his observations primarily by way of synthesis. Newton admitted that he was not interested in an "attempt to bring everything down to equations" (Whiteside 1981: 570–71) but in deriving a unified metaphysics of nature from the formulations of empirical observation (Guicciardini 2004: 324).

Einstein's methodology, on the other hand, is primarily analytical and not based on synthesis. For Newton, the various phenomena of nature observed in various experiments could yield complementary results in a single, universal frame of reference. For Einstein, symmetries between different experiments lead, at best, to the proposal of a general principle (Zahar 1989: 90). Whereas Newton's synthetic method sought to capture laws of nature based on a single reference frame and to apply them in the same manner to all parts of the universe, Einstein's analytical approach seeks to describe the theoretical properties of nature invariant to a particular frame of reference. The result of analysis instead of synthesis is a radically different perspective on nature and the cosmos. The theologian does not need to engage this difference mathematically in order to enter into dialogue with the physicist. What is needed is rather a clear understanding of the methodologies that stand at the root of the scientific enterprise at any given time.

Newton's synthetic method requires a number of particular elements that serve as the reference frame for the observation of nature. He located these elements in absolute time and space, which constitute for Newton the essential qualities that apply universally to all things (1999: 410). Absolute time and space are ontologically and epistemologically necessary for everything that exists, including God, who is eternal and omnipresent. This explanation led Newton to the conclusion that "there can be no truly empty times or places, since God is actually present with respect to all times and places whatsoever" (McGuire 1995: 5).[2] He labeled space and time as "modes" of existence universally, both created and divine (McGuire 1995: 10–12). Nevertheless, although eternity and infinity are therefore modes of God's existence, Newton denied that God is simply synonymous with these universal quantities: "He is not eternity and infinity, but eternal and infinite; he is not duration and space, but he endures and is present. He endures always and is present everywhere, and by existing always and everywhere he constitutes duration and space" (Newton 1999: 941). More precisely, for Newton, God is eternal in relation to time (not space), and ubiquitous in relation to space (not time). This distinction is important, because had Newton ascribed different times to different places, God's eternal duration would not be diffused equally throughout all places, things would exist differently in different parts of space (and, by inference, time), and Newton's entire philosophy of nature (and of God) would collapse.

In contrast, Einstein was confronted with the results of contemporary scientific experiment and the incongruence of Newton's synthetic approach. The general theory of relativity postulates that the properties of space and time are not independent of the material universe. In the place of absolute space and time, Einstein postulates a codependent spatiotemporal universe. He preserved the necessity of space and time, yet he rejected their absolute and independent character. Instead, the general theory of relativity intimately bound together the extension of space to the duration of time. Einstein maintained with Newton that space and time were epistemologically necessary for the existence of all things. Their ontological quality, however, was bound to each other as codetermining coordinates of the physical universe. In other words, God's eternity and ubiquity are "measured" in relation to how time and space relate to each other. Einstein could indeed ascribe different times to different places and, by inference, suggest that God's eternal duration is not diffused equally throughout all places.

The challenge of Newton's proposal is its inherent appeal to the equal diffusion of the divine presence in the cosmos through the ubiquity of space and time. This notion represents a particular obstacle to the trinitarian doctrine of God. Newton's main quarrel was with the patristic attempts to reconcile the one substance of God with the three divine persons (see Pfizenmaier 1997). After all, this doctrine suggests that God was present in a particular spatial and temporal manner in the person of Jesus Christ. Newton's position with regard to the person of Christ, however, resembled "the fourth century position of Eusebius and the Homoiousians who followed him" (Pfizenmaier 1997: 75). While the term *homoiousios* indicates a similarity in substance of Christ and the Father, it does not grant that both are of one (and the same) substance. Christ is thus not an exception to the presence of the divine being in the world but simply the manifestation of God's presence at one particular time and place.

While the Christian observer is confronted with Newton's semi-Arian position, the physicist is not challenged by Newton's proposal, since it can be seamlessly integrated in the overall framework of space and time. For pentecostals, however, Newton's proposal begs the question how the manifestation of God in Christ is different from other manifestations in the cosmos. Furthermore, Newton's perspective is silent on the presence of the Holy Spirit in the person of Christ. If the manifest presence of God is diffused equally throughout the universe, the foundation is withdrawn from the pentecostal-charismatic notion that the cosmos is experiencing an eschatological change in the *particular* presence of God's Spirit. In fact, if the presence of God in the universe must follow the same pattern in an absolute framework, then no argument can be made for the particular manifestation of God's Spirit in the life of the Christian.

Einstein's proposal offers a different but equally significant challenge to pentecostals. In general, Einstein's trajectory forbids the postulation of God as a personal being. He was convinced that the anthropomorphic conception of God presented the main source of conflicts between science and religion (see Einstein 1954: 47–48). In its place is found what Einstein called a "cosmic religious feeling" (1954: 38): "This firm belief, a belief bound up with deep feeling, in a superior mind that reveals itself in the world of experience, represents my conception of God. In common parlance this may be described as pantheistic" (Einstein 1954: 262). The chief theological postulate of Einstein's pantheism is: "The divine reveals itself in the physical world" (Rosenkranz 1998: 80). This meant, in the first place, that, like Newton, Einstein did not attribute any material attributes to God. However, unlike Newton, whose God is present in the absolute realm of space and time, Einstein's intimate connection of space-time and matter effectively places God (as person) outside the realm of physical reality.

Contrary to the Judeo-Christian concept of God, Einstein's pantheistic deity is present in the cosmos in a "superpersonal" manner (see Einstein 1954: 45). Although the theological development of the idea of divine personhood has also emphasized the analogical and often apophatic manner of understanding the divine "person," Einstein's "superpersonal" deity stands in particular contrast to the central Christian doctrine of the person of Christ and thereby to the trinitarian doctrine of God. From Einstein's pantheistic perspective, the presence of God is comprehensible but not observable. This notion provides a particular challenge to pentecostals and their assertions that God has manifested himself personally in their lives and that such a personal relationship with God forms the heart of the Christian life. The idea of a superpersonal relationship is irreconcilable with pentecostal spirituality and faith.

Nevertheless, the difficulties posed by both trajectories should not distract from the fact that the obstacles are fundamentally methodological in nature and not the result of pursuing a different content altogether. The question then arises, What kind of methodology is particularly suitable for the Christian who is also a physicist? The pentecostal-charismatic experience of the Holy Spirit suggests a spirit-oriented, or pneumatological approach to the presence of God in the physical universe.

### The Spirit and the Physical Universe

A pentecostal-charismatic view of the proposals of Newton and Einstein highlights that the methodology of both scientists is fundamentally oriented toward the notion of "spirit." In his attempt to relate his theological considerations to the scientific endeavors of his work, Newton leaves the reader with a surprising reference to a "spirit" pervading the natural world (1999: 943–44). The chief task in this endeavor is the explanation of this "spirit" as substantially situated in a spatiotemporal framework without being corporeally present in the natural world. Newton pursued the idea of a "subtle spirit" that operated in the natural world with particular fervor in his alchemical writings. The well-known concept of the "aether" provided the initial basis for Newton's idea of the spirit as an intermediary agent, since it was both uniform and universal, yet it continually resisted precise definition. More exactly, Newton proposed the existence of an internal aether dwelling within bodies and of a dense, external aether on the outside (see Cohen 1958: 250). At the same time, the aether exhibited both active and passive functions that led Newton to believe that "the aether is but a vehicle to some more active spirit. The bodies may be concreted of both together; they may imbibe aether as well as air in generation, and in that aether the spirit is entangled" (Dobbs 1991: 101–2).

Newton's choice of the term "spirit" reveals the difficulties in defining the properties of the aetherial medium. Although Newton understood God as the ultimate cause of everything that exists, the idea of a universally present, vital spirit offered the opportunity to show a more immediate cause for natural phenomena while maintaining the transcendence of God. In this way, Newton sought to avoid the dangers of atheism, deism, and pantheism. The struggle was whether this intermediate spirit was itself a divine or a created agent. Newton "called it a 'spirit,' as he had called God a 'spirit' . . . but seventeenth-century 'spirits' were notoriously ambiguous, existing in a broad gray area between solid matter and Deity" (Dobbs 1991: 95). Whereas Newton hesitated to draw the theological implications of his own view, the influence of Newton's thought on the theological schools of the eighteenth and nineteenth centuries is well attested.[3]

A closer look at the view of God exhibited in Newton's physics reveals that at the heart of the Newtonian philosophy of nature stands the possibility of a direct divine activity in creation (see Yong, chapter 3 in this volume), that is, at the least, a causal relationship between God's existence and the activity of the cosmos through a vital spirit. From a scientific perspective, "Newton concluded that only spirit could penetrate to the centers of bodies without causing retardation" (Dobbs 1991: 211). In this framework, "spirit" is responsible for the conformity and coherence of life, even if it is not possible to determine this pneumatological agent as the ultimate cause of all things. In summary, the following elements constitute Newton's understanding of the presence of spirit in the cosmos:

1) spirit is a necessary component for a philosophy of nature
2) spirit is an intermediate agent of the transcendent God in creation
3) spirit is a universal principle present in all natural phenomena
4) spirit is an internal medium of infinite duration (time) and extension (space)
5) spirit is a cohesive and conforming force in nature

In contrast, Einstein rejected the idea of the aether or an alchemical spirit. Explaining the advancement of physics, Einstein criticized the Newtonian mechanistic view of the cosmos for attempting to reduce all natural phenomena to forces acting between particles, which had formed the substance of Newton's aether theory (Einstein and Infeld 1938: 151). Although Einstein did not abandon the notion of the aether completely, for him it served "only to express some physical property of space" and "no longer stands for a medium built up of particles" (Einstein and Infeld 1938: 153). Instead, Einstein's special theory of relativity stripped the aether of its fundamental mechanical quality, immobility, and in so doing made the aether unnecessary (see Einstein 1989: 277).

Einstein's spirit-oriented approach takes a different direction. He suggested that "every one who is seriously involved in the pursuit of science becomes convinced that a spirit is manifest in the laws of the Universe—a spirit vastly superior to that of man" (Dukas and Hoffmann 1979: 33). However, here the term "spirit" has three primary functions that are different from those attributed to the spirit by Newton. First, Einstein's "spirit" (*Geist*) is the rationality of the cosmic order that lies at the basis of his cosmic religious feeling. Second, this spirit expresses a radically unitarian (not trinitarian) concept of the presence of God in the physical universe. Finally, the spirit who manifests in the laws of nature is a radically immanent entity that imbues the physical universe with meaning and order.

From a theological perspective, the abandonment of the aether effectively removed the basis for the continuing use of Newton's notion of "spirit." Einstein's scientific writings provide neither explicit theological observations nor references to an intermediary agent as in Newton's alchemical research. As a result, Einstein's cosmology provides no relative counterpart to Newton's proposal of a direct divine agent or a causal relationship of God and the physical universe. On the contrary, the "spirit" that Einstein admired was primarily synonymous with the rational order of the universe. Despite the similarities of a spirit-oriented methodology, the concept of spirit in Einstein's work differs radically from that of Newton. At the basis of a pneumatology in Einstein's universe stand the following elements:

1) spirit is a necessary component in the scientific endeavor
2) spirit is the rational order of the universe
3) spirit is a universal principle present in all natural phenomena
4) spirit is the symmetry of the space-time continuum
5) spirit has no physical, material reality

This summary of the spirit-oriented methodology in the works of Newton and Einstein illuminates the commonalities and differences between their scientific and theological approaches to the physical universe. The notion of "spirit" represents a unique opportunity in this situation to advance further our understanding of the cosmos from the perspectives of both physics and theology. The spirit-oriented scientist may be in a unique position to follow the quest for the Holy Spirit in the physical world. At the same time, the story of physics as it emerges from these two scientists carries significant implications for the laboratory.

First and foremost, both physicists considered the concept of spirit from a scientific perspective and for its implications of understanding the physical universe. This stands in sharp contrast to the general absence of a pneumatological perspective in the contemporary physics classroom, where "spirit" is generally considered the opposite of a physical quantity. Secondly, Newton's scientific pursuit, in particular, challenges the assumption that "spirit" is not experimentally verifiable—even if the experimental apparatus necessary leads to the fringes of what is considered orthodox scientific method. Moreover, the transition from Newtonian physics to Einstein, the forsaking of alchemy as a scientific practice, and the consequential turn to a rational perception of "spirit" highlights the significant influence of changing presuppositions and different experimental settings on the acceptability and verifiability of scientific phenomena. The departure from formerly acceptable systems and procedures under the auspices of new findings and scientific progress can impoverish the available experimental setup and jettison the pursuit of viable scientific projects altogether. A spirit-oriented approach may therefore lead to a reconsideration of the role of the laboratory in contemporary physics as well as the current methodology of data acquisition, conceptualization, and realization of laboratory experiments.

## Spirit, Physics, and Pentecostalism

We have seen that the methodology employed by some physicists has profound implications for addressing questions of faith, even if that was not the immediate intention of the scientific endeavor. The insight that the separation of theology and physics is largely the result of a neglect of method offers new opportunities for the Christian who is interested in the study of physics (Polkinghorne 2007: 23–47). The pentecostal-charismatic community is particularly suited for the pursuit of a spirit-oriented methodology due to its broad emphasis on the operation of the Holy Spirit in the cosmos, the world, and the human being. The question remains, however, what a contemporary pneumatological approach to physics might look like, and how it would function from a scientific perspective. To this end, we can paint a broad picture of pentecostal-charismatic approach to physics in the twenty-first century.

Among the immediate challenges a pentecostal who is also a physicist will likely encounter is the claim that "spirit" is not a category pursued in the study of physics. However, as we have seen above, the example of two of the most significant figures in the history of Western science shows that this argument is not entirely correct. It is more accurate to say that a spirit-oriented approach has not been central to the study of the physical universe and is not supported by contemporary experimental setup. Nonetheless, Newton and Einstein show that it is possible to make the methodological decision for including the notion of spirit in scientific inquiry.

It is accurate to say that the history of physics as a discipline of the natural sciences does not show a consistent pursuit of a spirit-oriented methodology. Much of the hesitancy is based on the difficulties to define spirit from a scientific perspective. Concerns among pentecostals may include that by adopting a spirit-oriented approach, their work might be considered unscientific. After all, at this time, there is no general agreement on what shape a spirit-oriented physics could take. Nonetheless, the pentecostal physicist might locate immediate resources in the recent revival of pneumatology in contemporary theology.

The traditional "cosmological argument" of modern theology shows the strong influence of a Newtonian worldview (Craig 1980). It postulates God as the first cause of creation who is then placed as absolutely transcendent above the created order. God is mover but not moved, the first cause but not the continuing cause of creation. In its place, pentecostals have repeatedly emphasized the importance of recognizing the operation of the Spirit *within* the created order and, if the concept of causality is maintained, *within* the causal relationship of the cosmos (see Yong 2005: 267–302). In pentecostal language, the Holy Spirit is "poured out," "sent," and "given"—a terminology that suggests that these actions originate from someone other than the Spirit. The Spirit is not "above" or "beyond" but "in" the cosmos, as intimate as the breath in the human being or the wind hovering over the waters, "groaning" with the pains and sufferings of creation.

The person of faith cannot afford to neglect the relational character of creation. Since a theology of the Holy Spirit emerges from the relations of the divine persons, more attention can be paid to how a relational universe exists in relation to itself and to the triune God. A perspective of the Spirit from a relational view should tell us not only about "God as God's self" but also about "God with us." A fruitful starting point among pentecostals in this regard is the notion of the self-giving (*kenosis*) of the Holy Spirit into creation.[4] In the Spirit, God has made a place for the divine presence in creation. Trinitarian concerns are certainly not the task of physics. Nonetheless, the pentecostal who pursues this discipline cannot avoid relational language, even if the goal is not primarily theological. Post-Newtonian physics had to abandon the view that the physical universe is an isolated system that functions consistently according to a set of inherent parameters. Instead, the contemporary physicist is confronted, among other things, with random processes, spontaneous changes, random motions, and non-causal relations (D'Espagnat 1999: 75–158) that have led to the formulation of new interpretations such as quantum physics (which emphasizes the relationship of nature on its smallest scale) and physical cosmology (which examines the relationship of nature on its largest scale) as well as theories that seek to explain the paradoxes exposed by those relational constructs. The spirit-oriented physicist can expect the pneumatological dimension in the relation of natural phenomena on any scale.

As an experimental discipline, the existence of relational variables in the physical universe is based on the rationality of natural phenomena (Davies 1993: 19–38). The physicist, however, can allocate a "place" for rationality only *between* natural phenomena, since these are not rational in themselves. To put it differently, the notion of reason has traditionally been attributed to God and the human being but not to nature in general. Western theology has linked the idea of rationality or intellect with the divine Word rather than the Spirit. The link of the former with the incarnation has further enhanced the distinction between spirit and flesh on the one hand, and between spirit and matter on the other hand. The implications of this dualism are particularly apparent in the attempt to ascertain the role of the divine Spirit at the creation. Pentecostals, by contrast, attribute the exercise of reason to the operation of the Holy Spirit. Wisdom and knowledge, prophecy and unknown tongues are gifts of the Spirit and not a product of the human intellect. The pentecostal-charismatic physicist faces the opportunity to confront the traditional dualistic tendencies and to involve, in the examination of physical processes, questions of the rationality and comprehensibility of nature that have rarely been the focus of scientific discussion. The goal of this endeavor is not simply to equate the divine Spirit with a cosmic rationality but to discover the role of the Spirit in the origin, availability, and distribution of reason in the physical universe.

Pentecostals can speak of what Thomas F. Torrance has called the "epistemological relevance of the Spirit" (1972: 165–92) in a twofold sense: as an agent of rationality, the Spirit is present in both the order and disorder within nature. From an epistemological perspective, moreover, knowledge of the natural phenomena necessitates a spiritual discernment by the scientist. Spirit-oriented physics is pneumatological not only in the sense of granting the Spirit a place in the cosmos but also in the sense of acknowledging that the exercise of the study of physics can in itself be an operation of the Spirit. Spiritual discernment must therefore speak of the Spirit's presence and activity as well as the Spirit's absence and withdrawal—in nature, in physics, and in the physicist.

From a pentecostal-charismatic perspective, we can then modify the cosmological argument by speaking of the Spirit, in particular, as the continuing cause for movement in creation. Although a full theological approach to the Spirit as movement has not yet been proposed, pentecostals have always described the Christian life as being moved by the Spirit. The notion of Spirit baptism is perhaps the prime analogy of the Spirit as movement. In this image, the Spirit can be seen as both mover and moved. From the pentecostal analogy of Spirit baptism, the "place" of God in the cosmos is best described not as a static location but as a form of movement. The movement of the Spirit in the physical universe can be seen as a movement of God away from God (and into that which is other than God) that nonetheless always seeks to return to God. The Spirit in creation does not move away from God but moves from God into creation in order to create and sustain that creation and eventually to return together with that creation to union with God. The implications of this view for an understanding of the presence of God in the physical universe have yet to be explored. While pentecostals may emphasize the importance of the notion of "sin" in the understanding of creation, the physicist may describe this theological concept scientifically as a movement of withdrawal by the Spirit, the absence of the Spirit, or a symmetry breaking (see Brading and Castellani 2003) in the cosmos. The doors are thus open to a pneumatological approach to physics—a methodological choice that is not only compatible with science but also invites the perspective of faith as an important dialogue partner in understanding the physical universe.

## Toward Spirit-Oriented Physics

A spirit-oriented physics encourages pentecostals not to relegate their pneumatological perspective to the realm of the so-called supernatural but to seek the spirit within the large and the small of the cosmos. As a person of faith, the scientist is encouraged to make room for the presence of God who is spirit in the experimental and empirical perspectives of physics. More immediately, this perception affects the way we see physics as a scientific discipline and, in the long run, influences the layout of the laboratory. The spirit-oriented perspective defines physics as a combination of experimental, philosophical, and spiritual dimensions that mutually inform each other. The physics lab is a connecting point for mechanics, chemistry, metallurgy, astronomy, and other elements that together comprise the experimental dimensions of nature. In the experimental, the philosophical and spiritual elements of physics come together as mutually complementary journeys toward a reality defined as much by human experience and reflection as by the presence and action of God.

For the pentecostal-charismatic Christian, the physical sciences do not have to be foreign territory. Both rationally and experimentally, the notion of "spirit" opens the doors for pentecostals to engage physics explicitly *as* pentecostals. The Spirit-filled physicist is perhaps the image that best represents the reconciled unity of physics and theology. In a sense, any physicist can adopt a spirit-oriented approach to describe the physical universe. The Spirit-filled physicist, however, will operate on a different level. Adapting the advice of the apostle Paul in 1 Corinthians, we may say that the "natural" and the "carnal" scientist are not able to discern the hidden things of the world, since those things are revealed only through the Spirit of God (1 Corinthians 2:10). The study of physics as a pentecostal depends not on the existence of spiritual things but on the acceptance and understanding of the things of the Spirit (v. 14) by the scientist.

In addition, the choice to study physics from a spirit-oriented perspective is not merely an epistemological decision but a reorientation in ontological focus. Simply put, the Spirit-filled physicist accepts the presence of "spirit" as an element of the physical universe. This means that physics as an engaging science is formed by a confluence of the experimental, philosophical, and spiritual dimensions that are each reflected in the pursuit of the other. Of course, just as not all theology is pneumatology, not all natural phenomena can be attributed to the function of the divine Spirit in creation. Nevertheless, a pneumatological perspective on the cosmos is not only consistent with contemporary theology but also continues the scientific tradition that emerges with Newton and Einstein. The paradigm for the spirit-oriented physicist is provided by the work of the Spirit, who calls attention not to himself but always to another, who directs the attention away from the human being and toward God and the fullness of God's creation. The pentecostal-charismatic existence, although defined by its Christian character, can therefore not be limited to theological concerns but is free to pursue the experience of God in the Holy Spirit as it becomes evident in physics as well as in other fields of scientific knowledge that reflect God's transformation of the whole of life.

On the other hand, a spirit-oriented approach to nature challenges those who intend to work in the physical sciences to be aware of the "pneumatological" categories that cannot be easily exorcised from their discipline. That "spirit" is an essential phenomenon in the study of nature not readily discernible in textbooks, lectures, and scholarly discussion. The notion of "spirit" has to be revived, in a sense, before it can be further implemented. The spirit-oriented approach therefore challenges those involved in physics to reexamine the discipline from both a methodological and an experimental perspective.

The way ahead for contemporary physics will likely lead pentecostals who work in the physical sciences toward dialogue with theology rather than away from the concerns of faith. This direction does not suggest, however, that theology provides answers to the questions of the physicist. Rather, the complementarity of both disciplines points to the influence each methodology has on the other. Pneumatology, as a methodological choice, is able to direct both the scientist and the theologian in the joint discovery and explanation of natural phenomena. In this way, the Spirit is able to unlock the mystery of creation from two different perspectives—a prospect that can lead the pentecostal-charismatic community to only one conclusion: both disciplines serve the glory of God.

# Notes

1. The term "spirit," as used by Einstein and Newton as well as in the remainder of this essay, is not capitalized unless I am using it explicitly as a reference to the Holy Spirit.
2. This foundational understanding of the presence of God in the universe formed the basis for Newton's interventionist concept of God that required the divine presence on behalf of what appeared to him as an imperfect solar system.
3. See Jammer 1957: 116–57; Austin 1970: 521–42; Quinn 1988: 176–92; Stangl 1991: 82–91; Force and Popkin 1999; McMullin 2001: 279–310; Ashworth 2003: 61–84 and 294–98.
4. See, for example, Bergmann 2005; Dabney 1997; Mühlen 1975.

# References

Ashworth, William B., Jr. 2003. "Christianity and the Mechanistic Universe." In David C. Lindberg and Ronald L. Numbers, eds., *When Science and Christianity Meet*. Chicago: University of Chicago Press, 61–84 and 294–98.

Austin, William H. 1970. "Isaac Newton on Science and Religion." *Journal of the History of Ideas* 31: 521–42.

Barr, Stephen M. 2006. *Modern Physics and Ancient Faith*. Notre Dame, Ind.: University of Notre Dame Press.

Bergmann, Sigurd. 2005. *Creation Set Free: The Spirit as Liberator of Nature*. Trans. Douglas Stott. Grand Rapids, Mich.: Eerdmans.

Brading, Katherine, and Elena Castellani. 2003. *Symmetries in Physics: Philosophical Reflections*. Cambridge: Cambridge University Press.

Cohen, I. Bernard, ed. 1958. *Isaac Newton's Papers and Letters on Natural Philosophy*. Cambridge, Mass.: Harvard University Press.

Craig, William Lane. 1980. *The Cosmological Argument from Plato to Leibniz*. New York: Barnes & Noble Books.

Dabney, D. Lyle. 1997. *Die Kenosis des Geistes: Kontinuität zwischen Schöpfung und Erlösung in Werk des Heiligen Geistes*. Neukirchener Beiträge zur systematischen Theologie 18. Neukirchen-Vlyun: Neukirchener Verlag.

Davies, Paul. 1993. *The Mind of God: The Scientific Basis for a Rational World*. New York: Simon & Schuster.

D'Espagnat, Bernard. 1999. *Conceptual Foundations of Quantum Mechanics*, 2nd ed. Reading, Mass., and New York: Westview Press.

Dobbs, Betty Jo Teeter. 1991. *The Janus Faces of Genius: The Role of Alchemy in Newton's Thought*. Cambridge: Cambridge University Press.

Dukas, Helen, and Banesh Hoffmann, eds. 1979. *Albert Einstein: The Human Side*. Princeton, N.J.: Princeton University Press.

Einstein, Albert. 1954. *Ideas and Opinions*. Trans. Sonja Bargmann. New York: Crown Publishers.

———. 1989. *The Collected Papers of Albert Einstein*, vol. 2, *The Swiss Years: Writings,*

*1900–1909.* Edited by Anna Beck and Peter Havas. Princeton, N.J.: Princeton University Press.

Einstein, Albert, and Leopold Infeld. 1938. *The Evolution of Physics: From Early Concepts to Relativity and Quanta.* New York: Simon & Schuster.

Force, James E., and Richard Henry Popkin, eds. 1999. *Newton and Religion: Context, Nature, and Influence.* Dordrecht: Kluwer Academic.

Guicciardini, Niccolò. 2004. "Analysis and Synthesis in Newton's Mathematical Work." In I. Bernard Cohen and George E. Smith, eds., *The Cambridge Companion to Newton.* Cambridge: Cambridge University Press, 308–28.

Jammer, Max. 1957. *Concepts of Force: A Study in the Foundation of Dynamics.* Cambridge, Mass.: Harvard University Press.

McGuire, J. E. 1995. *Tradition and Innovation: Newton's Metaphysics of Nature.* Dordrecht: Kluwer Academic.

McMullin, Ernan. 2001. "The Impact of Newton's Principia on the Philosophy of Science." *Philosophy of Science* 68: 279–310.

Mühlen, Heribert. 1975. "The Person of the Holy Spirit." In Kilian McDonnell, ed., *The Holy Spirit and Power: The Catholic Charismatic Renewal.* Garden City, N.Y.: Doubleday, 11–33.

Newton, Isaac. 1999. *The Principia: Mathematical Principles of Natural Philosophy.* Edited by I. Bernard Cohen and Anne Miller Whitman. Berkeley: University of California Press.

Pfizenmaier, Thomas C. 1997. "Was Isaac Newton an Arian?" *Journal of the History of Ideas* 58: 57–80.

Polkinghorne, John. 2007. *Quantum Physics and Theology: An Unexpected Kinship.* New Haven, Conn.: Yale University Press.

Quinn, Arthur. 1988. "On Reading Newton Apocalyptically." In Richard H. Popkin, ed., *Millenarianism and Messianism in English Literature and Thought 1650–1800.* Leiden: E. J. Brill, 176–92.

Rosenkranz, Ze'ev, ed. 1998. *Albert through the Looking-Glass: The Personal Papers of Albert Einstein.* Jerusalem: Jewish National and University Library.

Stangl, Walter. 1991. "Mutual Interaction: Newton's Science and Theology." *Perspectives on Science and Christian Faith* 43: 82–91.

Torrance, Thomas F. 1972. "Newton, Einstein and Scientific Theology." *Religious Studies* 8: 233–50.

Whiteside, D. T., ed. 1981. *The Mathematical Papers of Isaac Newton,* vol. 8, *1697–1722.* Cambridge: Cambridge University Press.

Yong, Amos. 2005. *The Spirit Poured Out on All Flesh: Pentecostalism and the Possibility of Global Theology.* Grand Rapids, Mich.: Baker Academic.

Zahar, Elie. 1989. *Einstein's Revolution: A Study in Heuristic.* La Salle, Ill.: Open Court.

## Recommended Readings

Chappell, Dorothy F., and E. David Cook, eds. 2005. *Not Just Science: Questions Where Christian Faith and Natural Science Intersect.* Grand Rapids, Mich.: Zondervan.

Davies, Paul. 1983. *God and the New Physics.* New York: Simon & Schuster.

Hodgson, Peter E. 2005. *Theology and Modern Physics.* Ashgate Science and Religion Series. Aldershot, UK: Ashgate.

Jammer, Max. 1999. *Einstein and Religion: Physics and Theology.* Princeton, N.J.: Princeton University Press.

Pannenberg, Wolfhart. 1993. *Toward a Theology of Nature: Essays on Science and Faith.* Edited by Ted Peters. Louisville, Ky.: Westminster/John Knox Press.

Polkinghorne, John. 1996. *The Faith of a Physicist: Reflections of a Bottom-up Thinker.* Minneapolis: Fortress.

Pugh, Jeffrey C. 2003. *Entertaining the Triune Mystery: God, Science, and the Space Between.* Harrisburg, Pa.: Trinity Press International.

Vondey, Wolfgang. 2005. "The Holy Spirit and Time in Catholic and Protestant Theology." *Scottish Journal of Theology* 58/4: 393–409.

———. 2009. "The Holy Spirit and the Physical Universe: The Impact of Scientific Paradigm Shifts on Contemporary Pneumatology." *Theological Studies* 70: 1–34.

Worthing, Mark William. 1996. *God, Creation, and Contemporary Physics.* Theology and the Sciences Series. Minneapolis: Fortress Press.

# 5 Does the Spirit Create through Evolutionary Processes? Pentecostals and Biological Evolution

*Steve Badger and Mike Tenneson*

*Three theistic perspectives on origins are followed by findings of two surveys that demonstrate that Pentecostal educators hold diverse opinions on the age of the universe and on macroevolution. Popular and scientific meanings of evolution are described along with arguments for and against macroevolution that clarify why this theory is so controversial. A synopsis of the historical development of evolutionary theory reveals that the scientific community has not unanimously embraced all parts of the theory. Intelligent design is presented as consistent with microevolution and some portions of macroevolution. A brief consideration of the genre and purpose of Genesis 1 follows a summary of how Pentecostals have historically responded to evolution. The positions of Pentecostal denominations and Pentecostal academicians are contrasted. Finally, suggestions are offered for an expanded Pentecostal participation in the conversation over origins.*

## Christian Evolutionist?

Ryan, a Pentecostal university student, is sitting in his biology professor's office. "I came to this university because I didn't want my faith destroyed by godless professors teaching evolution," he says. "A creation science expert at our church told us that we must choose between the Bible and Darwin. Dr. Price, why did you choose a textbook that presents evolution as *fact*? Can't you teach biology without evolution?"

Dr. Price listens silently to Ryan. She thinks: *How can I teach biology without weakening his faith in God and his confidence in the Bible? I'll need more than thirty minutes to answer his questions.*

"My girlfriend, Courtney, is majoring in biology. She's a Christian, but she believes in evolution. My parents told me to stop dating her. My roommate's a geology major who thinks the earth is billions of years old. He rarely goes to church and often breaks school rules. I doubt he's really a Christian. My theology professor warned us not to start down that 'slippery Darwinian slope.' He said first you accept a universe that is billions of years old, then you start to think maybe God directed evolution and call yourself a 'theistic evolutionist.' Finally, you become an atheist."

She thinks: *I don't want to get in a fight with my theologian colleagues!*

"I don't want to know all the arguments and evidences about origins. Just tell me what to think, what to believe."

She thinks: *Our denomination rejects theistic evolution. Some of our faculty hold different views, but I don't know what position our administrators take. I'm applying for tenure and promotion to full professor next year. If parents or pastors complain to the administration about my teaching, I might be passed over— or worse, they might not offer me a contract next year.*

"Dr. Price, I'm so confused. Can Pentecostals believe in evolution?"

She thinks: *Where do I begin?*

Although this scenario is fictional, the concerns of the two characters are quite real and recur frequently. A goal of this essay is to improve the dialogue between Pentecostals and scientists. Understanding where we agree and disagree can help us accomplish this goal. First, we describe three common Christian perspectives on origins, the results of surveys of Pentecostals about origins, the various meanings of the term *evolution,* and the historical development of evolutionary theory. Then we summarize the relationship between evolution and intelligent design (ID), the historical Pentecostal response to evolution, and Pentecostal denominational positions. Finally, we examine the Pentecostal academy, Pentecostal contributions, and search for a Pentecostal distinctive, concluding with suggestions for the future.

## Christian Perspectives

Westerners generally embrace one of five positions regarding origins, three of which are theistic. Since Christianity is antithetical to atheism and deism, we will not discuss the positions known as deistic evolution and atheistic evolution but will describe only the three theistic positions.[1]

*Young earth creationists* (YEC) are also known as fiat creationists or scientific creationists. They interpret the Genesis creation account as scientifically accurate historical narrative. They claim that both the Bible and scientific evidence support the conclusion that (1) God made the physical realm and life (2) out of nothing (3) in six consecutive 24-hour periods (4) about 6,000–10,000 years ago. They reject all theories of macroevolution and a universe that is billions of years old. They posit that geological strata are the result of a global flood in Noah's time.

While the works of theologian John Whitcomb and scientist Henry Morris (e.g., Whitcomb and Morris 1961) have greater notoriety, "Young Earth Creationism" by John Mark Reynolds and Paul Nelson in *Three Views on Creation and Evolution* presents a more evenhanded defense of YEC (Moreland and Reynolds 1999: 39–102). They are profoundly correct when they write, "Natural science at the moment seems to overwhelmingly point to an old cosmos. Though creationist scientists have suggested some evidence for a recent cosmos, none are widely accepted as true. It is safe to say that most recent creationists are motivated by religious concerns" (1999: 49).

Even those who fervently embrace a young earth model have been unable to provide convincing scientific evidence to confirm that position. A recent attempt by two influential recent creation advocacy groups failed to produce a coherent *scientific* case for a young earth. The RATE (radioisotopes and the age of the earth) project investigators, sponsored by the Institute of Creation Research (ICR) and the Creation Research Society (CRS), conceded that an overwhelming number of radioactive decay studies lead to the conclusion that the earth is more than 500 million years old (assuming uniformitarianism). They also claim, however, that several other scientific studies—along with their interpretation of the Genesis creation account—indicate a more recent creation. In an effort to present their findings as consistent with a recent creation, they posit that the rate of radioactive decay was at least a million times faster during the first three days of creation and the Genesis flood. However, they fail to provide a plausible mechanism for disposal of the massive amounts of heat and other radiation generated during this supposed decay rate acceleration (Vardiman et al. 2005). They consider their interpretation of Scripture to be more important than scientific evidences to the contrary.

*Old earth creationists* (OEC) accept the scientific evidences for a universe that is billions of years old, but most reject macroevolutionary theory and argue that God created everything—including life—by a series of creative acts. Adherents disagree on when each of these creative acts occurred, but they believe that God directly created life much as it is today. Creation accounts in Genesis are interpreted as historical narrative but not necessarily as a scientific explanation of how God created. Also known as progressive creation, this view has been advocated by theologian Bernard Ramm and scientist Hugh Ross.

Table 5.1. Self-Reported Position of Pentecostal Faculty

| Self-Reported Position | 2004 (n=224) | 2008 (n=70) |
|---|---|---|
| Young Earth Creationists | 34.8% | 24.3% |
| Old Earth Creationists | 30.8% | 38.6% |
| Evolutionary Creationists | 12.1% | 25.7% |
| Undecided and blank | 21.4% | 10.0% |
| Atheistic Evolutionists | 0.8% | 1.4% |

*Evolutionary creationists* (EC) attempt to harmonize theories of macroevolution with the biblical account of origins. Most think that the Genesis creation account is neither historical narrative nor scientifically accurate. They accept the scientific evidence for a universe that is billions of years old and embrace contemporary macroevolutionary theory, but they stress that God directed the evolution of existing life forms from the original life forms that he created. This position is also known as theistic evolution. Contemporary representatives of this position include scientists Howard van Till (1999), Kenneth Miller (2007), Francis Collins (2006), and Pentecostal theologian and scientist Denis Lamoureux (2008).

## Pentecostals and Evolution Today

Until the 1970s, Pentecostals were almost univocal in supporting the YEC position and rejecting all theories of macroevolution. However, Pentecostals today are much more diverse in their opinions on origins.

In 2004, the authors constructed, validated, and administered a 62-item online survey to students, professors, and administrators at Assemblies of God (AG) colleges and universities. In the summer of 2008 the authors constructed a 15-item online survey and invited more than 250 people who teach creation or evolution at a Pentecostal college or university to take it. In the 2004 survey, 5.4 percent of the respondents taught life sciences and 18.8 percent taught Bible courses. In the 2008 survey, the majority of respondents taught life sciences (24.3%) or Bible (44.3%). Table 5.1 summarizes with which camp Pentecostal faculty identified.

The two surveys and their results were different. In 2004, only faculty at AG schools were surveyed regarding many general beliefs vis-à-vis origins; the 2008 survey included faculty at AG and other Pentecostal institutions and specifically targeted what they believe and teach about evolution. The early survey included teachers in all disciplines; the later survey targeted only teachers of Bible and teachers of biology. These sample differences could account for the variations in the results above.

The 2008 survey showed that most of the respondents believe that the universe is billions of years old, that all life did not have a common ancestor, that one of the theistic positions has more support than the others, and that arguments for intelligent design (ID) are convincing. They were divided on whether new life has arisen since creation. Regarding their approaches to teaching origins, the respondents indicated that they cover ID, discuss the strengths and limitations of science, emphasize the different meanings of evolution, include theories of knowing, and emphasize God as creator—regardless of the method of creation. They are divided on teaching macroevolution as the unifying concept of biology.

In 2004, the AG life science professors (n=12) identified themselves primarily as OEC (41.7%) and secondarily as YEC (25.0%). In 2008, the responses of the Pentecostal life scientists (n=17) were more evenly distributed among the three theistic camps. Fewer differences were noticed among the biblical studies professors in both the 2004 and 2008 surveys. Almost half identified themselves as OEC, about one-fourth as YEC, and almost one-fifth as EC.[2]

### Evolution: Meanings

Differences in the use of the term *evolution* unnecessarily polarize people into opposing camps and intensify emotions among adherents, diminishing our ability to objectively evaluate the strengths and weaknesses of arguments. Some people confuse *evolutionary theory* (i.e., Darwinism) and *evolutionism* and warn that embracing the former leads to accepting the latter. The former is a biological theory that posits that changes in life forms are ateleological[3] and due primarily to natural selection. The latter is a philosophy that posits that evolution is the universal mode of change, both organic and inorganic, and is teleological (Medawar 1999: 294). A few other terms are often included in discussions of evolution. *Materialism* and *naturalism* assert that only the physical realm exists or that it is all we can know with any degree of certainty. *Scientism* claims that the methods of the natural sciences are the only paths to certain knowledge.

Evolutionary biologist Richard Dawkins's concept of evolution is atheistic and materialistic and falsely characterizes the origins debate as between Christianity and science (2006). Similarly, some popular creationists erroneously think only atheists embrace evolution. The large numbers of Christian biologists (e.g., Francis Collins, Kenneth Miller, Robert Bakker, and Michael Behe) who believe that God is the creator and also accept much macroevolutionary theory show this to be false.

Although some writers report that *biological evolution* is used with as many as six different meanings in biology textbooks (Meyer and Keas 2001: 1), we find *evolution* correctly used in two basic ways by scientists and the popular media: (1) evolution as genetic change with time, and (2) evolution as common descent (the famous "tree of life").[4]

## Evolution: Genetic Change over Time

The most basic and least controversial meaning of evolution is genetic change in a population over time (i.e., gene frequency changes). These measurable changes have been observed repeatedly and are thought to result in physical changes that affect survival and reproduction. For example, Dodd (1989) found that, after several generations, fruit fly populations grown with different food sources developed different digestive abilities and mate preferences.

We use *microevolution* to indicate small genetic change over time. The prefix *micro-* implies that the changes are so small that the individuals can still interbreed with the original population—a new type of organism has not formed. This noncontroversial meaning of evolution is almost unanimously accepted by both creationists and non-creationists.

The most often-cited example of observed natural selection is the 30-year study of beak thickness of ground finches on the Galapagos Islands (Grant and Grant 2002) in which the researchers concluded that the average beak thickness (top to bottom height measurement) was determined by the types of seeds available. During years of drought, the smaller and less-drought-tolerant plants produce fewer seeds. These easier-to-crush seeds are rare, leaving only the larger and harder-to-crack seeds from the drought-tolerant plants. Since thinner beaked finches are less successful at cracking larger seeds, they don't produce as many young as the thick-billed finches, and consequently the average beak thickness increases in the population. When rains are adequate, the smaller seeds become common again, and the average beak thickness decreases. Wells (2002: 174–75) points out that these studies have shown only a slight oscillation and that new species of finch have not evolved. Nevertheless, biologists see this example of natural selection as causing a change (albeit temporary) in population gene frequencies (evolution).

Evolution and natural selection are not synonymous, but it is thought to be the most significant mechanism driving evolution in natural populations. Natural selection has been observed hundreds of times (e.g., see Hoekstra et al. 2001). Although other processes can also cause genetic changes in populations (e.g., mutation, migration, and genetic drift), their effects are thought to be much less significant.

## Evolution: Common Descent with Modification

For some scientists, *evolution* means that all living things have a common ancestor, and this is offered as an interpretive paradigm of the fossil record and common biochemical and embryologic themes. In *The Origin of Species*, Darwin visualized this explanation as the "great tree of life" (1998: 170).[5] The base of the tree represents an ancient single original life form; the trunk and branches represent all subsequent life.

Common descent with modification is often condensed into the term *macroevolution*. Biologists think macroevolution results from the same processes that drive microevolution. The difference is that in macroevolution the genetic makeup of the population has changed enough that the daughter population can no longer interbreed with the original population—they are not the same species. This is why many writers use macroevolution and *speciation* (i.e., formation of a new species) synonymously.

Although biologists find it difficult to agree on a definition of *species*, the de facto standard is Ernst Mayr's (1942) "biological species" concept. Mayr posited that if individuals from two different populations can mate and produce fertile offspring, they are the same species, even if they do not appear similar. Notice that this definition cannot be applied to fossils or organisms that do not reproduce sexually.

### Macroevolution: The Controversy

The following five ideas are consistent with macroevolution. First, the vast majority of scientists agree that the earth is ancient. Although not a sufficient condition, an ancient earth is a necessary condition for macroevolution. The main mechanism of macroevolution is natural selection, which is usually thought to require long periods of time to produce new kinds of life. Second, the findings of the geographic distribution of living and fossil life are consistent with predictions of macroevolutionary theory. In addition, most geologists and paleontologists find the catastrophic Genesis flood an inadequate explanation of the distribution and abundance of fossils. Third, vestigial structures (features whose function is minimal or unknown) are thought to be ancestral remnants. Fourth, molecular biology and biochemistry have provided numerous biochemical correlates with ancestral relationships that were inferred from the fossil record. Fifth, many find macroevolution logical since it seems to fit the two common truth tests: correspondence and coherence.

Some theists find macroevolution controversial. Young earth creationists reject it because it depends on an ancient physical realm and on interpretations of the fossil, biochemical, and embryological data that presuppose uniformitarianism[6] and naturalism. Furthermore, it argues for species plasticity, that is, that life has speciated many times since the creation. Some old earth creationists also object to macroevolution. They claim that mutation has not been demonstrated to create new forms of life (Lester and Bohlin 1989), that God is the only Creator and his original life forms were ideal, and that any change since creation could only be negative (Bowler 1984: 120).

*Evolution: Historical Overview*

Broad acceptance of evolutionary theory required drastic changes in the geological and cosmological models in vogue in the 1800s (Bowler 1984: 4–5). The estimated age of the physical realm increased dramatically as a result of the works of geologists James Hutton and Charles Lyell. Geology and paleontology as interpreted further by Jean-Baptiste Lamarck and Georges Cuvier provided evidence that the earth and its inhabitants are not static monuments to God's creative acts but are constantly changing.

The scientific community adopted the philosophical premise that these changes were ateleological (non-goal-oriented). Naturalist philosophy's rejection of the supernatural had gained a strong foothold in the decades before Darwin. These ideas, along with economist and demographer Thomas Malthus's theories of human population limits and the resultant struggle for survival, produced a rich intellectual environment receptive to Darwin's novel ideas (Larson 2004).

Darwin's theories developed over decades of study. Observations of biology, geology, and paleontology during his circumnavigation of the globe on the H.M.S. *Beagle* (1831–36) led to the publication of his *Journal and Remarks* in 1839, establishing his reputation as a natural scientist. Darwin's theory of natural selection was an attempt to explain the geographic distribution of fossils and living flora and fauna. He had developed much of the theory by 1844 but was reluctant to publish it because of the expected public reaction. In 1858 Darwin read Alfred Russell Wallace's manuscript with a nearly identical theory derived from research in the Amazon basin and Malaysia. Alarmed, Darwin rapidly completed his writings and in 1859 published *On the Origin of Species* ahead of Wallace. This book established evolution through common descent as the dominant explanation for the unity and diversity of life.

By 1900 Darwin's theory had lost much of its preeminence. Field naturalists attempted to combine natural selection with Lamarck's theory of inheritance of acquired characteristics. While many paleontologists thought that evolution was teleological, experimental biologists began using the work of geneticist Gregor Mendel (rediscovered circa 1900) and posited that the environment played little or no role in evolution. For them, mutation ruled. In the 1920s these divided branches of evolutionary theory began to reconcile, and the merge was complete by 1940 when genetics and natural selection were combined in what is now called the *modern synthesis* (Bowler 1984: 289). Darwin's evolutionary theories returned to preeminence and remain so today.

Niles Eldredge and Stephen Jay Gould published a controversial paper in 1972 positing that evolution is not uniformly gradual as Darwin envisioned. Instead, they argued that evolution occurs in relatively brief, rapid bursts, interspersed with long periods of no evolution. They called it *punctuated equilibria,* and this idea remains contested. Evolutionary biologists also debate such ideas as the importance of mutation, horizontal gene transfer among microbes, sociobiology (evolutionary explanations of behavior, including human), and the Gaia theory (earth as a living thing).

## Intelligent Design

Could the unity and diversity of life be the result of both evolution and design? Many proponents of intelligent design (ID) answer "yes." They universally accept microevolution while rejecting ateleological macroevolution, and they often see ID and theistic teleological evolution as compatible.

William Paley hinted at ID in the early 1800s: "Intelligent causes are necessary to explain the complex, information-rich structures of biology and . . . these causes are empirically detectable" (1809: 1). Two of the best-known modern proponents of ID, mathematician and philosopher William Dembski and biochemist Michael Behe, have offered two main lines of support.

Specified complexity (Dembski) claims that living things are complex in ways that undirected random processes could never produce. Statistical analyses of DNA support this position. Dembski argues that chance alone can produce complex unspecified information and noncomplex specified information, but it cannot produce complex specified information. By this process of elimination, ID best explains the origin of complex specified information (Dembski 1999).

Behe presents irreducible complexity as another line of evidence. A single living system is composed of several (often many) interacting parts. Each part contributes to the function of the system. Removal of any one of the components causes the system to cease functioning. Furthermore, no functional intermediates that lack some of the parts are known. Behe (1996) illustrates this with the biochemistry of blood clotting and the structure and function of bacterial flagella (among others). Charles Darwin predicted this challenge to his theory: "If it could be demonstrated that any complex organ existed which could not possibly have been formed by numerous, successive, slight modifications, my theory would absolutely break down" (1998: 232).

Proponents of ID argue that materialistic biologists have failed to provide satisfactory natural explanations for the origin and development of these complex biological systems; thus, ID is presented as a better explanation than naturalistic evolution. ID also finds support in the "finely tuned universe" argument from physics (Ross 2001: 111–30). Scientists have long recognized that the physical constants of the universe have precisely the values essential for life. Small changes in these constants would correspond to a very different universe—one in which life as we know it could neither arise nor exist.

Intelligent design theories have little effect on which model of origins theists embrace, but they do support the notion of a creator. ID is defended by the Discovery Institute as a scientific approach (and not simply old-fashioned creationism masquerading as science) because it produces empirically testable hypotheses: (1) "Natural structures will be found that contain many parts arranged in intricate patterns that perform a specific function." (2) "Forms containing large amounts of novel information will appear in the fossil record suddenly and without similar precursors." (3) "Convergences will occur routinely. That is, genes and other functional parts will be re-used in different and unrelated organisms." (4) "Much 'junk DNA' will turn out to perform valuable functions" (Luskin 2007: 1).

Critics of ID raise several objections. The first is that ID is not science because it invokes supernatural factors. Since most scientists embrace a naturalistic philosophy that rejects the consideration of any supernatural agency, they reject the notion that science should ever include supernatural elements. Some creationists view it as being too watered down, since it doesn't explicitly name the designer as the God of the Bible, while others oppose it simply because some ID proponents accept macroevolution. Among creationists, the most serious objection is that ID is a "God of the gaps" approach, limiting itself to explaining only what science cannot. As our scientific knowledge expands, the gaps disappear and theological explanations are discarded, undermining the confidence people have in the Bible. Finally, some theistic biologists argue against ID on scientific grounds (e.g., Miller 2007).

Is ID science? While ID proponents say yes, the majority of biologists say no. Is evolution science? Everyone agrees that microevolution is science, and most biologists agree that macroevolution is also science. Your answers to these questions depend more on your definition of *science* than on empirical data.[7] Some theologians, philosophers of science, and scientists, however, argue that macroevolution is as much philosophy and speculation as it is empirical science. Evolutionist Michael Ruse, a philosopher of science, shocked his audience at the 1993 American Association for the Advancement of Science meeting when he said: "We should recognize, both historically and perhaps philosophically certainly that the science side *has certain metaphysical assumptions built into doing science,* which—it may not be a good thing to admit in a court of law—but I think that in honesty that we should recognize" it (Witham 2002: 86; italics ours).

## Pentecostals and Evolution

Pentecostal denominations trace their roots back to the last decade of the nineteenth century and the first decade of the twentieth century. In order to understand the response of these early Pentecostals to the idea of evolution, we should recognize who they were.[8] Very few of them were articulate or highly educated; indeed, many lacked a high school education. Further, as Amos Yong has observed, there was a "classical Pentecostal . . . distrust in philosophical and historical argumentation and human reason" (1997: 83).

During the very earliest years, Pentecostals largely ignored evolution, focusing primarily on salvation, sanctification, evangelism, healing, the Second Coming, and the baptism in the Holy Spirit. Ronald Numbers concluded that "the various Pentecostal churches, though instinctively opposed to evolution, devoted noticeably less attention to the question than Holiness folk and far less attention than Fundamentalists" (1992: 133). By about 1920, however, they had joined other Christians in vehemently rejecting evolutionary theory as contrary to the Bible. Early Pentecostal leaders considered themselves fundamentalists in opposition to the modernists and their "unprovable theories regarding the evolution of man" (Frodsham 1924: 4).

Christians who became Pentecostals often came from other Protestant denominations (e.g., Baptist, Lutheran, Methodist, Presbyterian) and often brought with them their anti-evolution views. Without question, evolutionary theories seemed to be irreconcilable to a plain reading of Genesis. Thus, it is not surprising that first-generation Pentecostals almost unanimously opposed evolution. Those who held other positions usually thought it prudent to keep their opinions private.

Because Pentecostals saw evolution as antithetical to the Genesis creation account, they perceived it as a threat to the authority of the Scriptures. How could humans have evolved into God's image? Embracing evolution produces other theological problems related to the inerrancy of the Scriptures, original sin and the fall, morality, and the unique relationship between humans and the Holy Spirit.

A survey of the twentieth-century religious literature finds much Pentecostal ink and paper invested in attacking Darwinian evolution.[9] The decades of the 1920s and 1930s were some of the most prolific (see King 2009). These early attacks were typically ad hominem arguments and frequently begged the question. Some were personal testimonies of people who had accepted evolution in public school or in college but had rejected this position upon conversion.

The Pentecostal revivals (1906–1909) that birthed the Pentecostal denominations occurred about fifty years after Darwin published *On the Origin of Species* (1859).[10] By the time of the formation of these denominations, several non-Pentecostal Protestant denominations were already aggressively debating creation-evolution. This feud reached a fever pitch in the mid-1920s when Tennessee high school teacher John Scopes was charged with and tried for teaching Darwinian evolution in a public school. The sensational trial showcased two famous lawyers: William Jennings Bryan prosecuted, while Clarence Darrow defended, Scopes.

Perhaps because of the notoriety of this trial, articles in Pentecostal literature attacking Darwinian evolution were most numerous in the late 1920s and early 1930s. Non-Pentecostals wrote some of these; for example, *The Latter Rain Evangel* reprinted an article entitled "Moses vs. Darwin: I Sent My Boy to

College a Christian and He Came Back an Atheist" by William Jennings Bryan (1923).

These early attempts to refute evolutionary theories were often illogical tirades. Georgie Robinson (1927) had a list of thirty-four examples of "The Bible's Answer to the Theory of Evolution." Not one item in this list actually addressed evolution. Another article in the *Pentecostal Evangel* (September 9, 1951) was guilty of both begging the question and appealing to authority: Mortimer J. Adler (a famous philosopher and author) "attacked the Darwinian hypothesis by stating that men and apes differ essentially in kind, not merely in degree" and that "there can be no intermediates and no common ancestor."

Both Pentecostal and non-Pentecostal detractors commonly claimed greater success at disproving evolution than they actually achieved. Through the years, titles like these were common: *The Evolution of Man Scientifically Disproved in 50 Arguments: Evolution Disproved* (Williams 1928), *Evolution–The Incredible Hoax* (G. Lindsay 1963), *The Dismantling of Evolutionism's Sacred Cow: Radiometric Dating* (D. Lindsay 1994), and "New Fossil Finding May Completely Disprove Darwin" (*Pentecostal Evangel*, May 6, 1956). But the only people who found these articles convincing were already convinced.

Occasionally, reports were inaccurate. For example, in January 1926, the *Latter Rain Evangel* printed as factual a fictitious account of the end of Darwin's life, "Darwin's Last Days," supposedly written by "Lady Hope" of Northfield, England, in which Darwin is said to have rejected the theory of evolution. This story is still being circulated even though anti-evolutionists admit that it lacks any historical support (Grigg 1995: 36–37).

The evolution debate intensified in 1961 when Whitcomb and Morris (non-Pentecostals) published *The Genesis Flood: The Biblical Record and Its Scientific Implications*. They argued that Noah's flood could explain the geological strata, giving the young earth theory scientific credence and spawning the *creation science* movement. It had the added effect of "dictating the terms of the debate over origins" (Numbers 1992: 145). From then on, arguments over origins began with the age of the universe, since an old earth is prerequisite to evolutionary theory.

Stanley Horton's *Systematic Theology: A Pentecostal Perspective* (1994), published by the Assemblies of God's Logion Press, included Timothy Munyon's "The Creation of the Universe and Humankind." Munyon presents four models that attempt to harmonize the Bible and scientific observations (1994: 223–33). First, Munyon dismisses *theistic evolution* (i.e., evolutionary creation) by saying that studying it "serves no useful purpose here because its proponents basically accept everything secular evolution proposes with the proviso that God was superintending the whole process" (223). Then he argues that the Hebrew of Genesis 1 does not allow for a gap of millions of years between the first and second verses (contra the gap theory).[11] Instead, this first verse "functions as an introductory summary statement of creation, upon which the rest of the chapter elaborates." He continues, arguing that "the gap theory is self-defeating" since accepting it rules out evidence for the global Genesis flood (226).

Third, Munyon discusses the claims of *fiat creationists* (YEC) that the earth is no more than ten thousand years old. Fiat creationists discount radiometric dating, maintain that the flood can account for all observations of geological strata and fossils, and claim that God created the universe "mature," with an appearance of age (228–29). He criticizes YEC for their "tendency to employ an overly strict interpretation of Scripture" and "the rejection of nonradiometric data that seem to indicate an older earth" (230). Finally, he describes *progressive creationists* (OEC) as rejecting macroevolution while accepting an old universe. He identifies three major weaknesses in the position of progressive creationists: that they "place too much stock in science's ability to recognize truth" (232–33); that their rejection of fiat creationism causes them to use a hermeneutic that is too dependent on contemporary science; and that this model is inconsistent with a global flood.

After listing six primary tenets that supporters of each of these four models can accept, Munyon ends by cautioning proponents of each view "that the Scriptures do not speak in support of their models with the degree of specificity they would like" (234). He leaves his readers with two acceptable options: fiat creationism (YEC) or progressive creationism (OEC).

## The Genre and Purpose of Genesis 1

Most of us tend to read Genesis 1 ethnocentrically—through the lenses of our culture. But since it was not written in English or to modern Westerners, we have some work to do if we hope to grasp what the author was trying to communicate and what the original audience understood.

Crucial to correctly understanding Genesis 1 is the identification of the literary form. Without question, it is narrative, but is it *historical* narrative? And does it portray a modern scientific worldview, or an ancient Hebrew worldview? Old Testament scholars have debated this for centuries. Moreover, while it is not poetry, it has poetical elements—for example, the events of the second three days mirror the events of the first three days. Waltke (1991: 5) sees God as *filling* on days four through six what he *formed* on days one through three.

A careful reading of Genesis is required to discover the author's purposes in writing. Old Testament scholar Bruce Waltke suggests that Moses wrote to address the "pagan mythologies about the creation [that] ever threatened to annihilate Israel's witness to ethical monotheism," and that Moses' creation story allowed "only one God, Creator of heaven and earth, who alone deserves worship, trust and obedience" (Waltke 1991: 2).[12] Neither God nor Moses intended to answer our contemporary scientific questions regarding creation.

Two sets of presuppositions generally determine which position a person will adopt vis-à-vis origins. One has to do with science, and the other with the Bible (or Genesis 1).

People who have confidence in the ability of the natural sciences to answer the questions of origins and who reject divine inspiration of the Bible (or Genesis 1) are not likely to embrace any creation model. People with less confidence in the ability of science to address origins and who embrace Genesis 1 as scientifically accurate historical narrative will typically embrace a recent creation. Furthermore, those who have confidence in the natural sciences, who believe the Bible is God's Word, but who see the Genesis creation account as reflecting an ancient Hebrew worldview (not a modern scientific worldview) will be more likely to adopt an ancient earth position. Finally, people who have a prior commitment to an origins camp (YEC, OEC, EC, etc.) will be inclined to adopt a view of the Scriptures and a view of the sciences that fits that position.

## Denominational Positions

A few Pentecostal groups have adopted an official position on creation. The second-largest Pentecostal group, the Church of God, published its stance on its Web site in a resolution titled "Creationism":

> WHEREAS secular humanism and anti-God philosophies are being taught in our public educational systems; and
> WHEREAS there is a need for God's people to unite against the teaching of evolution as a scientific fact;
> THEREFORE BE IT RESOLVED that we give our full support to the principle that where evolution is taught in our public schools, provision be made for teaching the Biblical alternative of creation (Church of God [Cleveland] 1980).

This resolution seems to leave room for teaching evolutionary theory in public schools as long as the Genesis creation account is given a hearing.

In 1977, the Assemblies of God, the largest Pentecostal denomination, adopted an official position on origins. Compared to early Pentecostal attacks, "The Doctrine of Creation" is a well-thought-out and articulated essay. However, the second paragraph states that the Bible "is as trustworthy in the area of science as when it speaks of any other subject" and later that the act of God breathing life into Adam "indicates that . . . God did not form Adam from some previously existing animal" (Assemblies of God 1977). The paper rejects evolution:

> This Bible record of creation thus rules out the evolutionary philosophy which states that all forms of life come into being by gradual, progressive evolution carried on by resident forces. It also rules out any evolutionary origin for the human

race, since no theory of evolution, including theistic evolution, can explain the origin of the male before the female, nor can it explain how a man could evolve into a woman. (Assemblies of God 1977)

The last statement is a "straw man," since no contemporary evolutionary theorist would suggest that "a man could evolve into a woman." The position paper is silent on the age of creation.

Another document published by the Assemblies of God offers commentary on this position paper. This shorter treatise asks,

However, by what means was His creative work accomplished? More specifically, did God employ a gradual process by which the world came into being? Did higher forms of life progress from lower forms of life? The advocates of gradual process are called theistic evolutionists. For them, God's creative days recorded in Genesis may well have been eons of time. (Assemblies of God 2006)

The three questions are left unanswered, but this document clearly calls evolution a fallacy while erroneously conflating OEC and EC.

Ken Horn, the managing editor of the *Today's Pentecostal Evangel* (AG), says theistic evolution (i.e., evolutionary creation) is unacceptable:

The Bible does not allow for "theistic evolution," the theory that evolution was not blind chance but the method God chose to make man. One would have to discount scriptural accounts in order to believe this, most notably God's specific creation of Adam and Eve.

In order to fit God into the evolutionary mold, one must sacrifice a high view of Scripture. The authority of God's Word and theistic evolution cannot coincide. (Horn 2006: 22–23)

In contrast, most contemporary origins researchers correctly consider adherents of YEC, OEC, and EC to be creationists as opposed to deistic and atheistic evolutionists.

Over the years, the AG weekly magazine published YEC news releases from the Institute for Creation Research and the Creation Research Society. As late as April 1996, the *Pentecostal Evangel* published an interview with YEC proponent Ken Ham, the director of "Answers in Genesis," who stated that people can either believe the Bible or science and that "if you believe the evolutionary theories of men, then you've just wiped out the basis of the gospel." Later, the *Pentecostal Evangel* had an article by OEC Hugh Ross who clearly rejected macroevolution (Ross 2003).

Wanda Brackett reported that "The Foursquare Church has not developed a contemporary denominational statement regarding evolution; the statement we have in regard to that issue is part of the doctrinal statements"[13] in the denomination's "Declaration of Faith."[14] A page on the Web site of Life Four-square Church (Angleton, Texas) describes several creation-evolution models. Although no position is embraced, readers are discouraged from accepting EC. Associate Pastor Sonny Bowman writes: "People who ask us about our creation viewpoint generally want to know what our official position is. Our official position is to not have an official position. There's simply not enough evidence to demand a verdict" (Bowman 2007).

The position of the Pentecostal Church of God is identical to that of the Assemblies of God.[15] No statement regarding origins was found in *Biblical Principles, Beliefs, and Doctrines of the Church of God of Prophecy* (Church of God of Prophecy 2008). No official position of the United Pentecostal Church was found; however, the Web site of the United Pentecostal Church of Pittsburg (California) has an article entitled "Creation versus Evolution" in which they affirm God as creator and reject "evolution" as unbelievable, but they do not specifically embrace a young earth position (United Pentecostal Church of Pittsburg 2008).

Finally, the Pentecostal editors of the notes in *The Full Life Study Bible*, which bills itself as "an international Bible for pentecostal and charismatic Christians," states that "Bible believing Christians must reject . . . *theistic evolution*" (Stamps 1992: 7; italics in original). This was repeated in the 2007 edition entitled *Fire Bible: Student Edition*.

## Pentecostals: The Academy

Early Pentecostals were typically not highly educated, thus the initial reactions to the theory of evolution were often superficial and poorly reasoned. However, many second- and third-generation Pentecostals were college graduates—some in the sciences—and their apologetic has been more measured and rational.[16]

During the 1970s, many Pentecostals abandoned YEC and the gap theory to espouse OEC or EC. For example, Myrtle Fleming, Ph.D., a biologist who taught at both Lee College (Church of God) and Emmanuel College (Pentecostal Holiness Church), "warned Pentecostal theologians not to be taken in by claims for a young earth. In writing and teaching about origins, she said, 'great care should be taken to distinguish between facts and theory, original works and philosophers' thinking'" (cited in Numbers 1992: 146). Through the years, a few professors (both of biology and of Bible) at Pentecostal colleges and universities were evolutionary creationists, "but these professors generally maintained a low profile to avoid becoming targets of a more conservative constituency" (Numbers 1992: 146).

In 1972 the Institute for Creation Research met at Evangel College (AG) for its first Summer Institute for Scientific Creationism (see Numbers 1992, 146).

None of Evangel's science faculty endorsed the YEC theories of the ICR flood geologists, and later a Bible professor and a biology professor held their own seminar using materials that advocated an old universe.[17]

Duane Thurman, a biology professor at Oral Roberts University, published *How to Think About Evolution* in 1977. Instead of the unconvincing arguments presented in earlier Pentecostal literature, Thurman carefully outlined the presuppositions and methods of the natural sciences and of biblical interpretation and concluded, significantly:

> In a time when some Christians call us to affirm their theory as the only one possible for a biblical Christian, it is important to refuse to be rushed into decisions. . . . We do not have enough evidence to say that one version of origins should with absolute certainty be espoused over another. We should listen to others, Christian and non-Christian alike. We should be wary of those who make one theory the test of whether one is truly a biblical Christian. (Thurman 1977: 136–37)

And, we might add, we should be wary of those who make affiliation in one camp or another the test of whether one is truly a legitimate scientist.

## Pentecostal Contributions

Pentecostals have not developed a distinctive theology of origins; instead, they have typically embraced any of the three theistic positions articulated by evangelicals and fundamentalists. But Pentecostals are now making some contributions to the conversation.

Amos Yong (2006) argues for integrating emergence theory with pneumatology. Emergence theory hypothesizes about how complex systems can arise from multiple simple interactions. Although usually presented as materialistic, the emergence theory of Clayton (2000, 2004) leaves room for a theistic influence. Yong argues that the biblical account of the emergence of creation from chaos can be explained as works of the Spirit that are dynamic and instill the creation with ongoing productive and reproductive abilities. He concludes that the Spirit may work in creation through evolutionary processes.

How does this model fit in the three common Western positions regarding origins? Yong suggests it fits the EC position, particularly as envisioned by Howard Van Till (1999), who espouses a teleological view of macroevolution with little ongoing divine intervention. Taken too far, this view sounds deistic. All OEC advocates see microevolution as an important process and view the Spirit as guiding creation; but unlike proponents of EC, they see the degree of change as limited. Those who believe in a recent creation agree with the initial creative work of the Spirit but reject macroevolution. Those who hold strongly to a fixed species concept would be even less open to this theory of emergence and the Spirit.

As educators, the authors have collaborated for years to further this conversation among Pentecostals. To accomplish this, we have surveyed the opinions of a large number of Pentecostals and published (Tenneson and Badger 2009) and presented our findings to a variety of academic and church audiences.

Pentecostals should seek and anticipate the guidance of the Holy Spirit as they participate in enterprises that attempt to integrate the truth revealed in God's Word with the truth revealed in God's creation (Romans 1:18–20). The Spirit may have played a greater creative role through evolutionary processes than we previously thought.

## Resolution: Ryan and Dr. Price

What can Pentecostal professors and students do to minimize the tension portrayed in the opening scenario? While there is no simple solution, we offer some suggestions. Biology teachers need to acknowledge the philosophical foundations of the scientific study of origins, as Ruse did in 1993 (Witham 2002). Furthermore, they should concede that we cannot and should not have the same confidence in the theories of historical science that we have in the conclusions of empirical science.[18] Students studying biology must realize that the majority of biology textbooks and teachers have the "Dobzhansky attitude": "Nothing in biology makes sense except in the light of evolution" (Dobzhansky 1973).[19] Students and teachers of biology must understand and use evolutionary theory—even if its reality is doubted.

All Pentecostals should agree that God is the creator; we are created in God's image to have fellowship with him; he is actively involved in his creation; and studying science is profitable since God's eternal power and divine nature are revealed in his creation (Romans 1:18–20). Surely the Holy Spirit can enable Pentecostals studying creation-evolution to fulfill the ancient saying "In essentials, unity. In nonessentials, liberty. In all things, charity."

## Desiderata

Advocates of YEC have so dominated the history of Pentecostalism that many educators may be unaware that the majority of their colleagues believe in an old earth (about 46% in the 2004 survey and 64% in the 2008 survey). The anti-evolution stance of Pentecostals has been so historically widespread that many do not realize that a significant number of Pentecostals embrace many aspects of macroevolutionary theory.

Should this shift to more diverse views vis-à-vis origins alarm Pentecostals? Should we insist on the traditional view? Should denominations reexamine their official positions? Or would any such move be more destructive than constructive—so controversial as to be divisive? Should educators and educational institutions (Bible colleges, universities, and seminaries) take the lead in this conversation? Or is this the role of pastors and denominational leaders? These are important questions that need to be addressed.

Pentecostals have not had problems with empirical science (e.g., chemistry, physics, medicine), but they have disagreed with the conclusions of historical sciences since they are based on disputed presuppositions. In fact, the tension between empirical and historical science may be unsolvable. So what contributions can Pentecostals make?

In Exodus 31:1–11, Yahweh tells Moses how he has empowered people with "skill, ability, and knowledge" by filling them with "the Spirit of God." We should anticipate that God can and will empower Pentecostals to contribute to the conversation on origins.

The idea of the Spirit breaking into the natural course of affairs is central to Pentecostal thinking, so we should not find the Spirit's actions through macro- and microevolution incredible, but an expression of God's immanence. The Scriptures support the Spirit's involvement in the development and maintenance of the physical creation (Genesis 1:1–2; Psalm 33:6; Psalm 104:30; Job 33:4). These passages and our Pentecostal experiences should encourage us to be open to an active, ongoing, creative role of the Holy Spirit in the physical realm.

Candid discourse on evolution can be hazardous because some influential people use their stance as the standard of orthodoxy. In private conversations with the authors, both science and theology colleagues have echoed this concern—even as they agreed with the need for dialogue. Pentecostals need a safe forum in which to discuss origins.

What is your goal in studying origins? Do you merely want to gain more support for your current position, or do you seek knowledge that will lead you to the most coherent view? Are you more interested in winning a debate or in dialoguing productively? If so, you might need to study more science, philosophy, and theology. Don't just read the works of advocates of your position, but study the writings of those who hold views contrary to yours.

The value of a broad knowledge of both science and theology in the life of a Christian can hardly be overstated. About sixteen centuries ago, St. Augustine addressed this issue:

Usually, even a non-Christian knows something about the earth, the heavens, and the other elements of this world, about the motion and orbit of the stars and even their size and relative positions, about the predictable eclipses of the sun and moon, the cycles of the years and the seasons, about the kinds of animals, shrubs, stones, and so forth, and this knowledge he holds to as being certain from reason and experience. Now, it is a disgraceful and dangerous thing for an infidel to hear a Christian, presumably giving the meaning of Holy Scripture, talking nonsense on these topics; and we should take all means to prevent such an embarrassing situation, in which people show up vast ignorance in a Christian and laugh it to scorn. The shame is not so much that an ignorant individual is derided, but that people outside the household of the faith think our sacred writers held such opinions, and, to the great loss of those for whose salvation we toil, the writers of our Scripture are criticized and rejected as unlearned men. If they find a Christian mistaken in a field which they themselves know well and hear him maintaining his foolish opinions about our books, how are they going to believe those books in matters concerning the resurrection of the dead, the hope of eternal life, and the kingdom of heaven, when they think their pages are full of falsehoods on facts which they themselves have learnt from experience and the light of reason? Reckless and incompetent expounders of Holy Scripture bring untold trouble and sorrow on their wiser brethren when they are caught in one of their mischievous false opinions and are taken to task by those who are not bound by the authority of our sacred books. For then, to defend their utterly foolish and obviously untrue statements, they will try to call upon Holy Scripture for proof and even recite from memory many passages which they think support their position, although *they understand neither what they say nor the things about which they make assertion.* (Augustine 1982: 42–43; italics in the original)

## Notes

1.  The categories we present are widely but not universally used. For an indepth presentation of the arguments for and against each of the three theistic positions elaborated here, see Moreland and Reynolds (1999).
2.  According to a May 2008 Gallup poll, most Americans are EC (45%), followed by YEC (35%) and AE (14%). (OEC was not an option in this poll, so individuals in this camp were probably split between YEC and EC camps.) A June 2005 Harris poll found that Americans were nearly evenly split on a belief in speciation (49% believe, 45% don't) and on the question of evolution through common descent (46% believe, 47% don't). Pentecostals seem to be shifting toward the cultural norm (Origin of Human Life 2008). Compare this to a 2005 survey of evangelical biologists at 67 schools of the Council of Christian Colleges and Universities: 25% identified themselves as YEC, 27% as theistic evolutionists; the other 48% were either OEC or declined to embrace a position (Sutherland 2005: 51).
3.  *Teleological* means progressing toward a goal; *ateleological* means not progressing toward a goal.
4.  Technically, the origin of life from nonlife (abiogenesis) is not part of biological evolution.
5.  The original 1859 title, *On the Origin of Species,* was changed in the 6th edition (1872) to *The Origin of Species.*
6.  Uniformitarianism posits that physical constants of the distant past were identical to what they are today. Thus the speed of light in a vacuum and rates of radioactive decay have not changed over the eons.

7. For an excellent discussion of the difficulty of defining *science* and *the scientific method,* see Moreland 1989.
8. For a brief overview of the cultural milieu of that era, see Kendrick 1993.
9. Much of the early Pentecostal literature is available online at the Flower Pentecostal Heritage Center at http://ifphc.org.
10. The Church of God of Prophecy in 1903, The Church of God (Cleveland) in 1907, the Assemblies of God in 1914, and The Foursquare Church in 1927, to cite a few.
11. This theory posits a long span of time between Genesis 1:1 and 1:2. Many Pentecostals embraced the gap theory because of the influence of the Schofield Reference Bible (published in 1909) and later (1963) by the first study Bible with notes written from a Pentecostal perspective by Finis Jennings Dake, an AG minister. The gap theory is no longer popular with theologians or scientists.
12. Interestingly, Waltke credits Dr. Francis Collins with helping him conclude that "the best harmonious synthesis of the special revelation of the Bible . . . and of science is the theory of theistic evolution" (2007: 202–203).
13. Wanda Brackett (Foursquare Church Communications office), telephone interview with Badger, 29 July 2008, followed by an email.
14. Available online at www.foursquare.org/landing_pages/4,3.html.
15. Aaron Wilson, vice president of development, Messenger College (Pentecostal Church of God, Joplin, Mo.), telephone interview by Badger, 14 July 2008, and subsequent email.
16. For an excellent example of a Pentecostal missionary with a rational approach, see Nañez 2005.
17. Turner Collins (professor emeritus, Evangel University), interview by the authors, 22 July 2008.
18. Empirical science deals with natural patterns and repeatable events. In contrast, historical science addresses past, non-repeating events. For an in-depth discussion, see Meyer 1990 and 2000.
19. For a thought-provoking response to Dobzhansky, see Edwards 2002: 614–15.

## References

Assemblies of God. 1977. "The Doctrine of Creation." www.ag.org/top/Beliefs/ Position_Papers/pp_4177_creation.cfm (accessed July 20, 2008).
———. 2006. "Creationism." In *Questions and Answers about General Christian Doctrines.* Springfield, Mo.: Gospel Publishing House, 28–30.
Augustine, Saint. 1982. *The Literal Meaning of Genesis.* 2 vols. Trans. J. H. Taylor. New York: Newman.
Behe, Michael J. 1996. *Darwin's Black Box: The Biochemical Challenge to Evolution.* New York: Free Press.
Bowler, Peter J. 1984. *Evolution: The History of an Idea.* Berkeley: University of California Press.
Bowman, Sonny. 2007. "An Overview of Creation Beliefs." www.life4square.com/ pdf/ creationoverview.pdf (accessed July 27, 2008).

Bryan, William Jennings. 1923. "Moses vs. Darwin: I Sent My Boy to College a Christian and He Came Back an Atheist." *Latter Rain Evangel*, 1 March, 2–7.

Church of God (Cleveland, Tenn.). 1980. "Creationism." http://churchofgod.org/resolutions/creationism.cfm (accessed July 20, 2008).

Church of God of Prophecy. 2008. *Biblical Principles, Beliefs, and Doctrines of the Church of God of Prophecy*. Cleveland, Tenn.: Church of God of Prophecy.

Clayton, Philip. 2000. "The Emergence of Spirit." *Center for Theology and the Natural Sciences Bulletin* 20/4: 3–20.

———. 2004. "Emerging God." *Christian Century* 121/1: 26–30.

Collins, Francis S. 2006. *The Language of God: A Scientist Presents Evidence for Belief.* New York: Free Press.

Darwin, Charles. [1859] 1998. *The Origin of Species: By Means of Natural Selection or the Preservation of the Favored Races in the Struggle for Life.* New York: Modern Library.

Dawkins, Richard. 2006. *The God Delusion.* Boston: Houghton Mifflin.

Dembski, William A. 1999. *Intelligent Design: The Bridge between Science and Theology.* Downers Grove, Ill.: InterVarsity Press.

Dobzhansky, Theodosius. 1973. "Nothing in Biology Makes Sense Except in the Light of Evolution." *American Biology Teacher,* March (1973): 125–29.

Dodd, D. M. B. 1989. "Reproductive Isolation as a Consequence of Adaptive Divergence in *Drosophila pseudoobscura.*" *Evolution* 43/6: 1308–11.

Edwards, John S. 2002. "Dobzhansky's Dangerous Epigram." *Science* 52/7: 614–15.

Eldredge, Niles, and Stephen Jay Gould. 1972. "Punctuated Equilibria: An Alternative to Phyletic Gradualism." In T. J. M. Schopf, ed., *Models of Paleobiology.* San Francisco: Freeman Cooper, 82–115.

Frodsham, Stanley H. 1924. "Fundamentalists Plus." *Pentecostal Evangel*, July 12, 4.

Grant, Peter R., and B. Rosemary Grant. 2002. "Unpredictable Evolution in a 30–Year Study of Darwin's Finches." *Science* 296/5568: 707–711.

Grigg, Russell M. 1995. "Did Darwin Recant?" *Creation Ex Nihilo* 18/1: 36–37.

Hoekstra, Hopi E., Jon M. Hoekstra, David Berrigan, Sacha N. Vignieri, Anhthu Hoang, Christopher E. Hill, Peter Beerli, and Joel G. Kingsolver. 2001. "Strength and Tempo of Directional Selection." *Proceedings of the National Academy of Sciences* 98/16: 9157–60.

Horn, Ken. 2006. "Theology in a Nutshell 9: Humanity." *Today's Pentecostal Evangel,* September 17, 22–23, 25, 27.

Kendrick, Klaude. 1993. "Background of the Modern Pentecostal Revival." *Paraclete* 7/2: 22–31.

King, Gerald W. 2009. "Evolving Paradigms: Creationism as Pentecostal Variation on a Fundamentalist Theme." In Amos Yong, ed., *The Spirit Renews the Face of the Earth: Pentecostal Forays into Science and Theology of Creation.* Eugene, Ore.: Pickwick Press.

Lamoureux, Denis O. 2008. *Evolutionary Creation: A Christian Approach to Evolution.* Eugene, Ore.: Wipf and Stock.

Larson, Edward J. 2004. *Evolution: The Remarkable History of a Scientific Theory.* New York: Modern Library.

Lester, Lane, and Raymond G. Bohlin. 1989. *The Natural Limits to Biological Change,* 2nd ed. Washington, D.C.: Probe Books.

Lindsay, Dennis Gordon. 1994. *The Dismantling of Evolutionism's Sacred Cow: Radiometric Dating.* Dallas, Tex.: Christ for the Nations.

Lindsay, Gordon. 1963. *Evolution—The Incredible Hoax.* Dallas, Tex.: Voice of Healing Publishing.

Luskin, C. 2007. "The Positive Case for Design." The Discovery Institute. www.discovery .org/scripts/viewDB/filesDB-download.php?command=download&id=546 (accessed July 22, 2008).

Mayr, Ernst. 1942. *Systematics and the Origin of Species, from the Viewpoint of a Zoologist.* Cambridge, Mass.: Harvard University Press.

Medawar, Peter. 1999. "Evolutionism." In Alan Bullock and Stephen Trombley, eds., *The New Fontana Dictionary of Modern Thought.* San Francisco: HarperCollins.

Meyer, Stephen C. 1990. "Of Clues and Causes: A Methodological Interpretation of Origin of Life Studies." Ph.D. thesis, Cambridge University.

———. 2000. "The Scientific Status of Intelligent Design: The Methodological Equivalence of Naturalistic and Non-naturalistic Origins Theories." In Michael J. Behe, William A. Dembski, and Stephen C. Meyer, eds., *Science and Evidence for Design in the Universe: Papers Presented at a Conference Sponsored by the Wethersfield Institute, New York City, September 25, 1999.* San Francisco: Ignatius Press.

Meyer, Stephen, and Michael Keas. 2001. "The Meanings of Evolution." The Discovery Institute. www.discovery.org/scripts/viewDB/filesDB-download.php?id=305 (accessed July 28, 2008).

Miller, Kenneth R. 2007. *Finding Darwin's God: A Scientist's Search for Common Ground between God and Evolution.* New York: Perennial.

Moreland, J. P. 1989. *Christianity and the Nature of Science.* Grand Rapids, Mich.: Baker Books.

Moreland, J. P., and John Mark Reynolds, eds. 1999. *Three Views on Creation and Evolution.* Grand Rapids, Mich.: Zondervan.

Munyon, Timothy. 1994. "The Creation of the Universe and Humankind." In Stanley M. Horton, ed., *Systematic Theology: A Pentecostal Perspective.* Springfield, Mo.: Logion Press, 215–53.

Nañez, Rick. 2005. *Full Gospel, Fractured Minds.* Grand Rapids, Mich.: Zondervan.

Numbers, Ronald L. 1992. "Creation, Evolution, and Holy Ghost Religion: Holiness and Pentecostal Responses to Darwinism." *Religion and American Culture* 2/2: 127–58.

Origin of Human Life. 2008. The Polling Report. www.pollingreport.com/science .htm (accessed July 28, 2008).

Paley, William. 1809. *Natural Theology; Or, Evidences for the Existence and Attributes of the Deity,* 12th ed. London: J. Fauldner.

Robinson, Georgie A. 1927. "The Bible's Answer to the Theory of Evolution." *Pentecostal Evangel,* August 20, 7.

Ross, Hugh. 2001. *The Creator and the Cosmos: How the Greatest Scientific Discoveries of the Century Reveal God,* 3rd ed. Colorado Springs, Colo.: NavPress.

———. 2003. "Evolution: It Doesn't Add Up." *Pentecostal Evangel,* November 30, 16.

Stamps, Donald C., gen. ed. 1992. *The Full Life Study Bible.* Grand Rapids, Mich.: Zondervan.

———. 2007. *Fire Bible: Student Edition.* Springfield, Mo.: Life Publishers.

Sutherland, John C. 2005. "Evangelical Biologists and Evolution." *Science,* July 1, 51.

Tenneson, Mike, and Steve Badger. 2009. "Teaching Origins to Pentecostal Students." In Amos Yong, ed., *The Spirit Renews the Face of the Earth: Pentecostal Forays in Science and Theology of Creation.* Eugene, Ore.: Pickwick Press, 210–31.

Thurman, L. Duane. 1977. *How to Think about Evolution and Other Bible Science Controversies.* Downers Grove, Ill.: InterVarsity Press.

United Pentecostal Church of Pittsburg (Calif.). 2008. "Creation Versus Evolution." www.geocities.com/upcpitt/Articles/evolution_vs_creation.html (accessed July 24, 2008).

Van Till, Howard J. 1999. "The Fully Gifted Creation ('Theistic Evolution')." In J. P. Moreland and John Mark Reynolds, eds., *Three Views on Creation and Evolution.* Grand Rapids, Mich.: Zondervan, 159–218.

Vardiman, Larry, Andrew A. Snelling, and Eugene F. Chaffin, eds. 2005. *Radioisotopes and the Age of the Earth,* Vol. 2. Waco, Tex.: Institute for Creation Research.

Waltke, Bruce K. 1991. "The Literary Genre of Genesis, Chapter One." *Crux* 27: 2–10.

———. 2007. *An Old Testament Theology: An Exegetical, Canonical, and Thematic Approach.* Grand Rapids, Mich.: Zondervan.

Wells, Jonathan. 2002. *Icons of Evolution.* Washington, D.C.: Regnery Publishing.

Whitcomb, John C., Jr., and Henry Morris. 1961. *The Genesis Flood: The Biblical Record and Its Scientific Implications.* Grand Rapids, Mich.: Baker Books.

Williams, William A., and Josephine Kaye Williams. 1928. *The Evolution of Man Scientifically Disproved in 50 Arguments: Evolution Disproved.* Camden, N.J.: W. A. Williams.

Witham, Larry A. 2002. *Where Darwin Meets the Bible: Creationists and Evolutionists in America.* New York: Oxford University Press.

Yong, Amos. 1997. "Oneness and the Trinity: The Theological and Ecumenical Implications of Creation Ex Nihilo for an Intra-Pentecostal Dispute." *PNEUMA: The Journal of the Society for Pentecostal Studies* 19/1: 81–107.

———. 2006. "*Ruach,* the Primordial Chaos, and the Breath of Life: Emergence Theory and the Creation Narratives in Pneumatological Perspective." In Michael Welker, ed., *The Work of the Spirit: Pneumatology and Pentecostalism.* Grand Rapids, Mich.: Eerdmans, 183–204.

## Recommended Reading

Alexander, Denis. 2001 *Rebuilding the Matrix: Science and Faith in the 21st Century.* Grand Rapids, Mich.: Zondervan.

Badger, Steve, and Mike Tenneson. 2007. *Christian Perspectives on Origins.* Revised and expanded edition. Springfield, Mo.: Evangel University [available from the authors].

Behe, Michael J. 1996. *Darwin's Black Box: The Biochemical Challenge to Evolution.* New York: Free Press.

Bube, Richard. 1995. *Putting It All Together: Seven Patterns for Relating Science and the Christian Faith.* Lanham, Md.: University Press of America.

Carlson, Richard F., ed. 2000. *Science and Christianity: Four Views.* Downers Grove, Ill.: InterVarsity Press.

Falk, Darrel R. 2004. *Coming to Peace with Science: Bridging the Worlds between Faith and Biology*. Downers Grove, Ill.: InterVarsity Press.

Fowler, Thomas B., and Daniel Kuebler. 2007. *The Evolution Controversy: A Survey of Competing Theories*. Grand Rapids, Mich.: Baker Academic.

Hagopian, David, ed. 2001. *The Genesis Debate: Three Views on the Days of Creation*. Mission Viejo, Calif.: Crux Press.

McGrath, Alister E. 1998. *The Foundations of Dialogue in Science and Religion*. Malden, Mass.: Blackwell.

Miller, Kenneth R. 2007. *Finding Darwin's God: A Scientist's Search for Common Ground between God and Evolution*. New York: Perennial.

Moreland, J. P., and John Mark Reynolds, eds. 1999. *Three Views on Creation and Evolution*. Grand Rapids, Mich.: Zondervan.

Pearcey, Nancy, and Charles Thaxton. 1994. *The Soul of Science: Christian Faith and Natural Philosophy*. Wheaton, Ill.: Crossway Books.

Ratzsch, Del. 1986. *Philosophy of Science: The Natural Sciences in Christian Perspective*. Downers Grove, Ill.: InterVarsity Press.

Ruse, Michael. 2001. *Can a Darwinian Be a Christian? The Relationship between Science and Religion*. Cambridge: Cambridge University Press.

Witham, Larry. 2003. *By Design: Science and the Search for God*. New York: Encounter Books.

Zimmer, Carl. 2001. *Evolution: The Triumph of an Idea*. San Francisco: HarperCollins.

# 6 Can Religious Experience Be Reduced to Brain Activity? The Place and Significance of Pentecostal Narrative

*Frederick L. Ware*

*Increasingly regarded as the seat of consciousness, the brain is now being viewed as a source for generating religious experience. Recent neuroimaging of brain activity in persons undergoing religious experiences demonstrates clearly that religious experience does involve neural processes. However, there is debate as to whether neuroimaging actually identifies the neural correlates of consciousness. A lot goes on in the brain. Yet a lot happens outside of the brain. A plausible study of consciousness must therefore be multifaceted, inclusive not only of studies of the brain but also of other methods of studying embodied experience. Phenomenology is one of these methods for studying consciousness and religious experience. Contesting the notion that phenomenology is value neutral and that reductive materialism offers the best set of values, the chapter identifies self-transcendence as a prominent feature in pentecostal religious narratives and an important goal toward which consciousness is directed, an aspect of experience not disclosed in or explained by brain scans.*

## The Head and Religious Experience

He lifted me to my feet and then the light of heaven fell upon me and burst into me filling me. Then God took charge of my tongue and I went to preaching in tongues. I could not change my tongue. The glory of God filled the temple. The gestures of my hands and movements of my body were His. Oh, it was marvelous and I thank God for giving it to me in His way. Such an indescribable peace and quietness went all through my flesh and into my very brain and has been there ever since. (C. H. Mason 1907: 4)

As Charles H. Mason (1866–1961) relates the story of his baptism in the Holy Spirit, he reports that he spoke in tongues and also felt something in his brain—in his head or mind. Is this—the goings-on in the head—normal in religious experience? Does this happen even if someone does not, as Mason did, feel it? How does one study or make sense of Mason's claims? Can experiences like his be replicated in laboratory settings? What would a brain scan reveal about his experience? Outside of the laboratory setting, how might his experience be studied?

A fascinating field of study surrounds investigation of brain activity during consciousness. Researchers are seeking to know what happens in the brain during religious experience, which is one of various forms of consciousness. Often in correlating brain activity with religious experience, it appears that religious experience is nothing more or less than a neurophysiological event.

Scientific studies of consciousness aimed at better understanding religious experience are promising are but fraught with challenges. These scientific studies provide pentecostals with a language for natural explanation of their religious experiences. The language of science is widely accepted and considered authoritative. Science is a crucial element in the achievement of cultural progress and technological development and innovation. Much of contemporary modern and global culture is attributable to science and technology. Especially where scientific studies are corroborating pentecostal testimony to a unique form of experience, pentecostals may now turn to science (in addition to their doctrinal teachings) in order to explain and justify their experiences in the Holy Spirit. Scientific studies of religious experience are also a means to communicate and engage persons beyond pentecostal and charismatic communities.

Yet reductionism, that is, the practice either of regarding mental states as nothing but neural processes or of establishing neuroscience as the standard for meaningful talk about consciousness, threatens the study of consciousness.[1] The first, reductive materialism, is the belief that consciousness can be explained mainly or only in terms of what happens in the brain. Mind is seen as simply a product of the brain. In the second type of reductionism, rather than functioning as one among several acceptable fields of discourse about consciousness, neuroscience becomes the basic science after which all studies of consciousness are modeled or evaluated.

In this chapter I am arguing, not for a rejection of neuroscience, but for the need to complement and balance it with other rigorous studies that may provide insights into the nature of consciousness. Though religious experience does involve neural processes, it is not reducible to brain activity. The brain plays a large role but not the only role in human experience. I begin with a brief overview of Andrew B. Newberg's recent neuroscientific study of pentecostal tongues speaking, showing the limitations of his study and of the project of neurotheology, that is, seeking explanation and justification of religion through neuroscience. Next there is a discussion of Alva Noë and Evan Thompson's criticisms of the research program for finding the content of neural correlates of consciousness, that is, the brain and nervous system activity and structures that are associated with and causing certain states of mind. Noë and Thompson are not opposed to Newberg's study and similar studies that uncover what happens in the brain and body during moments of religious experience, but they argue that there are some problematic philosophical assumptions upon which this research program is based. I then show how one may arrive at identification of self-transcendence as a prominent feature in narratives of pentecostal religious experience. Various metaphors are used to structure narratives of religious experience. These metaphors can be used for generating ideas and formulating hypotheses in scientific studies of consciousness. Self-transcendence may function as a telos of consciousness and thereby stand as an appropriate focus (reason and desirable outcome) for both theological reflection and scientific inquiry. Religious communities as well as cognitive neuroscience may be questioned about how well or poorly they understand the process and aid persons in the achievement of self-transcendence. The chapter concludes with a reminder that encounter with a living God in the Holy Spirit is at the center of pentecostalism. Cognitive neuroscience may aid, in various ways, in understanding pentecostal religious experience. However, it is doubtful that cognitive neuroscience will supply ultimate explanations. Pentecostal narrative is important for faith (witness and testimony) and scientific inquiry (investigation of self-reports of conscious experience).

## Neuroimaging of Tongue Speaking

Speaking in tongues—or glossolalia, as it is technically called—is regarded by many as one of the indications of the presence of the Holy Spirit in the life of a Christian. While pentecostal and charismatic churches are known for their acceptance of tongues speaking, not all believers in these churches practice or adhere to a doctrine of tongues speaking as infallible proof of baptism in the Holy Spirit or place tongues speaking above other manifestations of the Holy Spirit. In pentecostal and charismatic Christian communities, when tongues speaking does occur, it usually happens during private or personal devotional times when persons are worshipping or praying. Though some individuals may find tongues speaking to be incomprehensible and therefore meaningless, a considerable number of pentecostal and charismatic Christians believe that tongues speaking is a gift of God and is indicative of a mental and religious state where God is in control—willing, acting, and speaking through the believer.

In an effort to better understand this mental and religious state, Andrew B. Newberg took brain scans of persons who were engaged in tongues speaking (Newberg et al. 2006). He was able to recruit five persons for this laboratory study, women ranging from 38 to 52 years of age. Each woman identified herself as a pentecostal or charismatic Christian who had been practicing tongues speaking for more than five years. None of them had any documented psychiatric condition, neurological disorder, or medical problem affecting brain function. No woman was pregnant. The women were examined separately, and each was assigned a room where she would listen to gospel music. There was no chair in the room, so the women had to stand. Each woman was fitted to receive intravenous injections. After she began singing, each received an injection of Technetium Bicisate, a radiotracer that would later mark cerebral blood flow when a SPECT (single photon-computed emission tomography) was taken to detect brain activity during singing. After fifteen minutes of singing, each woman was subjected to a 40-minute brain scan (SPECT) and then taken back to the examination room. This time, when each woman spoke in tongues, she received an injection of Technetium Ethyl Cysteinate Dimer, a radiotracer that would later mark cerebral blood flow, when a SPECT is taken, to detect brain activity during tongues speaking. After fifteen continuous minutes of tongues speaking, each woman was subjected to a 30-minute brain scan.

The brain scans for singing and for tongues speaking were significantly different. The latter showed a decrease in blood flow in the frontal lobes (an area thought to be the control center) of the brain and a noticeable reduction of activity in the left caudate (an area of the brain for motor and emotional control). Areas of the brain regarded as language centers were relatively inactive on the scans for tongues speaking. Thus, the areas of the brain known to be active during normal speech, the exercise of motor and emotional control, and thinking (especially attention, concentration, and willing) were not as active among these pentecostal tongues-speakers. Newberg's study seems to corroborate what pentecostals have long claimed: that in this kind of mental and religious state, the Holy Spirit enables the person to speak in tongues.

Notwithstanding, several criticisms may be made about Newberg's neuroscientific study of tongues speaking. First, the study involved a very small number of human subjects and thus conclusions drawn may represent too-hasty generalizations of pentecostal religious experience. While it is true that the results of the experiment are consistent over this small group of test subjects, a larger test group, one diversified by gender, race, and ethnicity, may show a different pattern of results. What is true of the small test group may not be true of pentecostal and charismatic experience as a whole. Secondly, there is no consensus among pentecostal and charismatic Christians about the meaning of tongues speaking. While pentecostals affirm and accept tongues speaking, not all pentecostals subscribe to a doctrine of tongues speaking as initial evidence or infallible proof of baptism in the Holy Spirit or place it above other charismatic manifestations of the Holy Spirit (Walston 2005). Among themselves and between other Christian groups, pentecostal and charismatic Christians wrestle with the question of whether encounter with God (life in the Spirit) is expressed ultimately or most profoundly in tongues speaking. Thirdly, Newberg's study tends to mislead persons into the practice of making theological judgments on the basis of data collected through scientific experimentation. Newberg is an advocate of neurotheology, the study of theology from a neuropsychological perspective of how brain and mind make possible human religious experience. According to Newberg, his neural imaging research on the brain proves the existence of absolute unitary being, an altered state of consciousness where all boundaries and differentiations in being cease (D'Aquili and Newberg 1999: 200). This absolute unitary being may be described as God. While this may be assuring to some Christians, neurotheology puts Christian faith on an unsure foundation, that of SPECT scans. Finally, neurotheology is not theology proper. Theology is concerned not only about the explanation of belief but also about its logical consistency and coherence with sources like Scripture, doctrine, tradition, and experience that are authoritative for Christian communities. In neurotheology, the concept and reality of divine transcendence as a primary focus of reflection is lost. In theology proper, God is Person, One who is radically other. Encounter with a living God beyond nature and other human categories is fundamental in, as well as for, understanding Christianity (Delio 2003).

## Problematic Assumptions in the Search for Neural Correlates of Consciousness

According to Alva Noë and Evan Thompson (2004a), in studies like Newberg's neuroimaging of tongues speaking, there are explanatory gaps between consciousness and the neuroimages used to represent these human experiences. Noë and Thompson argue that research on the neural correlates of consciousness, the project of identifying the brain and nervous system activity and structures that are causally related to certain states of mind, is based on very questionable philosophical presuppositions.[2] The philosophical presupposition on which Noë and Thompson concentrate is the "matching-content doctrine" (2004a: 4). This is the view that for every act of perception, there is a distinct pattern of activity in the brain and nervous system such that this pattern is a sufficient explanation and cause of the perception. The perception and pattern are believed to be essentially the same. The content (i.e., most substantive or meaningful part) that constitutes one matches the content of the other.

Noë and Thompson state that there are no known examples of matches but many doubts as to whether a neural image can match the content of a conscious experience (2004a: 25). A neural image is not the total neural event. Also, the neural event is not identical to the experience. Even then, not all neural events are mappable (Azari 2006: 45). Moreover, there is no good reason to take one neural process as opposed to another as the correlate to consciousness (Noë and Thompson 2004b: 88). Newberg focuses on decrease (lack) of blood flow in certain areas of the brain as bearing significance for the explanation of tongues speaking. He does not identify for further investigation those areas of the brain where there is substantial blood flow during tongues speaking. He regards tongues speaking as something that is ultimately explainable by lack, not by any positive material event. For the most part, Newberg deals with tongues speaking relative to previous established studies that have shown correlations between neural activity and experience. The neural processes that may actually be correlated with tongues speaking are ignored.

As Noë and Thompson correctly assert, human behavior is quite complex. A more realistic approach to the study of consciousness would be to regard neural activity as something that may enable, but by itself does not constitute, embodied mental life (2004a: 18–19). They do not deny that there is some correspondence between neural events and experience; they seek to maintain appropriate emphasis on the fact that some causes and influences on human behavior are outside of the brain (2004b: 93). In the study of consciousness, there is a need for a multifaceted approach and openness to a variety of methods, like self-reporting and narrative, that can enrich insight into embodied experience.

## Phenomenology of Consciousness and Religious Experience

Daniel C. Dennett argues that cognitive neuroscience must take the path of phenomenology in order to achieve greater understanding of consciousness (1991: 71; 2003: 19–20, 27). Phenomenology is a movement in the history of philosophy emerging from the work of Edmund Husserl and its reinterpretation by Martin Heidegger, Maurice Merleau-Ponty, Jean-Paul Sartre, and Paul Ricoeur. Husserl conceived of phenomenology as rigorous, holistic inquiry—as a return to the traditional aim of philosophy. According to Husserl, ancient Greek philosophers sought not only facts about nature but also understanding of their representations and attitudes about the world (1965: 153). Their study of reality was inclusive of their self-introspection of consciousness. For Husserl, consciousness is not just another substance among many others in nature. Consciousness is constituted by the self (lived-body), awareness of self, and phenomena (objects about which the self is aware) (Stewart and Mickunas 1990: 37). Consciousness, emerging from the lived-body, is the center from which everything is observed (Stewart and Micku-nas 1990: 97). Given this centrality of consciousness, the natural sciences and humanities presuppose and are products of consciousness (Husserl 1965: 154–55). Husserl is especially critical of naturalism (the reduction of conscious-ness to a sensible object in nature) and psychologism (the reduction of con-sciousness to an inner mental life separate from physical nature) in the natural sciences and human sciences (1965: 80, 85). If these disciplines are to achieve a genuine philosophical dimension, then they must become phenomenologi-cal, studying their objects in light of consciousness. Cognitive neuroscience is not exempt from following this principle.

Dennett claims that his method of phenomenology (heterophenomenology) is value-neutral (1991: 95–98). Heterophenomenology is a third-person per-spective (phenomenology of another person, not oneself) that takes seriously first-person reporting (2003: 21–22). This concept of phenomenology is not truly value neutral, however. Dennett privileges the prevailing scientific para-digm. He reasons that after all, if we want to do science, then we must ad-here strictly to the canons of modern science. Science operates successfully using a third-person methodology. Because Dennett fails to take first-person accounts of religion seriously, he ends up with a pejorative view of religion. Based on his application of Darwinism to cultural ideas and his selective read-ing of various anthropologists, Dennett explains religion (religious belief) in terms of memes, patterns of cultural thought that are replicated for their own sake and antithetical to human survival and fulfillment (Dennett 2006: 78, 398).

For Dennett, religion is merely an object for study, not a source for insight. He is closed to the prospect of finding in the thing he studies (i.e., religion) anything that may challenge or alter his orientation to inquiry. Dennett seems unaware that breakthroughs in science are not always the result of ideas in-ternally generated from within science. Cognitive thinking, in every field of human endeavor, is facilitated by metaphors, several of which are basic and readily available to many persons in a culture (Gerhart and Russell 1984: 183). In fact, historians of science do acknowledge that major advancements in their disciplines have come through the use of common metaphors.[3] Thus, re-ligious language, plentiful in metaphor, has the potential of enriching scien-tific inquiry.

A phenomenological study of consciousness and religion does not have to be construed in the way Dennett does. The scholar may draw norms from sev-eral places, provided that he or she recognizes that, in the academic setting, norms are always subject to challenge, negotiation, and revision. While the data of a religion are not normative in the study of that religion, in the thing being studied (i.e., religion), the scholar may find something that will challenge or alter his or her orientation to inquiry. The scholar does not have to draw upon religion as a source of norms. Yet the scholar is not prohibited from this. If it is advantageous, and I think that in the case of study of consciousness it is, scholars may test the norms found in religious stories narrating subjective experience. As a recurrent feature in pentecostal religious narrative and valued aspect of human life, self-transcendence may function as a norm for both theological reflection and scientific inquiry.

As I have attempted to show, scientific studies of consciousness aimed at better understanding religious experience are promising but fraught with difficulty. Newberg's neuroimaging of tongues speaking corroborates pentecostal and charismatic Christians' claims to be under the influence and control of the Holy Spirit when they speak in tongues. Newberg's scientific experiment provides pentecostal and charismatic Christians with natural explanation and justification of their religious practices. However, as Noë and Thompson point out, attempts to plot the neural correlates of consciousness, such as Newberg's experiment, rest upon questionable assumptions (i.e., the matching-content doctrine). The neural correlation of consciousness, as a research program, is not infallible. A small but increasing minority of scholars are critical of the reductive materialism in the cognitive neuroscience of religion.

I am not rejecting neuroscience or neuroimaging. Like Noë and Thompson, I am advocating a multifaceted approach to the study of consciousness. This acceptance and acknowledgment of multiple approaches requires inclusion of different methods. One of these approaches is phenomenology, a method first proposed by Edmund Husserl for the study of consciousness. Dennett is a leading contemporary proponent of phenomenological method; however, his concept of phenomenology is not the only possible construal of phenomenological method. Still, I agree with Dennett's emphasis on narrative. Humans tell stories. Consciousness is understood and conveyed by stories of experiences. As a tool available to most persons, narrative is used to process and convey meanings arising from conscious experiences. This shift to an examination of narrative is not a retreat from science but rather a turn to a form of inquiry that can be just as rigorous as neuroimaging.

Newberg chose to study pentecostal religious experience using neuroimaging, which reveals a distinct pattern of activity in the brain while persons are having these experiences. But is his method of study capable of establishing the sort of factual information required by science? Science requires the findings be confirmed in repeated experimentation. Another question that looms large over Newberg's approach to the study of pentecostal religious experience is, Can religious experience be replicated in laboratory settings? Pentecostal religious experience usually occurs in worship settings and is reported in narratives. Where neuroimaging technology cannot capture these religious experiences in social settings, other disciplines for studying behavior, social interaction, and language may disclose important aspects of pentecostal religious experience like self-transcendence.

## Self-Transcendence in Pentecostal Narrative

Charles Mason's spiritual autobiography portrays pentecostal religious experience as integrative (i.e., resulting in wholeness and union with God) and liberating (i.e., freeing him from limiting aspects of his previous conception of self). This is an approach that seems quite appropriate for a study of pentecostal religious experience. There is already use and appreciation of phenomenology in the study of religious story as well as other dimensions of religion. Moreover, narrative is the way pentecostals most often talk about, think about, evaluate, and communicate their experiences. Storytelling is central in pentecostalism. In personal accounts and spiritual testimony, pentecostals tell stories of having had unique experiences—conversion, baptism in the Holy Spirit, healing and other miracles, and moments marked by bursts of insight.

Mason's baptism in the Holy Spirit is a symbol of self-transcendence, a recurrent event often told in black religious narrative. Self-transcendence is a change in the self that becomes foundational for new constructions of identity, apprehension of one's purpose, and successful engagement with other selves in one's social and cultural environments. In self-transcendence, the person has an awareness of self that goes beyond any of his or her past and present conceptions of self and immediate circumstances. There is a change in self-identity, the way one images oneself. In the person's attempt to reconcile him- or herself to newly perceived identity and potential, self-transcendence becomes a form of self-realization.

Mason claims that his deepest and most life-altering religious experience was his baptism in the Holy Spirit. In 1907, at 40 years of age and after having heard about a great revival with charismatic manifestations of the Holy Spirit, Mason traveled from Memphis, Tennessee, to the Azusa Street Mission in Los Angeles, California. He later recalled the following events that occurred at the revival:

> Then I began to seek for the baptism of the Holy Ghost according to Acts 2:44, which readeth thus: "Then they that gladly received His word were baptized." Then I saw that I had a right to be glad and not sad. . . . There came a reason in my mind which said, "Were you sad when you were going to marry?" I said, "No, I was glad." It said that this meant wedlock to Christ.
>
> Then the enemy said to me, "There may be something wrong with you." Then a voice spoke to me and said, "If there is anything wrong with you, Christ will take it away and marry you, at any rate, and will not break the vow." More light came and my heart rejoiced!

The sound of a mighty wind was in me and my soul cried, "Jesus, only, none like you." My soul cried and soon I began to die. It seemed that I heard the groaning of Christ on the Cross dying for me. . . . The sound stopped for a little while. My soul cried out, "Oh, God, finish your work in me." Then the sound broke out in me again. Then I felt something raising me out of my seat without any effort of my own. I said, "It may be my imagination." Then I looked down to see if it was really so. I saw that I was rising. Then I gave up, for the Lord to have His way within me. So, there came a wave of glory into me, and all my being was filled with the glory of the Lord. So when He had gotten me straight on my feet, there came a light which enveloped my entire being above the brightness of the sun. When I opened my mouth to say "Glory," a flame touched my tongue [and] ran down in me. My language changed and no word could I speak in my own tongue. Oh, I was filled with the glory of the Lord. My soul was then satisfied. I rejoiced in Jesus my Savior, whom I love so dearly. And from that day until now there has been an overflowing joy of the glory of the Lord in my heart. (M. Mason [1924] 1987: 29–30)

After this incident, Mason stayed at the Azusa Street Mission in Los Angeles for a period of five weeks before returning home to Memphis.

The quotation above is taken from an account of Mason's spiritual biography published in 1924 (M. Mason 1987). It is possible that Mason may have taken the liberty to embellish his narrative in order to magnify and heighten the drama of his experience of Spirit baptism. His narrative involves the exercise of memory in recall of details about a past event. The first published account of Mason's Spirit baptism is a very short article in the February–March 1907 issue of the Azusa Street Mission newspaper (C. Mason 1999). While Mason's 1924 recollection does not contradict the 1907 version, the latter account is noticeably longer and richer in detail.

Mason claims to be forever a changed man. He is not describing a conversion in the sense of an experience of how he becomes a Christian. Yet he confesses a change of ideas. His Azusa experience is preceded by his shift from a figurative to a literal biblical interpretation of tongues speaking (C. Mason [1907] 1999: 27). He had experienced divine healing but had never spoken in tongues in the ways described in the New Testament. Mason originally thought that tongues speaking meant righteous speech, that one ceased from cursing, swearing, and use of profanity. He decided to regard and seek an experience of tongues speaking as ecstatic utterances and ability to speak foreign languages.

After this experience, Mason said that he now was "full of the power." Everything was new. He had a new approach to ministry. In addition to this sense of renewal, other results following this experience of Spirit baptism included inspiration for composing new songs, the ability to interpret tongues (his and others), discernment of spiritual writing, greater manifestation of divine healing, cessation of troubling dreams and visions like he had during

childhood and previous to his Spirit baptism, and boldness in his proclama-
tion of the gospel. He was emboldened with courage to cross the color line,
addressing the ungodliness of all peoples, and even protesting against war
(C. Mason [1924] 1987: 31–34).

Mason's narrative exhibits structure. He uses the metaphor of marriage
in order to achieve as well as describe his experience of Spirit baptism (Lakoff and Johnson 1980: 14). Using this metaphor, he employs concepts like joy,
mutual acceptance, surrender, and consummation in order to describe what
was happening to him. In explanation of the outcome, Mason uses a metaphor of causation: *the object* (the glory of the Lord) *comes out of the substance*
(baptism in the Spirit) (1980: 73). Spirit functions as a *container* (Lakoff and
Johnson 1980: 30–31). He interprets various things as either being in or coming out of the Spirit. For Mason, glory is majestic beauty and splendor, itself
a metaphor based on the optical phenomenon where light is scattered back toward its source. Mason claims to have experienced a state of being that reflects God's presence and power.

In addition to the metaphors used to structure Mason's narrative, other
features of his story are worth noting. His experience occurs during middle
adulthood and in the context of the public religious meeting, a revival or
church meeting involving the practice of "tarrying," a religious ritual to in-
duce the ecstatic experience of Spirit baptism (Bruner 1998: 101–103, 113,
125–26; Daniels 2000: 299–301). For non-pentecostals, and even for some pentecostals, Mason's narrative raises the question of whether tongues speaking
is infallible proof of baptism in the Spirit or if dramatic charismatic manifestations, if possible, are required for all Christians (Walston 2005). His experience occurred at the initial moment of Spirit baptism and involved tongues
speaking. His autobiography does not address later experiences that come
many years after the initial experience of Spirit baptism.

In stark contrast to Mason's narrative, Elizabeth Dabney's *What It Means to
Pray Through* (1945/1987), a spiritual autobiography that enjoys a wide circulation within the Church of God in Christ, contains no references to tongues
speaking in the recollection of her religious experiences. Dabney's emphasis is
on her mystical experiences and empowerment through prayer. Mason's narrative entails a metaphysics presupposing the existence of a spiritual realm
populated by God, the risen Christ, the Holy Spirit, Satan, and spirits. Also, his
narrative presupposes an epistemology in which knowledge emerges from religious experience.

Since Mason is founder of the Church of God in Christ, his narrative is
widely known and regarded as paradigmatic in the denomination. Even when
his narrative has not been read, it is retold in oral tradition. Thus, members
of the denomination who have not read Mason's autobiography know about
his spiritual experiences. His narrative has achieved normative status, serv-

ing as inspiration for and model of religious experience in the Church of God in Christ. Persons desirous of baptism in or empowerment by the Holy Spirit emulate Mason.

Self-transcendence is an important feature of Mason's narrative. There may be a lot happening in Mason's brain, yet much is happening outside of his brain as well. He rose from obscurity to national and international prominence, from itinerant pastor to leader of the Church of God in Christ, the largest Pentecostal denomination in the United States. His spiritual experience recalled from memory is a foundational event, a turning point, a new basis for self-understanding and apprehension of his purpose in life. His self-conception is changed. He transcends one identity, achieves a new identity, and experiences success in his social environments.

## Conclusion

In this chapter, I have argued for the need to complement and balance cognitive neuroscience with other rigorous studies of consciousness such as narrative analysis, which may be interpreted as a form of phenomenology. A potential threat to studies of consciousness is reductionism, that is, the practice of either regarding mental states as nothing but neural processes or establishing neuroscience as the standard for meaningful talk about consciousness. In order to unsettle the dominance of neuroscience and materialism in studies of consciousness, I pointed out the limitations of Andrew Newberg's neuroimaging of pentecostal tongues speaking and provided an overview of Alva Noë and Evan Thompson's criticism of philosophical assumptions underlying research programs like Newberg's that seek to match brain activity with mental states. Next, I argued that if one takes the path of phenomenology as Daniel Dennett claims is the best way to study consciousness, one's formulation of phenomenology does not have to be materialist. I illustrated this kind of alternative formulation of phenomenology in my analysis of Charles Mason's spiritual autobiography. In Mason's narrative, one may find metaphors by which he structures and recalls his religious experience as well as the priority that he places on self-transcendence. Neuroimaging on its own will not yield this kind of insight into pentecostal religious experience, and materialism will not even pursue this line of inquiry.

The move toward the multifaceted approach that I am suggesting requires: (1) abandonment of reductive materialism; (2) acknowledgment of the significance of narrative, something quite like self-reporting in that it involves first-person comment on mental states; and (3) openness to the testing of hypotheses formed in light of metaphors and other structures disclosed in narratives of conscious experiences.

For some neuroscientists, this move may be difficult. Even if one is not committed wholly to or convinced of the truth of reductive materialism, there are pressures to conform to the reigning idea that the mind is a product of the brain. Complicating this move is the ongoing debate about the reliability of introspective reporting in studies of consciousness (Hulbert and Schwitzgebel 2007). Thus narrative, as a form of self-reporting, may prove to be as risky and problematic as neuroimaging. Narrative analysis may not provide ultimate explanations either.

Still, this is a move that should be taken. Neuroscientists cannot resist the enlargement of the scientific enterprise resulting from the acceptance and interchange of multiple approaches. The ethos of modern science invites and thrives on this type of pluralism in the search for truth.

The study of consciousness in general, and of religious consciousness in particular, if it is to be done properly and comprehensively, will involve attention to narratives. The advancement of neuroscientific imaging techniques for showing and correlating brain activity with human experience will contribute to our self-understanding as embodied beings. Moreover, neuroscience has the potential of enriching religious communities' deliberations about which kinds of experience best represent their beliefs and values. These communities may want to exclude those experiences associated with dysfunctions in the brain. Still, there is much that happens outside of the brain that influences human life. Cognitive neuroscience will supply us with *good* explanations but probably not *ultimate* explanations.

While neuroscience provides pentecostal and charismatic Christians with a form of natural explanation of their spiritual experiences, they should be wary of the use of science for justification of religion. As easily as one finds scientific studies that corroborate religious experience, one may find also scientific studies that contest religious experience. Encounter with a living God in the Holy Spirit is at the center of pentecostal-charismatic Christianity. Mason's narrative and the similar stories of pentecostal and charismatic Christians bear witness to this encounter and the subsequent changes that occur in people's lives. Pentecostal narrative is important both for religious testimony and, as a source of self-reporting, for scientific investigations that welcome introspection of conscious experience.

## Notes

1. Major publications oriented toward reductive materialism include Atran 2002; Crick 1994; D'Aquili and Newberg 1999; D'Aquili, Newberg, and Rause 2001; Dennett 1991 and 2006; Koch 2004; Newberg and Waldman 2006 and 2007; Persinger 1987. The increasing minority of works challenging the materialist assumptions of the cognitive science of religion include: Searle 1992; David Chalmers 1996; Schwartz and Begley 2002; and Beauregard and O'Leary 2007.

2. Critical interactions with Noë and Thompson's perspective and Noë and

Thompson's replies to their critics are published in *Journal of Consciousness Studies* 11/1 (2004): 29–86 and 87–98.

3.     For example, Stephen J. Gould points out that geologists moved from belief about the age of the earth as thousands of years to belief about the earth as millions of years using metaphor. This shift in thinking occurred from the late seventeenth through the mid-nineteenth centuries and without the quality of empirical observation enjoyed in the latter twentieth century (Gould 1987: 4, 15). That geologists formed this proposition many years before empirical data confirmed their hypothesis shows how narrative facilitates science's pursuit of knowledge. According to Gould, the use of metaphors such as "time as an arrow" and "time as a circle" led to the development of the ideas of linear history and immanent laws (1987: 191). Using the metaphor of arrow, early geologists came to understand time as linear, a history that is irreversible and unrepeatable (1987: 10, 194). Using the metaphor of cycle, they came to understand time as non-directional, a repetition of series occurring because of fixed laws (or stable patterns) within nature (1987: 11, 196). The dialectical tension of these metaphors (the manner in which they are related) results in greater insight about "deep time," temporal aspects of the both the earth and universe, whose origins and early development reaches far back into a period not immediately observable to human beings (1987: 199–200). Arrows and cycles are metaphors used not only by scientists but by other persons in society in order to understand time (1987: 194).

## References

Atran, Scott. 2002. *In Gods We Trust: The Evolutionary Landscape of Religion*. New York: Oxford University Press.

Azari, Nina P. 2006. "Neuroimaging Studies of Religious Experience: A Critical Review." In Patrick McNamara, ed., *Where God and Science Meet: How Brain and Evolutionary Studies Alter Our Understanding of Religion*. Westport, Conn.: Praeger, 33–54.

Beauregard, Mario, and Denyse O'Leary. 2007. *The Spiritual Brain: A Neuroscientist's Case for the Existence of the Soul*. New York: HarperCollins.

Bruner, Frederick D. 1998. *A Theology of the Holy Spirit: The Pentecostal Experience and the New Testament Witness*. Eugene, Ore.: Wipf and Stock.

Chalmers, David. 1996. *The Conscious Mind: In Search of a Fundamental Theory*. New York: Oxford University Press.

Crick, Francis. 1994. *The Astonishing Hypothesis: The Scientific Search for the Soul*. New York: Touchstone/Simon & Schuster.

Dabney, Elizabeth J. [1945]1987. *What It Means to Pray Through*. Repr. Memphis, Tenn.: Church of God in Christ Publishing Board.

Daniels, David D. 2000. "'Live So You Can Use Me, Lord, Anywhere': Theological Education in the Church of God in Christ, 1970 to 1997." *Asian Journal of Pentecostal Studies* 3/2: 295–310.

D'Aquili, Eugene G., and Andrew B. Newberg. 1999. *The Mystical Mind: Probing the Biology of Religious Experience*. Minneapolis: Fortress Press.

Delio, Ilia. 2003. "Brain Science and the Biology of Belief: A Theological Response."
    *Zygon: The Journal of Religion and Science* 38/2: 573–85.
Dennett, Daniel C. 1991. *Consciousness Explained*. Boston: Little, Brown, and Co.
———. 2003. "Who's on First? Heterophenomenology Explained." *Journal of Conscious-
    ness Studies* 10/9–10: 19–30.
———. 2006. *Breaking the Spell: Religion as a Natural Phenomenon*. New York: Viking.
Gerhart, Mary, and Allan Russell. 1984. *Metaphoric Process: The Creation of Scientific
    and Religious Understanding*. Fort Worth: Texas Christian University Press.
Gould, Stephen J. 1987. *Time's Arrow, Time's Cycle: Myth and Metaphor in the Discov-
    ery of Geological Time*. Cambridge, Mass.: Harvard University Press.
Hulbert, Russell T., and Eric Schwitzgebel. 2007. *Describing Inner Experience? Propo-
    nent Meets Skeptic*. Cambridge, Mass.: MIT Press.
Husserl, Edmund. 1965. *Phenomenology and the Crisis of Philosophy*. Trans. with notes
    and intro. by Quentin Lauer. New York: Harper Torchbooks.
Koch, Christof. 2004. *The Quest for Consciousness: A Neurobiological Approach*. Engle-
    wood, Colo.: Roberts and Co.
Lakoff, George, and Mark Johnson. 1980. *Metaphors We Live By*. Chicago: University
    of Chicago Press.
Mason, Charles H. [1907] 1999. "Tennessee Evangelist Witnesses," *Apostolic Faith*
    (February–March 1907); repr. in Larry Martin, ed., *Azusa Street: The True
    Believers: Part 2*. Joplin, Mo.: Christian Life Books, 27–29.
Mason, Mary, ed. [1924] 1987. *History and Life Work of Elder C. H. Mason, Chief
    Apostle, and His Co-Laborers*. Repr. Memphis, Tenn.: Church of God in Christ
    Publishing House.
Newberg, Andrew B., and Mark Robert Waldman. 2006. *Why We Believe What We
    Believe: Uncovering Our Biological Need for Meaning, Spirituality, and Truth*.
    New York: Free Press/Simon & Schuster.
———. 2007. *Born to Believe: God, Science, and the Origin of Ordinary and Extraordi-
    nary Beliefs*. New York: Free Press/Simon and Schuster.
Newberg, Andrew B., Eugene G. D'Aquili, and Vince Rause. 2001. *Why God Won't Go
    Away: Brain Science and the Biology of Belief*. New York: Ballantine Books/
    Random House.
Newberg, Andrew B., Nancy A. Wintering, Donna Morgan, and Mark R. Waldman.
    2006. "The Measurement of Regional Cerebral Blood Flow during Glosso-
    lalia: A Preliminary SPECT Study." *Psychiatry Research: Neuroimaging* 148:
    67–71.
Noë, Alva, and Evan Thompson. 2004a. "Are There Neural Correlates of Conscious-
    ness?" *Journal of Consciousness Studies* 11/1: 3–28.
———. 2004b. "Sorting Out the Neural Basis of Consciousness: Authors' Replies to
    Commentators." *Journal of Consciousness Studies* 11/1: 87–98.
Persinger, Michael A. 1987. *Neuropsychological Bases of God Beliefs*. New York: Praeger.
Schwartz, Jeffrey, and Sharon Begley. 2002. *The Mind and the Brain: Neuroplasticity
    and the Power of Mental Force*. New York: Regan Books.
Searle, John R. 1992. *The Rediscovery of the Mind*. Cambridge, Mass.: MIT Press.
Stewart, David, and Algis Mickunas. 1990. *Exploring Phenomenology: A Guide to the
    Field and Its Literature*. Athens: Ohio University Press.

Walston, Rick. 2005. *The Speaking in Tongues Controversy: The Initial, Physical Evidence of the Baptism in the Holy Spirit Debate.* Eugene, Ore.: Wipf and Stock.

## Recommended Reading

Alexander, Estrelda. 2005. *The Women of Azusa Street.* Cleveland, Ohio: Pilgrim Press.

Bruner, Jerome. 1991. "The Narrative Construction of Reality." *Critical Inquiry* 18: 1–21.

Cox, James L. 2006. *A Guide to the Phenomenology of Religion: Key Figures, Formative Influences, and Subsequent Debates.* New York: Continuum.

Goff, James R., and Grant Wacker, eds. 2002. *Portraits of a Generation: Early Pentecostal Leaders.* Fayetteville: University of Arkansas Press.

Hefner, Philip J., ed. 2001. "Engaging D'Aquili and Newberg's *The Mystical Mind.*" *Zygon: The Journal of Religion and Science* 36/3: 477–507.

James, William. 1929. *Varieties of Religious Experience: A Study in Human Nature.* New York: Random House/Modern Library.

Kress, Gunther. 1990. "Critical Discourse Analysis." *Annual Review of Applied Linguistics* 11: 84–99.

Martin, Larry, ed. 1998. *Holy Ghost Revival on Azusa Street: The True Believers: Eye Witness Accounts.* Pensacola, Fla.: Christian Life Books.

——, ed. 1999. *Holy Ghost Revival on Azusa Street: The True Believers: Part Two: More Eyewitness Accounts.* Joplin, Mo.: Christian Life Books.

McNamara, Patrick, ed. 2006. *Where God and Science Meet: How Brain and Evolutionary Studies Alter Our Understanding of Religion.* Westport, Conn.: Praeger.

Metzinger, Thomas, ed. 2000. *Neural Correlates of Consciousness: Empirical and Conceptual Questions.* Cambridge, Mass.: MIT Press.

Riessman, Catherine Kohler. 1993. *Narrative Analysis.* Newbury Park, Calif.: Sage.

——. 2007. *Narrative Methods for the Human Sciences.* Newbury Park, Calif.: Sage.

Schiffrin, Deborah S., Deborah Tannen, and Heidi E. Hamilton, eds. 2003. *The Handbook of Discourse Analysis.* Malden, Mass.: Wiley-Blackwell.

Teske, John A. 2006. "Neuromythology: Brains and Stories." *Zygon: The Journal of Religion and Science* 41/1: 169–95.

# 7   Serotonin and Spirit: Can There Be a Holistic Pentecostal Approach to Mental Illness?

*Donald F. Calbreath*

*The pentecostal/charismatic community has long had a distrust of the field of psychiatry. In return, psychiatrists have often considered some pentecostal/charismatic practices and beliefs to be a form of psychopathology. We are seeing a coming together of the two camps in more recent years. This chapter explores the issue of depression from both medical and religious perspectives. Biochemical causes of depression are developed and critiqued. Treatment approaches are explained and evaluated. An integrated model for depression is proposed that links neurochemistry, psychiatry, and religion, especially pentecostal/charismatic beliefs and practices. Information is provided to help the student and the pastor reconcile possible conflicts and become more informed about the various options available to those dealing with depression.*

## Seeing the World Differently

It was a chance conversation with a colleague I had not seen for awhile. When asked how I was spending my retirement, I described my project dealing with the interface between science and pentecostal/charismatic theology. His response was immediate and bitter. "I have no use for charismatics. They destroyed my marriage."

He went on to describe the treatment he and his wife had received from the pastor of the independent charismatic church they attended. His wife was severely depressed. Their logical first step was to look to their spiritual leader for advice and counsel. What they received was "a lot of Bible verses and prayer. They even tried to cast a demon out of my wife. Then they told her she had made a choice to be depressed and she needed to choose not to be depressed." There was apparently no effort made to get the couple into professional counseling of any sort. The depression continued and intensified. Eventually the marriage fell apart.

Why did this situation take place? What was it about the pastor that made him resistant to getting this couple into professional psychotherapy or other form of counseling? Would treatment with antidepressants have helped this man's wife? To try to answer these questions, we need to explore two related issues. First, what tensions exist between modern psychiatry and pentecostals (in particular, with regard to depression) and why do they exist? Second, may pentecostals use psychiatry (either various forms of psychological counseling/therapy, drug therapy, or both) as a means of healing for depression? As we explore these issues, we need to keep in mind that the issues go beyond the pentecostal/charismatic community. To some extent, many conservative Christians share these beliefs and attitudes.

## Possible Conflicts between Psychiatry and Spirit-Filled Christianity

The story that began this chapter highlights some of the differences seen in the ways modern psychiatry and pentecostal theology approach the issue of mental illness. The reluctance of Spirit-filled Christians to embrace modern psychiatric thinking has several possible origins.

First, psychiatry and pentecostalism differ in their concepts of the causes and treatment of depression. Psychiatry sees mental illness as some sort of organic problem, with abnormal biochemical processes occurring in the brain and (often) altered brain structure as a result of the changes in neurochemistry. Traditional pentecostal theology has taken a very different view of mental illness, usually preferring an explanation that relies heavily on a concept of sin and the possibility of demon possession. These issues will be explored in more detail later.

Second, there is also the perennial antagonism between psychiatry and religion. Until fairly recently, psychiatry has often been reluctant to give credence to the benefits of religious faith and has been quick to attack faith as "abnormal" in many cases. This antagonism toward religion on the part of mental heath professionals has been a serious detriment to developing beneficial alliances between psychiatry and pastors (a false dichotomy often seen with many conservative evangelicals in general, not just pentecostals and charismatics).

Dobbins (2001) provides a very useful overview of pentecostal history, theology, and attitudes toward mental health professionals. In addition to providing a good survey of the major streams of pentecostal/charismatic theology and history, he looks at the historic reluctance of Pentecostal leaders to embrace modern psychology/psychiatry: "Leaders have often been suspicious of the behavioral sciences and opposed to any kind of counseling or therapy that is not strictly Biblical" (Dobbins 2001: 168).

Dobbins points to one of the essential tenets of pentecostal theology in understanding this suspicion. Pentecostals believe that healing (both physical and emotional) should come through prayer and the laying on of hands. In addition, there is the sense of personal failure (and guilt) in needing professional treatment. Finally, there is a concern (often a very valid one) that the patient's spiritual beliefs are not going to be respected by the therapist. He then goes on to outline several approaches to counseling with pentecostal patients that are sensitive to their theological stance and also deal with issues that are likely to arise.

In one of his books on religion and mental health, Koenig (2005) traces briefly the thinking on mental illness throughout various periods of history. Using a mix of literature sources, personal experience, and anecdotal evidence, this Duke University Medical Center psychiatrist describes the uneasy alliance between mental health professionals and religious institutions as they entered the early 1900s. However, early in the twentieth century, the influential Sigmund Freud led the way in smashing whatever bridges existed between the two groups. He began by comparing the act of prayer to the obsessive-compulsive behavior of neurotics. Some of his further work attempted to demonstrate the various debilitating and destabilizing effects of religion on mental health.

Koenig points out that by 1980 essentially all religious influences had been removed from most academic institutions that delivered treatment to psychiatric patients. At his own Duke University (a Methodist-affiliated institution with a well-known divinity school), visits to psychiatric patients by clergymen or even by the hospital chaplain had to be explicitly authorized by the attending physician on the psychiatric unit.[1] To illustrate the strong antagonism of mental health professionals against religion, Koenig cites a 1992 statement by Dr. Wendell Waters (psychiatry professor at McMaster University):

> Evidence that religion is not only irrelevant but actually harmful to human beings should be of interest, not only to other behavioral scientists, but to anyone who finds it difficult to live an unexamined life. Finally, the argument advanced in this volume should stir the political decision makers who complain abut the high cost of health care even while continuing to subsidize that very institution that may be actually making the public sick." (Koenig 2005: 26)

A third reason why Spirit-filled Christians may be reluctant to embrace psychiatry is the discipline's history of "psychologizing" pentecostal practice, specifically that of speaking in tongues. A number of early research studies on the phenomenon tended to conclude that people who demonstrated glossolalia were mentally disturbed and/or poorly educated and easily suggestible. There has been a slow acceptance on the part of the psychiatric profession that these early impressions were not correct and that speaking in tongues is a real phenomenon and has some beneficial impact on those who engaged in the practice.

Pattison (1967) summarizes a large number of psychiatric studies dealing with glossolalia. He describes the practice in a variety of non-Christian religions and traces the history of speaking in tongues in Christian thought and practice through the centuries. Early studies on the phenomenon described the practitioners as having "personality instability." Some reports suggested that most people who spoke in tongues were mentally ill or at least compensating for some personal or social lack in their lives. Pentecostals from lower-class settings were often thought to show "overt psychopathology of a sociopathic, hysterical, or hypochondriacal nature."

In more recent years, there has been a shift in the thinking of many in the psychiatric profession. There is no longer an attitude that praying in tongues demonstrates an abnormal psychological state (Castelein 1984; Francis and Robbins 2003). In addition, the benefits of glossolalia have begun to be recognized. However, the seeds of distrust were sown over many years, and the healing of the rift between psychiatry and pentecostals/charismatics will take time.

Finally, pentecostals have been reluctant to adopt psychiatry because of their suspicion of modern science. With a theology that emphasizes the role of the supernatural in everyday life, pentecostals have long been suspicious of modern scientific explanations. Yong (2005) points out the tendency of pentecostals to disavow modern science constructs such as scientific materialism and methodological naturalism. These approaches accept only natural explanations for all physical events—the supernatural is explicitly rejected.

Trice and Bjork (2006) point out the historic reluctance of pentecostals to embrace higher education. This education was often seen as a hindrance to the empowerment of the individual by the Holy Spirit. In the realm of mental illness, this antipathy certainly was held toward psychiatry. These authors also point out the widespread doubts among pentecostals (and many evangelicals) about the effectiveness of secular therapy.

## How Pentecostals View Depression

Trying to establish a pentecostal/charismatic view of depression or any mental illness is tricky business. There are some published studies that examine specific groups (such as college students or pastors). Several studies are probably outdated since the demographics of the pentecostal population have changed markedly over the last forty or so years from a predominantly lower-class and low-income population to a very diverse blend of believers from a wide variety of educational and socioeconomic groupings. In addition, much of the mainstream pentecostal thinking on depression (and mental illness in general) is shared by a significant number of more conservative evangelicals.

One useful summary of pentecostal thinking comes from Belcher and Hall (2001). These researchers describe the diversity in thinking among pentecostals: "While healing was incorporated into many of the doctrinal statements of the different factions of the Pentecostal movement, a singular view of healing that all the different denominations and factions of the movement could agree upon has yet to surface" (2001: 68).

These writers point out that illness (either physical or psychological) could come from God, the devil and/or demons, or from "natural causes." At least one Pentecostal denomination (Assemblies of God) explicitly acknowledges the possibility of "natural causes" contributing to mental illness. While there may not be written policies or position papers, other denominations frequently refer their members to professional mental health services when needed.

Official denominational statements about mental illness in general, and depression in particular, are hard to find. The Assemblies of God (AG) Web site (http://ag.org/top) contains a statement on counseling and psychology that says:

When people struggle mentally and emotionally, the hurt and anguish often can be extremely painful. It is important that these individuals receive immediate help. If they are in risk of physical danger because of extreme depression, suicidal thinking, or some form of severe mental anguish it is imperative that the individual see a medical doctor to determine if the problem is caused by physical deficiencies such as a chemical imbalance. In such cases a doctor often can stabilize or remedy the situation through proper diagnosis and prescription. Depending on the need, a counselor (preferably Christian) or pastor should also be prepared to come alongside to administer healing through compassion, listening, counsel, support, encouragement, and prayer. . . .

In situations not caused by physical deficiency, but that are either relational or emotional in origin, a counselor may prove helpful. A Christian should be concerned with a counselor's personal belief system. It is best to choose a counselor who is a Christian (one who has accepted Christ as Savior, lives for Him, and recognizes the Bible as God's guide for mankind).

If the counselor does not believe one can have a personal relationship with God, and instead approaches life strictly from a humanistic point of view, the advice and counseling approach will be devoid of an essential component of true healing—God. While some help may be received without reference to faith, a counselor who recognizes the centrality and importance of God's Word and power of His Spirit can deal with the whole person more readily. A pastor often will be able to team with a physician to bring a more complete healing process into focus by addressing the spiritual needs of the individual.

The danger in selecting a secular counselor who employs strictly a humanistic worldview is seen at its worst when the counselors go so far as to assume that the cause of psychological problems is religious beliefs.

Pastoral care and reliance on the Bible and prayer for healing offer a better alternative than anti-religious counseling provided physical deficiencies have been eliminated by medical doctors. God knows what help is available to us for our well-being, and He can lead us to proper resources that recognize His existence.

This statement suggests a blending of traditional pentecostal practices with an increasing realization that contemporary psychiatric might sometimes be appropriate. But note that the statement, located within a section of the Web site called "Counseling and Psychology," contains the following imprimatur: "This document reflects commonly held beliefs based on scripture which have been endorsed by the church's Commission on Doctrinal Purity and the Executive Presbytery."

In personal correspondence in 2008 with past and present members of the denomination's Commission on Doctrinal Purity, I was told that these perspectives do not represent official church policy and practice as would the doctrinal statement. They merely reflect a stream of thinking that is now prevalent within the AG leadership. This particular statement shows the tension between more longtime members of the church and those who have become more comfortable with the use of modern medical and psychiatric tools. The acknowledgement by AG individuals who had been involved in drafting and reviewing these perspectives over the years is that the use of physicians, psychiatrists, and other health professionals has become widely accepted in that denomination. Both the older group and the more modern members fully recognize God's role in healing and see professionals as one possible means of that healing.

## Depression—Psychiatric/Psychological Issues and Causes

How do these issues apply to depression? What is depression? Does modern psychiatric treatment of depression (especially the wide-spread use of antidepressant drugs) come into conflict with traditional pentecostal/charismatic approaches to the problem? We need first to define the problem and then look at psychiatric explanations of depression and its causes.

### Statistics and Diagnostic Criteria

Depression is the most common psychiatric disorder in the United States. Major depressive disorder (the most severe form of depression) is seen in some 14.8 million Americans 18 years of age and older, while dysthymic disorder (a chronic but milder form of depression) is observed in another 3.3 million American adults.[2] Although both males and females show a similar incidence of depression during childhood, more than twice as many females demonstrate symptoms of depression during adolescence and into adulthood (Weissman and Olfson 1995; Kessler et al. 2003, 2005a, 2005b). However, this apparent gender difference is being reevaluated in light of current data suggesting that depression in men may be seriously underreported (Scelfo 2007).

The *DSM-IV* (1994) lists the following criteria for a major depressive disorder. At least five of the symptoms must be present, they must be seen together for at least two weeks, and the symptoms have to indicate a significant change from a previous level of functioning:

- depressed mood almost every day
- significant decrease in interest in everyday activities
- noticeable weight loss in the absence of dieting, or significant weight gain or some change in appetite
- either insomnia or marked increase in the number of hours slept every night
- increased tiredness or energy loss
- strong sense of worthlessness and/or guilt
- inability to concentrate or make decisions
- sense of agitation or decreased responsiveness to physical environment
- increase in thoughts about death or recurrent suicidal thoughts.

### Causes of Depression

There are a variety of explanations for the cause(s) of depression. In line with many other scientists, R. A. Remick (2002) argues that depression is a result of the disruption of normal brain neurochemistry. This neurochemical approach is in keeping with a strong trend within the field of psychiatry to attribute biochemical phenomena as primary causes of mental disorders.

An example of a broader perspective is offered by O'Keane (2000). Here there is an interplay among developmental, environmental, and physiological components of depression. Each factor contributes something to the development and outcome of the depressive disorder. The connecting theme seems to be the activation of stress responsors, a concept we will return to later.

One of the leading researchers in the field of spirituality and mental health proposes that "depression is a whole-person disorder with biological, psychological, social, and spiritual roots. Addressing only one or two of them does not solve the problem. And there is no magic cure" (Biebel and Koenig 2004: 9). Unraveling the root cause(s) of depression will allow more informed and more effective treatment for this complex disorder.

## The Biochemistry of Depression

Major contributors to our current understanding of the etiology and treatment of depression have been studies of neurotransmitters. A primary role has long been ascribed to certain neurotransmitters such as serotonin, with secondary emphasis being given to norepinephrine (structurally related to serotonin). The hypothalamic-pituitary-adrenal (HPA) axis has been implicated, since altered levels of cortisol and an abnormal diurnal rhythm of cortisol release have often been seen in depressed patients. We will explore these two factors in some detail. However, as we shall see, sorting out whether a particular biochemical process is the *cause* of the disorder or the *result* of the disorder represents a real challenge today.

The monoamine group of neurotransmitters consists of serotonin, norepinephrine, and dopamine. The process of neurotransmission involves the movement of an electrical impulse down the nerve fiber, illustrated at right.

Decreases in the brain levels of serotonin (and norepinephrine) have long been implicated in the etiology of unipolar depression. The major pharmacological interventions are all based on somehow restoring the normal brain concentrations of these neurotransmitters, thus relieving the depressive symptoms.

The neurotransmitter hypothesis holds that a decrease in brain serotonin concentrations is believed to be the primary factor in depression (Meltzer 1990; Risch and Nemeroff 1992; Mahli et al. 2005). Brain serotonin concentrations exert significant influences on a number of behavioral entities such as mood, sleep, eating, and sexual behavior. Unfortunately, we do not have a clear understanding at present as to how this neurochemical actually influences the listed behaviors.

A variety of studies also implicate low concentrations of norepinephrine in the brain as being linked with depression (Dinan 1996; Ressler and Nemeroff 2000). Brain norepinephrine appears to be primarily associated with alertness and awareness of the surrounding environment. Many of the antidepressants commonly used affect norepinephrine levels in the brain along with serotonin.

Increases in the amount of cortisol produced and alterations of the diurnal cycle of cortisol production have long been implicated in depression (Sachar et al. 1970; Carroll et al. 1976; Ettigi and Brown 1977). Corticotropin-releasing factor (CRF) (also known as corticotropin-releasing hormone or CRH) from the hypothalamus stimulates the pituitary to release adrenocorticotropin (ACTH). Cortisol is released from the adrenal cortex in response to stimulation from pituitary ACTH. As the concentration of cortisol increases, the rising level of the steroid produces negative feedback inhibition of both the hypothalamus and the pituitary. This negative feedback causes a decrease in the production of CRF and ACTH, leading to a diminished output of cortisol. The alterations of cortisol production in depressed patients are currently

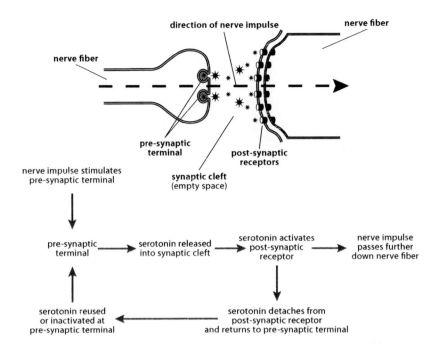

direction of nerve impulse

nerve fiber

nerve fiber

pre-synaptic
terminal

post-synaptic
receptors

nerve impulse stimulates
pre-synaptic terminal

synaptic cleft
(empty space)

pre-synaptic → serotonin released → serotonin activates → nerve impulse
terminal      into synaptic cleft   post-synaptic        passes further
                                    receptor             down nerve fiber

serotonin reused ← serotonin detaches from
or inactivated at   post-synaptic receptor
pre-synaptic terminal and returns to pre-synaptic terminal

believed to be a result of the depressed state and not a primary cause (Gillespie and Nemeroff 2005).

### Treating Depression: Pharmacological and Non-pharmacological Treatments

The most common strategies for treating depression are the use of drugs or by employing "talk therapy." The former is more prevalent, with the majority of patients being treated via some sort of antidepressant drug. The antidepressant can be divided into three broad classes: monoamine oxidase inhibitors (MAOI), tricyclics, and selective serotonin reuptake inhibitors (SSRI) (Fawcett 1994, Rush and Ryan 2002). The brief description of each class of drugs will be drawn from information cited in these two references.

Pharmacological treatment of depression has focused on increasing the level of a specific neurotransmitter (generally serotonin) at the synaptic cleft so it can continue to trigger nerve impulses. This increase can be generated either by inhibiting the inactivation of serotonin or by blocking the reuptake of the molecule back into the pre-synaptic system for reuse.

Monoamine oxidase is the enzyme that inactivates serotonin (and norepinephrine) after the neurotransmitter has been released from its post-synaptic receptor. Inhibition of monoamine oxidase allows the neurotransmitter to remain longer in the synaptic cleft, providing more opportunity for its interaction with the post-synaptic receptor and stimulation of more nerve impulses. The first successful antidepressants worked on this enzyme inhibition mechanism. By blocking the oxidation of serotonin to its inactive product, the active concentration of serotonin was higher and could trigger further neurotransmission. Even though the MAOIs were the first class of antidepressants to be developed and have been somewhat superseded by newer classes, they are still extremely effective in a large number of cases.

The tricyclic antidepressants (named because of their molecular structure) increase the synaptic cleft concentrations of both norepinephrine and serotonin by blocking the reuptake of the molecule by specific proteins in the pre-synaptic system. These antidepressants affect reuptake of both molecules, so tend to be less selective than newer drugs.

Blocking the reuptake of serotonin alone is accomplished with the use of selective serotonin reuptake inhibitors. This newer category of antidepressants allows a more focused treatment that often has proven to be much more effective than the two older classes of drugs.

However, it should be noted that there are a number of questions and concerns associated with the use of antidepressants (Rush and Ryan 2002). The placebo effect for most drugs is fairly high (sometimes as much as 25–35% of a control group will show relief of depressive symptoms in contrast to 50–60% of the medicated group). Often the effects of the medication are not seen for a couple of weeks after treatment has been initiated. Lacking a clear understanding of the biochemical changes associated with depression, it is difficult to predict accurately which specific drug will be most effective in a given patient. Finally, there have been a number of recent reports implicating some SSRIs with an increase in adolescent suicide (Valuck et al. 2004).

Not surprisingly, the most common treatment for depression is with the use of antidepressant drugs. The American Psychiatric Association guidelines for treatment (2005) suggest that pharmacological intervention appears to be most effective. But the ideal effect of the drug is to elevate the mood to a point where the patient can begin to look realistically at the psychological issues producing the depression. Sadly, drug treatment is often undertaken as an initial approach with no therapy used as follow-up. It is very common for family physicians (who are usually not trained in either psychotherapy or in proper use of antidepressant medications) to prescribe these drugs and have little or no psychological counseling over the course of the next year.

Various forms of non-pharmaceutical therapies are proving to be fairly successful, especially in combination with drug treatment. Cognitive-behavioral therapy, for example, has shown to be beneficial in a wide range of settings (Kuyken et al. 2007). This, as well as a variety of other "talk therapies," has proven effective in dealing with depression. Unfortunately, these forms of therapy are labor intensive and are usually not covered for long-term treatment by most health insurance plans.

In some important respects, these forms of therapy can resemble the pastoral counseling that is often provided by skilled ministers. The essential features of non-drug treatments usually involve some mix of looking at what triggers depressive attitudes, challenging negative beliefs, and developing strategies to help the individual "rethink" their lives and reprogram their thoughts. Unfortunately, there is often not enough time in a medical setting for really effective therapy. In pastoral counseling, the minister too often lets theology drive the counseling (as seen in our opening example) instead of trying to discern what the issues really are.

These guidelines also point out some problems in assessing the effectiveness of these psychotherapies. There are many therapies in use, with different approaches taken by different practitioners. Few controlled studies of treatment efficacy appear in the professional literature. Questions of frequency of treatment (number of times per week or month), duration of treatment, and the continuing inability to distinguish clearly among the various subtypes of depression complicate our understanding of these forms of therapy for depression. Obviously, more carefully designed studies are needed to shed light on these questions.

## Toward a New Paradigm for Dealing with Depression

There appears to be a dilemma for pentecostal/charismatic Christians. Do they engage in modern psychiatric treatment with its heavy emphasis on medications, or do they rely on church resources, using staff members who frequently have little or no training in counseling? There are at least two recent developments that suggestion a growing rapprochement. The first deals with the increasing awareness of the value of religious belief to mental health. The second involves formulating a more holistic approach to depression that takes into account some of the non-biochemical issues (like the role of environmental stress and existential guilt) related to depression.

Much recent research in psychiatry clearly demonstrates the beneficial impact of religion on mental health. The Center for Spirituality, Theology and Health at Duke University, under the able leadership of Harold Koenig, M.D., has been at the forefront of studies in this area. Growing numbers of publications in books and psychiatric journals attest to the fact that people for whom religion is a regular part of their lives have better mental health than others. Koenig's *Faith and Mental Health* (2005) and Plante and Sherman's *Faith and Health* (2001) both are valuable resources for this topic. The *Handbook of Psychotherapy and Religious Diversity*, edited by Richards and Bergin (2001) shows the interest on the part of the American Psychological Association in working effectively with religious patients. The "war" between psychiatry and religion may well be over. What impact these findings will have on any pentecostal/charismatic theology of mental illness remains a subject for further study.

### Depression, Stress, and Guilt

In considering the cause (or causes) of depression, there seems to be a return to an earlier model that implicated stress as a major precipitator of the disorder. An early two-part study in the *New England Journal of Medicine* laid out the clear links between stress and depression (Gold et al. 1988). The writers describe the clinical and biochemical processes operative in depression and tie them to changes in both behavior and biochemistry seen in stress situations. Arborelius and colleagues explored the relationship between stress and depression stating, "Stressful events often precede the onset of depression and stress has also been associated with the severity of the illness. . . . Moreover, stressful life events in childhood have been shown to predispose an individual for development of mood and anxiety disorders in adulthood" (Arborelius et al. 1999: 1). Many other studies could also be cited.

One of the major stressors frequently encountered in depression is guilt. The DSM lists excessive feelings of unworthiness and/or guilt as one of the diagnostic criteria for depression. Guilt (real or otherwise) can place tremendous stresses on an individual.

The link between depression and guilt has been widely explored in Christian thinking. Particularly in evangelical circles, there is a longstanding belief that unresolved sin can lead to depression. This sin must be dealt with in some way before the depression will decrease. The well-known physician and psychiatrist Paul Tournier explored the relationship between guilt and depression in sections of several books (1962, 1964, 1965, 1966). The theme has also been developed by other Christian psychologists such as Paul Meier and his colleagues (1982). Jay Adams explored this issue in depth in his (somewhat controversial) books *Competent to Counsel* (1970) and *The Christian Counselor's Manual* (1973). Richard Dobbins suggests that pentecostals often bring guilt issues into their therapy (2001). An earlier, more academic paper looking at the question of spiritual imbalance and depression suggests that the issue of sin can be significant for many Christians who experience depression, but the author rightly warns against placing undue emphasis on this aspect of the problem (Johnson 1980).

The literature covering the links between depression and guilt is voluminous. We find guilt and depression linked in individuals in a wide variety of situations. These range from the seemingly trivial to the very serious. Table 7.1 summarizes some of the situations that result in both depression and a

Table 7.1

Situations Linking Guilt and Depression

| Affected Individuals | Situation | Reference |
|---|---|---|
| women on diets | looking at candy pictures | Fletcher et al. 2007 |
| chocolate addicts | eating chocolate | Macdiarmid and Hethering-ton 1995 |
| women | physical abuse | Street and Arias 2001 |
| nurses | participating in abortions | Mokgethi et al. 2006 |
| couples | experiencing infertility | Hart 2002 |
| women | sexual abuse | Gorey et al. 2001 |
| women | miscarriage | Stirtzinger et al. 1999 |
| mothers | severely injured child | Fukunishi 1998 |
| parents | children with birth defects | Dolger-Hafner et al. 1997 |

strong sense of guilt in the depressed individual. The references listed are not comprehensive but give a sense of the extensive literature on this subject.

### An Integrative View of Depression

We have approached the problem of depression from several different fronts. Many psychiatrists argue that this disorder is primarily a problem of neurochemical imbalance. Their treatment involves restoring those imbalances through pharmacological means. Many pentecostals and other conservative religious persons see the issue mainly as one of incorrect beliefs and behaviors. Others present a model that looks primarily at events that produce severe stress in the individual, with this stress often being very long-lasting.

I propose the following model that integrates the biochemical issues (both neurochemical and endocrine), the psychological problems, and a role for spiritual healing. The precipitating event in depression is some sort of external stress (divorce, physical abuse, rape, and severe financial crisis, among others) (Wong and Licino 2001). The stress could be direct (happening to the person) or indirect (e.g., one's parents get a divorce). The individual experiences a strong sense of guilt (either real or assumed). The psychological stress gives rise to disturbances in both the neurotransmitter system and the endocrine system (there is a complex interplay between the two). Although the antidepressants may alleviate some of the symptoms, the underlying stress has not been resolved. If the guilt is real, the stress needs to be resolved by repentance and seeking forgiveness. Through cognitive-behavioral therapy (a form of counseling that has its counterpart in pastoral ministry), the individual learns to recognize triggers to depressive behavior and develops successful coping strategies (changes in behavior). The patient acknowledges wrong-doing and seeks to resolve the situation. If the guilt is assumed (as I suspect it is in the majority of cases to which this idea might apply), resolution comes when the person understands the erroneous source of the guilt and finds healing from that mistaken idea.

This model certainly will not apply to all cases of depression. Let me suggest that the mostly likely population for which this idea is immediately applicable is women, especially teens and younger adults (a sizable percentage of the population that experiences depression). Women experience depression at rates over twice that of men. Many of the adverse events of life (especially physical and sexual abuse) are inflicted much more often on women than on men. During adolescence, many of the psychological issues that seem to be much more prevalent in girls include a sense of personal failure, not measuring up to some standard (usually of physical beauty or self-imposed idea of "proper" body image) or those coming out of an abusive relationship (which could be physical, sexual, emotional, or some combination of the three).

As mentioned earlier, stress produces hormonal changes that cause the adrenal cortex to produce greater than normal amounts of cortisol (Gold et al. 1988). In depression, these same endocrine changes are often seen (Arborelius et al. 1999). Many studies indicate that the ACTH and cortisol levels drop back to normal after clinical recovery. Therefore, it is possible that more attention should be given to regulation of cortisol in treating depression.

So where does this leave serotonin and norepinephrine (the two major neurotransmitters said to be involved in depression)? The primary pharmacological treatments are antidepressants that produce increases of one or both of these molecules at the synapse. However, many studies have questioned the efficacy of most of these treatments. Hindmarch (2002) argues that the focus on serotonin has hindered the development of possibly more effective drugs that would alter other biochemical processes, including the HPA axis. Some studies suggest that serotonin and norepinephrine may have a role in the regulation of ACTH production by the pituitary (Dinan 1996). Therefore, it is becoming increasingly apparent that both alterations in the HPA axis biochemistry and in the amounts of neurotransmitters available at the synapse are state functions (a result of the primary precipitating event in depression) and not trait functions (a cause of the depression). These data may help explain the confusing literature on the therapeutic effectiveness of various antidepressants and could help us better understand the high placebo effect seen in studies of drugs used to treat depression.

### The Religious Dimension of the Model

If depression arises from a stress environment of some sort, those stresses need to be discovered. Professional counselors (psychiatrists and psychologists who are trained to do this type of counseling) have the skills both to look for and to uncover the stresses present. Many lay counselors (and I include most pastors in this category) are not trained to do counseling and quite often will miss significant issues. In addition, the managed-care system so prevalent in medicine these days works against the detailed discovery of the underlying issues in many cases.

The religious component in depression is often downplayed or ignored. If it is incorporated into the diagnosis and treatment, the spiritual aspect usually involves some sort of search for personal sin in a person's life and the need to change the lifestyle to remove that sin. The "assumed guilt" model draws upon this strand of therapeutic intervention, but the major focus here is to help patients realize that they have not done anything wrong and they are not guilty of any specific sin that they have taken on through the stress event.

There are at least two components of the healing process that will be effective in these situations. First, individuals need (in a sense) to forgive themselves. Forgiveness has been shown to be a very effective approach to dealing with many issues in depression where someone else has done the wrong (and that may be yet another avenue that needs to be explored—letting go of the stress event and not revisiting it). Several works have been published exploring the role of forgiveness in depression and related disorders (Worthington 1998; Plante and Sherman 2001; Biebel and Koenig 2004). Secondly, the individual needs to experience the power of forgiveness and the cleansing of the soul that comes from being truly forgiven. Pargament and Rye (1998) describe the process of dealing with forgiveness issues. While the initial means of coping involves anger, fear, and related emotions, the transformational aspects involve a reframing of the experience, an empathetic approach, a reappraisal of what has happened, and ultimately a sense of peace.

How is this awareness of assumed guilt to be achieved? Certainly, counseling will be very helpful, especially if the counselor is on the lookout for the possibility that the client has taken on guilt for something that he or she had no control over. By careful questioning, clients perhaps can see that the roots of the issues that precipitated the depression may well be outside of themselves—they are simply innocent victims of someone else's behavior and are not at all responsible for what has happened. This awareness can free them from the guilt they have assumed or internalized.

### The Holy Spirit and the Healing of Depression

In addition, Christians in general, and pentecostal and charismatic Christians in particular, can draw upon the power of the Holy Spirit for enlightenment. Romans 8:26 tells us "In the same way the Spirit also helps our weakness; for we do not know how to pray as we should, but the Spirit Himself intercedes for us with groanings too deep for words." Although this passage is dealing with prayer, I believe we can reasonably take it to suggest that whatever is deep within us, whatever cannot be articulated by the person, that issue can be illuminated by the Holy Spirit. When Paul speaks in Ephesians 4:23 of the "renewing of your mind." he says this in a context of a person coming out of their "former life" (presumably their non-Christian past). We could also see that passage as a suggestion that our minds can be renewed in a variety of situations while we are believers, including times of depression.

This renewal has an interesting and promising medical basis. Paul tells us in Romans 12:2, "And do not be conformed to this world, but be transformed by the renewing of your mind." Cognitive behavioral therapy (mentioned above) and its spiritual counterpart in effective pastoral counseling can literally renew the brain. There is a growing body of literature that suggests actual regeneration of brain tissue after treatment for various disorders including depression (see Roffman et al. 2005; and Frewen et al. 2008 for reviews of studies). This renewing of brain tissue accompanies the alleviation of the depression. Certainly, much more research is needed in this important area.

The other avenue of healing is direct intervention by the Holy Spirit. The Holy Spirit can reveal the inner workings of our heart, as mentioned above. In addition, the Spirit can bring direct healing, not just of the body but also of the mind. The attitudes of the mind can be changed. The person can receive insights into the reality of the situation. An understanding of the nature of the guilt taken on by the individual can then be extended to an experience of healing, both in terms of freedom from the pain of the stress experience and the acceptance of forgiveness for the assumed guilt. These roles of the Holy Spirit are integral to pentecostal/charismatic theology and are part of the ministry that we can bring to this segment of depressed individuals.

## Notes

1. The hospital chaplain at the community hospital in Durham where I directed the clinical chemistry lab (which had a teaching affiliation with Duke University) told me in 1982 that the worst physicians she had to work with were the psychiatrists—they did not appear to want any involvement at all from the religious community.
2. The National Institute of Mental Health has current statistics at their Web site: www.nimh.nih.gov.

## References

Adams, J. E. 1970. *Competent to Counsel*. Nutley, N.J.: Presbyterian and Reformed Publishing Co.
———. 1973. *The Christian Counselor's Manual*. Nutley, N.J.: Presbyterian and Reformed Publishing Co.
American Psychiatric Association, 2005. "Practice Guidelines for the Treatment of

Patients with Major Depressive Disorder (Revision)." *American Journal of Psychiatry* 157/4, April supplement: 1–45.

Arborelius, L., et al. 1999. "The Role of Corticotropin-Releasing Factor in Depression and Anxiety Disorders." *Journal of Endocrinology* 160: 1–12.

Belcher, J. R., and S. M. Hall. 2001. "Healing and Psychotherapy: The Pentecostal Tradition." *Pastoral Psychology* 50/2: 63–75.

Biebel, D. B., and H. G. Koenig. 2004. *New Light on Depression.* Grand Rapids, Mich.: Zondervan/Christian Medical Association.

Carroll, B. J., et al. 1976. "Neuroendocrine Regulation in Depression. II: Discrimination of Depressed from Nondepressed Patients." *Archives of General Psychiatry* 33: 1051–58.

Castelein, J. D. 1984. "Glossolalia and the Psychology of the Self and Narcissism." *Journal of Religion and Health* 23/1: 47–62.

Dinan, T. G. 1996. "Noradrenergic and Serotonergic Abnormalities in Depression: Stress-Induced Dysfunction?" *Journal of Clinical Psychiatry* 57/supplement 4: 14–18.

Dobbins, R. 2001 "Psychotherapy with Pentecostal Protestants." In P. S. Richards and A. E. Bergin, eds., *Handbook for Psychotherapy and Religious Diversity.* Washington, D.C.: American Psychological Association, 155–84.

Dolger-Hafner, M., et al. 1997. "Parental Reactions Following the Birth of a Cleft Child." *Journal of Orthofacial Orthopedics* 58/2: 124–33.

*DSM-IV, the Diagnostic and Statistical Manual of Mental Disorders.* 1994. 4th ed. Arlington, Va.: American Psychiatric Association.

Ettigi, P. K., and G. M. Brown. 1977 "Psychoneuroendrocrinology of Affective Disorder: An Overview." *American Journal of Psychiatry* 134/5: 493–501.

Fawcett, J. 1994. "Overview of Mood Disorders: Diagnosis, Classification, and Management." *Clinical Chemistry* 40/2: 273–78.

Fletcher, B. C., et al. 2007. "How Visual Images of Chocolate Affect the Craving and Guilt of Female Dieters." *Appetite* 48/2: 211–17.

Francis, L. J., and M. Robbins. 2003. "Personality and Glossolalia: A Study among Male Evangelical Clergy." *Pastoral Psychology* 51/5: 391–96.

Frewen, P. A., et al. 2008. "Neuroimaging Studies of Psychological Interventions for Mood and Anxiety Disorders: Empirical and Methodological Review." *Clinical Psychology Review* 28/2: 228–46.

Fukunishi, I. 1998. "Posttraumatic Stress Symptoms and Depression in Mothers of Children with Severe Burn Injuries." *Psychological Report* 83/1: 331–35.

Gillespie, C. F., and C. B. Nemeroff. 2005. "Hypercortisolemia and Depression." *Psychosomatic Medicine* 67/supplement 1: S26–S28.

Gold, P. W., et al. 1988. "Clinical and Biochemical Manifestations of Depression—Relation to the Neurobiology of Stress." *New England Journal of Medicine* 319: part 1, 348–53, and part 2, 413–20.

Gorey, K. M., et al. 2001. "Guilt, Isolation and Hopelessness among Female Survivors of Childhood Sexual Abuse: Effectiveness of Group Work Intervention." *Child Abuse and Neglect* 25/3: 347–55.

Hart, V. A. 2002. "Infertility and the Role of Psychotherapy." *Issues in Mental Health Nursing* 23/1: 31–41.

Hindmarch, I. 2002. "Beyond the Monoamine Hypothesis: Mechanisms, Molecules and Methods." *European Psychiatry* 17/ supplement 3: 294–99.

Johnson, W. C. 1980. "Depression: Biochemical Abnormality or Spiritual Backsliding?" *Journal of the American Scientific Affiliation* 32/1: 18–27.

Kessler, R. C., et al. 2003. "The Epidemiology of Major Depressive Disorder: Results from the National Comorbidity Survey Replication (NCS-R)." *Journal of the American Medical Association* 289/23: 3095–3105.

———. 2005a. "Prevalence, Severity, and Comorbidity of Twelve-month DSM-IV Disorders in the National Comorbidity Survey Replication (NCS-R)." *Archives of General Psychiatry* 62/6: 617–27.

———. 2005b. "Lifetime Prevalence and Age-of-onset Distributions of DSM-IV Disorders in the National Comorbidity Survey Replication (NCS-R)." *Archives of General Psychiatry* 62/6: 593–602.

Koenig, Harold G. 2005. *Faith and Mental Health: Religious Resources for Healing.* Philadelphia: Templeton Foundation Press.

Kuyken, W., et al. 2007. "Advances in Cognitive-Behavioural Therapy for Unipolar Depression." *Canadian Journal of Psychiatry* 52/1: 5–13.

Macdiarmid, J. I., and M. M. Hetherington. 1995. "Mood Modulation by Food: An Exploration of Affect and Cravings in 'Chocolate Addicts.'" *British Journal of Clinical Psychology* 34/1: 129–38.

Mahli, G. S., et al. 2005. "Structural and Functional Models of Depression: From Subtypes to Substrates." *Acta Psychiatrica. Scandinavica* 111: 94–105.

Meier, P. D., et al. 1982. *Introduction to Psychology and Counseling.* Grand Rapids, Mich.: Baker Book House.

Meltzer, H. Y. 1990. "Role of Serotonin in Depression." *Annals of the New York Academy of Science* 600: 486–99.

Mokgethi, N. E., et al. 2006. "Professional Nurses' Attitudes towards Providing Termination of Pregnancy Services in a Tertiary Hospital in the North West Province of South Africa." *Curationis* 29/1: 32–39.

O'Keane, V. 2000. "Evolving Model of Depression as an Expression of Multiple Interacting Risk Factors." *British Journal of Psychiatry* 177: 482–83.

Pargament, K. I., and M. S. Rye. 1998. "Forgiveness as a Method of Religious Coping." In E. L. Worthington Jr., ed., *Dimensions of Forgiveness: Psychological Research and Theological Perspectives.* Philadelphia: Templeton Foundation Press, 59–78.

Pattison, E. Mansell. 1968. "Behavioral Science Research on the Nature of Glossolalia." *Journal of the American Scientific Affiliation* 20: 73–86.

Plante, T. G., and A. C. Sherman, eds. 2001. *Faith and Health: Psychological Perspectives.* New York: Guilford Press.

Remick, R. A. 2002. "Diagnosis and Management of Depression in Primary Care: A Clinical Update and Review." *Canadian Medical Association Journal* 167/11: 1253–60.

Ressler, K. J., and C. B. Nemeroff. 2000. "Role of Serotonergic and Noradrenergic Systems in the Pathophysiology and Depression and Anxiety Disorders." *Depression and Anxiety* 12/supplement 1: 2–19.

Richards, P. S., and A. E. Bergin, eds. *Handbook for Psychotherapy and Religious Diversity.* Washington, D.C.: American Psychological Association.

Risch, S. Craig, and C. B. Nemeroff. 1992. "Neurochemical Alterations of Serotonergic Neuronal Systems in Depression." *Journal of Clinical Psychiatry* 53/10, supplement: 3–7.

Roffman, J. L., et al. 2005. "Neuroimaging and the Functional Neuroanatomy of Psychotherapy." *Psychological Medicine* 35/10: 1385–98.

Rush, A. J., and N. D. Ryan, 2002. "Current and Emerging Therapeutics for Depression." In K. L. Davis et al., eds., *Neuropsychopharmacology: The Fifth Generation of Progress.* Nashville, Tenn.: American College of Neuropsychopharmacology, 1081–95.

Sachar, E. J., et al. 1970. "Cortisol Production in Depressive Illness: A Clinical and Biochemical Clarification." *Archives of General Psychiatry* 23: 289–98.

Scelfo, Julie. 2007. "Men and Depression: Facing Darkness." *Newsweek* 149/8: 42.

Stirtzinger, R. M., et al. 1999. "Parameters of Grieving in Spontaneous Abortion." *International Journal of Psychiatry and Medicine* 29/2: 235–49.

Street, A. E., and I. Arias. 2001. "Psychological Abuse and Posttraumatic Stress Disorder in Battered Women: Examining the Roles of Shame and Guilt." *Violence and Victims* 16/1: 65–78.

Tournier, P. 1962. *Guilt and Grace.* Trans A. W. Heathcocke. New York: Harper and Row.

———. 1964. *The Whole Person in a Broken World.* Trans. John and Helen Doberstein. New York: Harper and Row.

———. 1965. *The Healing of Persons.* Trans. E. Hudson. New York: Harper and Row.

———. 1966. *The Person Reborn.* Trans. E. Hudson. New York: Harper and Row.

Trice, N. D., and J. C. Bjork. 2006. "Pentecostal Perspectives on Causes and Cures of Depression." *Professional Psychology Research and Practice* 37/3: 283–94.

Valuck, R. J., et al. 2004. "Antidepressant Treatment and Risk of Suicide Attempt by Adolescents with Major Depressive Disorder: A Propensity-Adjusted Retrospective Cohort Study." *CNS Drugs* 18/15: 1119–32.

Weissman, M. M., and M. Olfson. 1995. "Depression in Women: Implications for Health Care Research." *Science* 269: 799–801.

Wong, M.-L., and J. Licinio. 2001. "Research and Treatment Approaches to Depression." *Nature Reviews Neuroscience* 2: 343–51.

Worthington, E. L., Jr., ed. 1998. *Dimensions of Forgiveness: Psychological Research and Theological Perspectives.* Philadelphia: Templeton Foundation Press.

Yong, Amos. 2005. "Academic Glossolalia: Pentecostal Scholarship, Multidisciplinarity, and the Science-Religion Conversation." *Journal of Pentecostal Theology* 14/1: 61–80.

## Recommended Reading

Blazer, D. 1998. *Freud versus God.* Downers Grove, Ill.: InterVarsity Press.

Corr, P. 2006. *Understanding Biological Psychology.* Malden, Mass.: Blackwell.

Glenmullen, J. 2000. *Prozac Backlash: Overcoming the Dangers of Prozac, Zoloft, Paxil, and Other Antidepressants with Safe, Effective Alternatives.* New York: Simon and Schuster.

Jeeves, M. 2006. *Human Nature: Reflections on the Integration of Psychology and Christianity.* Philadelphia: Templeton Foundation Press.

Johnson, E. L., and S. L. Jones, eds. 2000. *Psychology and Christianity: Four Views.* Downers Grove, Ill.: InterVarsity Press.

Kandel, E. R., et al. 2000. *Principles of Neuroscience,* 4th ed. New York: McGraw-Hill.

Lajtha, A., and E. S. Vizi, eds. 2008. *Handbook of Neurochemistry and Molecular Neurobiology: Neurotransmitter Systems,* 3rd ed. Philadelphia: Springer.

McMinn, M. R., and C. D. Campbell. 2007. *Integrative Psychotherapy: Toward a Comprehensive Christian Approach.* Downers Grove, Ill.: InterVarsity Press.

Menninger, K. 1973. *Whatever Became of Sin?* New York: Hawthorn Books.

Siegel, G. J., et al., eds. 2006. *Basic Neurochemistry: Molecular, Cellular and Medical Aspects,* 7th ed. Burlington, Mass.: Elsevier Academic Press.

# PART THREE

## The Human Spirit

*Questions and Possibilities
in the Social and
Technological Sciences*

# 8  Can Social Scientists Dance? Participating in Science, Spirit, and Social Reconstruction as an Anthropologist and Afropentecostal

*Craig Scandrett-Leatherman*

*When the Spirit informed Peter through a vision that cultures are not "unclean" and that he was to go talk and eat with Gentiles, he was inducted into the participatory methods of anthropology and the Spirit. Science is often characterized by a critical perspective and disinterested objective method that denies the reality of anything that is not verifiable by repeatable experimentation. On the other hand, Afropentecostal practice is characterized by emotive and embodied participation. But together, the scientific philosophy of Michael Polanyi, the methodology of anthropology, and the ritual theory of Victor Turner suggest that scientific and Afropentecostal knowledge may not be so neatly characterized and compartmentalized. Science and ritual both seek knowledge through participation. Because participation involves multidirectional influences between objects in fields of energy, it challenges conceptions of a closed universe. Neither social nor subatomic realities are completely predictable because they exist in inter-participating fields of energy. The discipline of cultural anthropology and the rituals of Afropentecostal worship both emphasize participatory epistemology. Social science specializes in discerning social patterns; religious ritual, in discerning social poten-*

*tial. Discerning social patterns and possibilities together, through caring participation, may increase the possibility of social re-imagination and transformation.*

## Can Social Scientists Dance?

In all of my academic studies, from college through graduate school, the hardest class I took, by far, was African Dance. The difficulty was due to my lack of experience. I began my life in a Free Methodist parsonage where holiness and dancing didn't go together—not at all. I learned this one day after school when I was about seven years old. My friend Lucy invited me over to her house to dance with a small bunch of second-graders. Without a thought, I went. Then—when we were dancing to Peter, Paul, and Mary singing "Puff, the Magic Dragon"—my brother's head appeared in the small basement window, saying, "You need to come home right now!" He was ten years older. His tone suggested that I'd better hurry, so I did. When I got outside, he said, "Man, are you going to get it." I asked, "For what?" He thought my question was a bluff. "For dancing, that's for what." Members of holiness churches didn't dance.

I didn't dance much in the forty-something years after that event, so by the time I got to my class on African Dance, I was way out of practice. And my first question, Can a scientist dance? was accompanied by other questions like, What on earth am I doing in this class with a djembe drummer and a bunch of young co-eds, dance majors who clearly *can* dance?

Why would an anthropologist studying Afropentecostalism take an African dance class? you might be asking. Here's the story in short form. In Chicago I was an addiction counselor in a residential recovery program; the program became more effective when we hired African American counselors and they connected us to African American churches and worship. I visited those churches, had a sense that there were African roots to the worship, and began to regularly attend an Afropentecostal church. Eventually, my family and I joined Calvary Church of God in Christ Church (COGIC), and I used anthropology as a discipline of participating, observing, and understanding. The anthropology story is longer.

*Cultural anthropology* is a social science that focuses on the perspectives and social patterns of people groups—the way that they perceive, think, know, communicate, and relate to each other and to the world.[1] People's cultures form a common way of living and being that is not usually discussed or even noticed. Rather, culture is taken for granted: fish presume water; Frenchman think its nosey to ask questions of a stranger; Indians presume that their parents will find them a spouse. But such assumptions are shaken when we are thrown out of the water. We become aware of our own culture by contact with a different culture, like when someone moves next door who plays strange music and invites us to strange funerals. We become aware of culture when we know another people well enough to know that their "strange" actions or way of thinking are part of a comprehensive and cohesive way of life. Cultural anthropologists intentionally immerse themselves in another people's way of life to gain such understanding.

Anthropology is a science because its methods are systematic: it discerns social patterns and represents that its work claims at least plausibility and also universal validity. In other words, though it describes a particular people, its purpose is not to provide a personal account of cross-cultural food and friendship (though it might include that) but to describe a way of life so that "outsiders" (and maybe "insiders" too) might understand the cohesiveness or comprehensiveness of a people group. It aims to expand cross-cultural understanding and relationships by interpreting culture. In short, anthropology is a science because its method is systematic and it aims at universal validity, but it is different from the ideal of "hard" sciences because its method emphasizes participation. Understanding cultural variation requires it. Since the main method of cultural anthropology is participation, I thought taking a dance class would enhance my participation in my COGIC church where dancing was common.

Both anthropologists and pentecostals value participation as a method of knowing. In this chapter, and with the help of Frank Cushing, Michael Polanyi, Victor Turner, and Afropentecostal participation, I hope to show that: (1) science involves participation; (2) participation modifies the notion of closed systems; and (3) practicing anthropology and Afropentecostalism together may promote transformative social participation. Often spiritual and social participation is segregated, but the life of the Spirit can integrate both. I believe that those who participate in both spiritual and cross-cultural realities will make new and important discoveries; they will participate in powers that transform persons and societies; and they will know that life is not stagnant but dynamic—like dancing in the Spirit. In short, pentecostal dance might make us better anthropologists; and the cross-cultural practice of anthropology might make us better pentecostals.

## Frank Cushing: Participant Observation as a Way of Knowing

Anthropology as an academic discipline developed in Britain and the United States in the 1880s. In Britain, E. B. Tylor wrote *Researches into the Early History of Mankind* (1865) and *Religion in Primitive Cultures* (1871). Both were based on third-hand information from traveling observers who were communicating through translators.[2] On the American side, Lewis Henry

Morgan advanced anthropological method from third-hand to second-hand observation when he entered "the field" himself and hired a bilingual informant, Ely S. Parker. Parker, a Seneca Indian, interpreted the ceremonies to Morgan, who then wrote these as *League of the Ho-de-no-sau-nee or Iroquois* (1851). Eventually, Parker got hold of Morgan's book, but his review was not positive. "There's nothing actually wrong in what he says, but it isn't right either. He doesn't really understand what he is talking about" (Turner 1977: 2). Morgan took anthropology to "the field," but the sit-and-observe method still left the anthropologist as a detached outsider who didn't really "get it."

In 1879 anthropology's second-hand and stand-offish method took a turn for the better when a Zuni elder invited an anthropologist, Frank Hamilton Cushing, to participate in Zuni life:

> Little brother, you may be a Washington man, but it seems that you are very poor. Now, if you do as we tell you, and will only make up your mind to be a Zuni, you shall be rich, for you shall have fathers and mothers, brothers and sisters, and the best food in the world. But if you do not do as we tell you, you will be very, very, very poor, indeed. (Green 1979: 68)

Being a Washington man meant he had ongoing political, financial, and military support—national power and privilege—behind him. But despite all of this "wealth," the elder thought Cushing was poor because he didn't know how to do anything: he didn't know how to act right, talk right, eat right; he didn't know how to participate in rituals; and he didn't know how to hunt. By this time, Cushing had been hanging around Zuni people long enough to be impressed with their manners, ethos, perspectives, and skills. He must have agreed that he was poor in their wisdom and ways, because he accepted the elder's invitation to become Zuni. According to Jesse Green, this was the point at which Cushing became the first anthropologist to practice *participant* observation: to enter another people's way of life. He lived with the Zuni Native Americans for five years from 1879 to 1884.

Cushing's participation was consummated through an initiation that involved pain and a four-day fast. It continued through many months of language learning, and it involved learning to hunt, weave, and make pottery. Cushing's greatest challenge was to maintain his observations. The Zuni did not appreciate his note-taking and writing, especially after he was initiated. But when someone approached him with a knife to take away his books and journals, Cushing brandished his own knife and eventually won the skirmish. The chief congratulated him, and he got back to his note-taking (Green 1979: 72–74). By attention, desire, and invitation Cushing experienced *being* a Zuni.

Having learned so much and been so accepted, Cushing had a strong hunch that he was involved in something important. In a letter to a friend, he wrote, "My ability may not be as great as those who preceded me but my method must succeed" (Green 1979: 136). What Cushing discovered was that he was changed by his cross-cultural experience. His method was not only gathering information *about* other people; it was also *being changed by participating in their daily lives.* He was discovering another way of life, another way of being in the world.[3] Because of this, Cushing was distinguished from his predecessors by conveying "a sense of the presence of living people and real things" (Green 1979: 19). This sense was the result of his living presence with the people and their reality. It was the result not only of his keen observation but also of his full bodily participation.

In most social scientific discourse, observations and subjective experience are distinguished, and the latter is devalued and delimited. But Cushing's method began to undermine this distinction. It would take another century before another scientist, from another continent and science, Michael Polanyi, would reverse the devaluing of participant knowledge. He would affirm participation as a way of science and discovery.

## Michael Polanyi: The Tacit Dimension as Participation and Discovery

Michael Polanyi was an accomplished physical chemist at research institutes in Berlin and then at Manchester University, where he began to philosophize on scientific knowledge, and then on knowing in general. His work is developed most comprehensively in *Personal Knowledge: Toward a Post-Critical Philosophy* (1958). I will summarize the book in two theses: (1) we know more than we can say; and (2) knowledge involves participation.

*We know more than we can say.* On the one hand, this statement seems like common sense. Based on this straightforward assumption, people have been practicing apprenticeships for millennium. On the other hand, this statement is the antithesis of modernity with its almost exclusive focus on explicit knowledge, whose thesis seems to be *If you can't say it, you don't know it.*

Polanyi's "we know more than we can say" thesis is illustrated in two examples from daily life: learning to ride a bicycle, and recognizing a friend's face in a crowd. A physicist is able to analyze mechanical forces, balances, and vectors in such a way that she could tell a would-be bicyclist that one balances a bicycle through a combination of centrifugal force, weight balance, and minor force-vector changes that are accomplished by steering in the direction of the tilt. But this will be of little use in teaching someone to ride a bike. The process of learning to ride a bicycle usually goes something like this: the potential learner sees others riding bicycles and becomes interested in and then passionate about learning to ride; a lesson is requested or offered; an experienced bicyclist gives basic instructions and offers support; the learner tries, wobbles, falls, gets up, tries again, makes adjustments, practices, and eventually becomes a bicyclist. Because we know more than we can say, the knowledge of bicycling is passed on with very few explicit words. A parent would be a fool by trying to teach a child how to ride a bike with a physicist's explicit explanation.

Another example of knowing more than we can say is face recognition. We can easily recognize a friend in a crowd, but it is very difficult to give someone else a description of a person's face so that he or she will recognize that person in a crowd. We know more than we can say.

According to Polanyi, people wouldn't get very far in life or learning if they didn't act before they explicitly understood the principles that support action. People wouldn't drink until they understood gravity, liquids, vacuums, nutrition, calorie needs, and so forth. People wouldn't drive until they understood fuel and its explosive qualities, electricity, and the physics of bearings, wheels, gears, and pulleys, and until they understood the physics of bridges on which they and their cars depend. People wouldn't marry before they fully understand the opposite sex. So all of us—bicyclists, philosophers, eaters, scientists, drivers, and lovers—travel by the knowledge demonstrated by experts and elders. Some of that knowledge is spoken, but we all know more than we can say, and we all learn by the "more" as much as by what words convey.

It follows, then, that *knowledge involves participation.* In a way similar to the way people learn to ride bicycles, mechanics, carpenters, bakers, steelworkers, florists, guitarists, painters, cooks, and artisans learn their skills by participating in their arts by practice and instruction, by watching and doing, by apprenticeship. Children learn language by participating in communication. But do scientists learn by participating in science? Polanyi argues that even the most objective of scientists learn by participation. In his field of chemistry, people do not learn their discipline by explicit knowledge being transferred to their minds. Instead, students bring themselves into the presence and under the discipline of experts. Knowledge is gained not only through books and lectures but also by association with experts whose assumptions are trusted. Students spend hours in labs learning techniques, habits, and practices which give them confidence in trusting the communal cosmology of chemists and chemistry.

Though some scientists still suggest that their every assumption and theory is explicit and is critically reviewed and tested, Polanyi argues that, in the economy of time, scientists spend very little time critically testing their theories or assumptions or those of their predecessors. "The articulate contents of science are successfully taught all over the world in hundreds of new universities, [but] the unspecifiable art of scientific research has not yet penetrated to many of these" (Polanyi 1958: 53). The art of research is learned by participating in the discipline—by participating in the practice and habits of thought and activity of experts. So even in the hard sciences, Polanyi argues, the ways of knowledge and discovery are taught, not by explicit knowledge that can be passed on through books and the Internet, but by *participating* in the ways and disciplines of elder experts.

Polanyi is critiquing the idea that knowledge is primarily explicit and objective. He is saying that infants and artisans learn by participation, and so do scientists and philosophers. All human disciplines of knowledge involve not only explicit knowledge but also participation. Unlike those scientists who reduce knowledge to that which can be discerned by observation, Polanyi grounds knowledge on a broad epistemology that is not positivistic but human; it is personal knowledge based on participation in a tradition and community of knowledge. Cushing's anthropological method of participation is supported by Polanyi's epistemology. As we move toward Afropentecostal participation, we turn to Victor Turner, an anthropologist who came to see society not only as a self-perpetuating social structure but also as an open social field whose dynamism could be accentuated by ritual participation.

## Victor Turner: Ritual Liminality and Social Potentialities

As Michael Polanyi described scientific inquiry as "an imaginative thrust toward discovering potentialities" (1967: 89) based in the physical realm, Victor Turner discovered and articulated these dynamics in the social realm. The significance of Turner's work must be seen as a revision of the positivist social science that was dominated by a theory called "structuralism." So we begin with the significant work of Émile Durkheim, who was one of Turner's predecessors in the social sciences.[4]

Durkheim (1912) agreed with his mentor Fustel De Coulanges about the intimate relationship between religion and society, but where Fustel De Coulanges (1965[1864]: 90) saw religion in dynamic *relation* with society, Durkheim saw religion as a *reflection* of social order, and social science as the analysis of social order. For him, the only way to transform society was to replace the embodied and emotional dynamics of religion with the analysis and reason of social science.

But as an anthropologist in Zambia, Victor Turner saw a community crisis, and he saw doctors of the community intervene with a communal ritual. Members did not survive by their reason but by strengthening social bonds. They did not address the problem only through rational discourse but by activity. Turner saw a communal prescription in which social roles and divisions were suspended while persons became active, their bodies moved, and in the process, it seemed, relationality itself was accentuated. So in response to community crisis, the community intervened with ritual that neither reinforced an existing social structure nor sought further social rationalizations. Instead, the ritual became an enactment of social bonds through the embodied participation of members.

At the center of this healing/strengthening ritual, Turner described a state of "liminality" or "anti-structure" characterized by suspension of social roles and status, reenactment of relationality, and active bodily participation. Among the Ndembu of northwestern Zambia, the crisis was that a woman had given birth to twins. This was a sign of fruitfulness but also a sign of great challenge and burden to the woman, the couple, and society. Such an event would challenge the role divisions between men and women. The intervening ritual involved dancing and gender jesting between the sexes. The liminal center was not characterized by the controls of reason, reasonable will, or social structure, but by the traditions, imaginations, movements, and innovations of ritual leaders and participants. Though liminality is informed and interpreted by communal teaching, it is also characterized by creative (large) muscle movements, active bodies, and accentuated emotions.

Victor Turner argued that liminality does not permanently replace social structure (1977: 129, 139, 203), but it does have the capacity to revise the social order. Society is a process in which any living, relatively well-bonded human group alternates between fixed and floating, or liminal, worlds. Liminal worlds allow the interplay of thought, feeling, and will; and in these worlds new models are generated, "some of which may have sufficient power and plausibility to replace eventually the force-backed political and jural models that control the centers of a society's ongoing life" (Turner 1977: vii). Turner agreed with his mentor, Max Gluckman, that social structure usually maintains a kind of equilibrium, but where the equilibrium model seems not to allow for change (Gluckman 1940: 172–73), and where change is urgent, Turner suggests that liminality or ritual anti-structure may transform personal participation into social dynamism. He observes that ritual is "not only *transition* but also *potentiality,* not only 'going to be' but also 'what may be'" (Turner and Turner 1978: 3; emphasis in original).

Victor Turner sought to revise Durkheim's theory because it could not account for situations where social structure was altered by religious rituals. He argued that the social science about religion would be advanced if the imaginative, emotive, and strange aspects of rituals were perceived as the core of religion's social contribution rather than its embarrassing hype (1977: 2). Turner observed, then argued, that a potential for social transformation is concentrated in the liminal center of rituals. He observed this in rites of passage for individuals or cohorts and in pilgrimages, carnivals, and twin ceremonies. In biblical terms, liminality is "wilderness." Liminal spaces were places and processes where social groups set aside their normal roles and structures; where new perspectives, new resources, and new powers were revised for challenges of a new season of life for a person or community.

Embodied rituals are not only events that complement social structure and serve as a distraction from critical consciousness, but they may also be the furnace where power is gained to overcome oppressive circumstances. Power is gained through the revision of identity, through communal connectivity to people (contemporaries and ancestors), through hearing testifiers say how they survived, through the emotions of joy that produce the strength of hope, through blood flowing to feet and brain, through a drum as a rhythm of life and dance, through the sight of someone leaping, through the warming of the heart and flow of joyful tears—through the indeterminate life of the Spirit. Powers to overcome personal and social diseases are concentrated in ritualizations that accentuate indeterminacy—experience that is not determined by social structure but is open to an undetermined and unimagined future.

While explicit knowledge (referential symbols) "grow with formal elaboration in the conscious," ritualization "strikes deeper and deeper roots in the unconscious, and diffuses its emotional quality to types of behavior and situations" (Sapir 1934: 494). When people practice rituals (worship), they do something different than when they talk with words that have fixed referents. "The efficacy of symbols lies in their ability to release a response" (Lewis 1980: 117, 112, 116).[5] Through a diversity of multisensory arts such as pilgrimage, feasts, drama, story, metaphor, poetry, narrative or testimony, glossolalia, music, drumming, and dance, social structures are suspended, social indeterminacy and imagination is accentuated, and new social possibilities are promoted.[6]

Rituals are most likely to transform society when they cut loose from social structure—when they evolve in a liminal ritual field. While "traditional" Western healing is characterized by a passive body in the doctor's office or the psychiatrist's couch, ritual liminality involves the dynamic interplay between personal and social fields. Participation is a means not only of knowing but also of shaping reality. Participation is not only a passive acceptance of a closed system. Participation is active. So is Afropentecostal worship.

## Afropentecostal Ritual: Embodied Participation in Social-Spiritual Potentialities

Medical research suggests that aerobic exercise increases quantity of life, but Afropentecostal practice suggests a belief that body-engaged worship increases the quality of life. Afropentecostal ritual often involves bodily exercise. A good service is not characterized by relaxed effort, calm or monotone voice, quiet music, or consistent rhythm. Afropentecostals promote worship and prayer that use large muscles, varying vocal volume, and driving polyrhythms. We start by kneeling and end by walking, but in between the kneeling and the walking is "the shout," which is the climax of body-active worship and the height of body-active prayer. The body-talk starts between members and with God: arms reach, hug, and raise; hands clap and gesture; heads tilt, rock back and forth, or protrude in and out; feet tap. But at the center of

worship, when friends have been greeted, Scripture has been read, and testimonies of hardship and victory are joined with songs, organ, and drums,
someone will get happy about Jesus and let the Spirit have her way with his or
her body.

The shout may start with the voice or a dance, but one form almost always
follows the other. A church mother may bend back and let out a belly yell:
"*Glory!*" or "Halle-*lu*-ia" or "Tha-ank *you* Je-sus." Or the shout may start with
someone stomping, running, or dancing. In dance, it is not only body extremi-
ties that are in motion, but the largest leg and shoulder muscles. The center
of the body moves. Torsos twist, curve side to side, or bend over dancing legs.
Knees bend and kick. Feet twist, stomp, and jump. Others join. If "the shout"
started with yells, bodies join in. If it started with bodies dancing, voices join
in, yelling some kind of awe or thanks to God.

Voices are used not only to convey meanings but to declare reality, "What a
wonder!" And to create reality: "Satan, be bound." To declare emotion, "So glad
to be walkin' in your way." To create emotion: "Lord, you are *so* good." Oftentimes inflections and varieties of voice and sounds—cadence and rhythms—
take precedence over words and meaning. The human body and the Spirit join
together to utter and make something new. New, by the soul being filled to
overflowing. New, in the body and tongue let loose.

A person can stop the Spirit's flow and can say no. A person could imitate or
fake another's Spirit-filling, but there is little pattern to copy. Afropentecostal
worship has a consistent structure, and the testimonies have a pattern in their
frame: It begins with "Giving honor to God and to the Pastor" and ends with
"pray my strength in the Lord." But the core of the testimony includes thanksgiving for being baptized by the Holy Ghost and with fire—and that fire does
not have a standard form of reproduction. The fire frees the person—body,
soul, and mind—through an aesthetic ritual experience of sensing and being
overcome by Jesus. Nobody knows what the Spirit-yielded soul will feel. Nobody knows what the Spirit-yielded body will do. There is no standard emotion, though emotions are characterized by joy. There is no standard body
style, though a filled body is likely to move in some kind of way. No standard
expression, though some kind of testimony is given. The soul and the Spirit
meet and play differently in each person. The Spirit takes the pain of suffer-
ing and transforms it through an encounter with the holy. This is the fire. But
the fire of the Spirit does not yield a homogenous gray ash. It does not make
a standard color. By the flame, each sanctified saint shines differently—and
each testifies differently to the beauty of the soul, the beauty of the Spirit, and
the beauty of their combustion. These aspects of beauty are experienced and
expressed in some bodily expression.

Rather than present such ritual as objective observation, I am, as a social
scientist, attempting to give an aesthetic representation of participation. An-

thropology is science by its systematic method. But anthropology is also aesthetic because it involves the senses and thus representation of data must take some aesthetic form (whether metaphor or chart).[7] Dictionaries define the word *aesthetic* in three ways: as pertaining to perceptions by the senses, as pertaining to a sense of the beautiful, and as concerning sensation and emotion. In a way similar to the way love-making involves aesthetic participation, so also does Afropentecostal worship. At the core of this religion is an encounter with the holy that is felt in the center of the person and sensed again in the person's expressive body. Afropentecostal worship has to do with the beautiful because the perceptions of the holy are known and expressed in forms that are orderly and enjoyable to behold. Afropentecostal worship is emotional because the body and emotions are primary in relationships, and Afropentecostalism is a relational religion—a way to participate in reality.

Aesthetic rituals disengage symptoms from the sign system of the world of affliction and realign them under powers aimed at life.[8] Afropentecostal communities aim at life through rituals of liminality that are characterized by indeterminacy. Even its vernacular language is indeterminate.

Pentecostal glossolalia had been interpreted as a result of trance or altered states of consciousness (Goodman 1972), as a means of commitment to a peripheral religious group (Gerlach and Hine 1970), or as a religious community's ritualized speech act (Samarin 1972). But Csordas interprets glossolalia as an embodied phenomenon. The practice of speaking in tongues challenges the canons of taken-for-granted talk "and intelligibility, and . . . [calls] into question conventions of . . . logic and authority" (Csordas 1990: 24). By taking up sounds and tones without syntactic, phonetic, or grammatical rules, glossolalia accentuates the existential grounding of language as a bodily act. "Just as vernacular speech facilitates and is the embodiment of verbal thought, so glossolalia facilitates and is the embodiment of nonverbal thought. . . . In glossolalia the physical experience of utterance (*parole*) comes into balance with the intellectual experience of language (*langue*)" (Csordas 1990: 24–26). In Polanyi's language, tacit or embodied knowledge takes primacy over verbal or explicit knowledge. Glossolalia is both the body's most primitive communicative act and an esoteric spiritual language.

One Afropentecostal described glossolalia as a language that flows like living water from the belly.[9] And as described above, Afropentecostals sing about the same. Communication begins in the inner person with a desire to connect to the other and to the attributes and resources of the other—as with a baby wanting to nurse. Communication expands its repertoire with gesture, utterance, and verbal message; but it remains grounded in the body. The body's request and invitation is not only for contact and connection but also for the flow of nurturing relationship. Among pentecostal adults, glossolalia renews and prioritizes the body's total gesture toward life-giving resources.

Thomas Csordas (1990) lays out an anthropological paradigm of embodiment largely through phenomenology, which does not deny that objects exist but insists that they are, to us, always indeterminate and dependent upon human perception (1990: 38).[10] "Such a perspective is essential," writes Csordas,

> for understanding movements that resist hegemony and, in particular, religions that recast the taken-for-granted world of disease and injustice. The phenomenological perspective is essential to explore a pentecostal movement which does not exist in a taken-for-granted world but in a world where indeterminacy holds sway. Here the religious practice exploits the preobjective to produce new, sacred objectifications . . . the sacred reorchestrates dispositions that constitute sense and the locus of sacred ritual is the body. (1990: 39)

Csordas is reiterating the idea that ritualization not only transfers information but transforms dispositions. Afropentecostal testimony and healing services accentuate the indeterminacy within ritual liminality. Indeterminacy is crucial for healing and revising oppressive social orders. The broad order of service and the individual orders of each testimony create a frame around a liminal and refining core that allows and promotes aesthetic recreation through all the senses of the body in discourse with the saints and the Spirit.

The practice of religion in general and Afropentecostal worship in particular is a participation in the realities of potentiality. If the world were a closed system, then each part would also be closed; but reality is relational, and relationality is not a closed system. Relationality invites full participation of emotion, body, mind, spirit, imagination; participation in materiality, in social life, and in the Spirit. Even God is known and shaped by such participation.

## Conclusion

Throughout this chapter I have sought to revise the modern notion that we know primarily in our minds by observing and thinking about reality. I have argued that participation is the dominant human way of both knowing and being in the world and that this is true for both pentecostalism and anthropology—for discerning and shaping social and spiritual realities through participatory anthropology and worship. In contrast to the eye and book-based research of Tylor, Morgan, and Durkheim, Frank Cushing lived with a Zuni tribe for five years and was initiated through the learning of practical social skills and through a ritual process. In contrast to the positivist science of hypothesis testing, Michael Polanyi, based on the intuition that we know more than we can tell, argued for the priority of tacit knowledge, which is implicit knowledge derived from the body's practice in the world. In contrast to the social science positivism inherently represented in the theory of structuralism, Victor Turner argued for a dynamic under-standing of society, where humanizing and healing powers soften and revise social structure. Ritual studies confirm that rituals are capable of strengthen-ing persons and communities in their pursuit of life even through great suf-fering and challenge. Turner argued that such rituals have the potential not only to transform the community but to create experiences of and imagi-nations about communal potentialities—and that these occasionally impinge on social structure. In contrast to the material-spiritual divide of Cartesian-based modernity, Afropentecostalism integrates materiality and spirituality by hopeful participation.

I also gave an aesthetic account of my experience in Afropentecostal wor-ship. Though African American pentecostals participate in the world of sci-ence, Afropentecostal rituals bypass a whole set of modern dualisms based on unembodied notions of knowledge. Because Afropentecostal rituals pre-cede and supercede modern dualisms, they bear postmodern significance. The mixing of races and embodied rituals of Azusa was itself a reaction to moder-nity that still has relevance for our segregated postmodern society (Scandrett-Leatherman 2005).

The pentecostalism of the Azusa Street revival grew out of a sober assess-ment of racial segregation. It represented, not necessarily an explicit or aca-demic knowledge of racism, but an outworking of and reaction to the tacitly felt bodily experiences of oppression and exclusion. Like the day of Pentecost of Acts 2, and Peter's cross-cultural calling (Acts 10:15–45),[11] the Azusa re-vival led to the mixing and mingling of cultures and then to a reassessment of "crude," "profane," or "unclean" cultural judgments. One critic, Charles Par-ham wrote:

> There was a beautiful outpouring of the Holy Spirit in Los Angeles. . . . Then they pulled off all the stunts common in old camp meetings among colored folks. . . . That is the way they worship God, but what makes my soul sick, and make[s] me sick at my stomach is to see white people imitating unintelligent, crude negro-ism of the Southland, and laying it on the Holy Ghost. (Parham 1925, cited in Anderson 1979: 190)

Jim Crow segregation had been legally instituted by *Plessy vs. Ferguson* in 1896. It represented a reformulation of the "clean" and "unclean" perspective in modern forms of social Darwinism and black-white dualisms. But that segregation and the evaluation of black culture as "unclean" was cast off by those who participated in the "crude negroisms of the Southland." Partici-pation in the rituals of "unclean cultures" and in the Spirit whose creation knows nothing unclean birthed a multicultural movement, the fastest growing religious movement of the twentieth century, and unleashed the aesthetic experience of and imagination for a new society—a new city, whose architect, builder, and lover is Christ.

Afropentecostal rituals shook up early-twentieth-century social structures with their race-based status and roles, overturning the aesthetics of segregation in the process. Afropentecostals viewed society in light of the ends identified by God (Revelation 21–22) and thus according to its potential rather by its givenness. And all this shaking and mixing and potentiality involved or began with active participation. Participation involves a perspective that the world is open. Practice itself bears that tacit assumption. Afropentecostals could push anthropologists to acknowledge this assumption. And anthropologists could push Afropentecostals to acknowledge static systems of injustice. Participation is central to both anthropology and Afropentecostalism. Participating in the world of injustice and the open world of the Spirit embodies a hope of in the transformation of people and society.

Passivity is an expression of doubt that the world can be changed. Modernist self-assertion is an expression of belief that an individual (or a mind) can change the world. But participation is an expression of hope that the world is being changed by our cooperation. The paradox of faith is that God's activity in the world requires persons to participate in the faith that they already know, and yet by this to discover the world as it is emerging. The purpose of the Spirit is to empower people to participate in reality. That certainly includes social reality.

I won't ever dance on Broadway. My dancing didn't improve much by taking the African Dance class, but I dance in worship now. I dance against the dichotomies of body and mind, science and Spirit, black and white. Dance is a way to participate in the lives of a people and the life of the Spirit.

Participation is the way of anthropologists and Afropentecostals. It is a disciplined way of knowing social reality and being real. Participating in anthropology and Afropentecostal worship is a way to know the present and the potential of society.

## Notes

1.    The word *anthropology* comes from the Greek *anthropos,* which means human, so it is the study of humankind. The broad discipline of anthropology includes such subdisciplines as linguistics, ethnomusicology, and biological anthropology, but as a cultural anthropologist, I sometimes use the word *anthropology* as a shorthand for the discipline.

2.    A summary of the history of anthropology might include ancient cross-cultural encounters including the work of Abū Rayhān Bīrūnī in the eleventh century through the work of Ibn Khaldun in the fourteenth century (Ahmed 1984), and the work of early Jesuit missionaries, Le Clerca, Le Jeune, and Sagard in Canada in the seventeenth century. In England the

Aborigines Protection Society, which became the Anthropological Institute of Great Britain, was established in London in 1838 by evangelical Christians and anthropologists. On the U.S. side, Franz Boas became the founder of American anthropology. Boas lived near the Inuit on Baffin Island in 1883 and began teaching anthropology at Clark University that same year. He then moved to Columbia University in 1892, where he founded the first U.S. anthropology department. Bronislaw Malinowski was exiled to the Trobriand Islands at the outbreak of World War I, earned a doctorate in anthropology, and was the first anthropologist to promote participant observation as a critical method for cross-cultural understanding and social theory. For further reading in history of anthropology see Asad (1973); Barth et al. (2005); Patterson (2001); Reining (1962); Stocking (1968, 1987, 1992); see also "anthropology" and "history of anthropology" on Wikipedia.

3.    Many of Cushing's methodological descendents have made similar discoveries. See Young and Goulet 1994.

4.    Of course Émile Durkheim also made significant discoveries and revisions to the social science that he inherited, but the focus of this project is how understanding Afropentecostalism requires the postmodern revision in anthropology, epistemology, and ritual theory.

5.    Jackson says that participation in "external independent agencies or powers seems to be a necessary precondition for people to achieve their own responsibilities for their own situations and destinies" (1989: 60). Turner says that rituals are a "fusion of the powers . . . a mobilization of energies as well as meanings" (1973: 1102). Geertz says that religious symbols "establish powerful, pervasive, and long-lasting moods and motivations" (1973: 90). Durkheim writes that the ritualizing person "is *stronger*. He feels within him more force, either to endure the trials of existence or to conquer them" (1965: 464). Comaroff argues that the orchestration of signs and bodies imprints "its logic upon action in the everyday world" so that daily habits are transformed (1985: 44). Energies are strengthened within the body as they are applied to and through all the senses of the body.

6.    See, respectively, regarding narrative or testimony: Jackson 1989, Janzen 1992, Gelisen et al. 1994, Mattingly 1994; music: Blacking 1995; drumming: Friedson 1996, 2000; dance: Comaroff 1985, Janzen 1992, Schumaker 2000; glossolalia: Malinowski 1935, Csordas 1994; metaphors: Jackson 1989, 142ff., Sontag 1978, Janzen 2002, 180ff.; poetry: Jackson 1989, 154ff.; drama: Janzen 1982, Kapferer 1991; pilgrimage: Turner and Turner 1978; and feasts: Visser 1991.

7.    Unless we are to exclude human beings from systematic research and theorizing, a science of humans cannot exclude human aesthetics, emotions, and rituals because they are clearly universal human features. Since they are *uniquely* human, such features are critical to social science.

8.    Charles Mason, founder of the Church of God in Christ, promoted not only the aesthetic forms of drum and dance but also of oil and icons used in healing. Pictures of roots are prominent in early COGIC histories. Mary Mason's 1924 book, *The Life Work of Elder C. H. Mason and his Co-Laborers,* has one

picture of Charles H. Mason alone, holding a hand-like root; six other pictures of roots are printed in the first several pages of the book, while pictures of his co-laborers don't show up until page 100 of the 140-page book. A publicity photo used to announce "Founders Day, May 31, 1953" shows Bishop Charles Harrison Mason behind a desk with a dozen or more roots spread before him. In Afro-Pentecostalism, aesthetic presentation promotes active aesthetic participation in healing, society, and life.

9.    Drawn from the testimony of a woman at Moore Temple Church of God in Christ (March 21, 2003). COGIC glossolalia tends to flow from ecstatic experience, a flood of joy. The woman sang a song based on Jesus and the Samaritan woman at the well: "Jesus said it [repeated 3 times] . . . believe on me [repeated] . . . outa your belly [repeated] . . . flow [repeated] . . . living water . . . flow living water [repeated]." Two saxophones joined: one with the woman's call, the other with the woman's response. Then trumpet, guitar, drums, and tambourines throughout the room also joined. People danced, shouted and spoke in tongues. The next testimony was about a woman whose refrigerator had been filled by members when she wasn't able to feed her family. Within and between the testimonies was a dynamic relationship between earthly existence (belly/body, a birthday, provision of food, etc.) and exuberant thanksgiving.

10.    Phenomenology was founded by German philosopher Edmund Husserl (1859–1938) and significantly developed by France's philosopher Merleau-Ponty (1907–1961).

11.    Peter was called from Jewish monoculturalism into cross-cultural participation by the Holy Spirit. In that participation he discovered the character of God and the culture-crossing generosity of the Holy Spirit: " 'You yourselves know that it is unlawful for a Jew to associate with or to visit a Gentile; but God has shown me that I should not call anyone profane or unclean. . . . I truly understand that God shows no partiality' . . . While Peter was still speaking, the Holy Spirit fell on all who heard the word. . . . Peter was astounded that the gift of the Holy Spirit had been poured out even on the Gentiles" (Acts 10:28, 34, 44–45).

# References

Ahmed, Akbar S. 1984. "Al-Beruni: The First Anthropologist." *RAIN* 60: 9–11.

Anderson, Robert Mapes. 1979. *Vision of the Disinherited: The Making of American Pentecostalism.* New York: Oxford University Press.

Asad, Talal. 1973. *Anthropology and the Colonial Encounter.* New York: Humanities Press.

Barth, Fredrik, Andre Gingrich, Robert Parkin, and Sydel Silverman. 2005. *One Discipline, Four Ways: British, German, French, and American Anthropology.* Chicago: University of Chicago Press.

Blacking, John. 1995. *Music, Culture, and Experience.* Edited by Reginald Byron. Chicago: University of Chicago Press.

Comaroff, Jean. 1985. *Body of Power Spirit of Resistance: The Cultural and History of a South African People.* Chicago: University of Chicago Press.

Csordas, Thomas J. 1990. "Embodiment as a Paradigm for Anthropology." *Ethos* 18/1: 5–47.

———. 1994. *The Sacred Self: A Cultural Phenomenology of Charismatic Healing.* Los Angeles: University of California Press.

Durkheim, Émile. 1965 [1912]. *The Elementary Forms of the Religious Life.* Trans. Joseph Ward Swain. New York: Free Press.

Friedson, Steven M. 1996. *Dancing Prophets: Musical Experience in Tumbuka Healing.* Chicago: University of Chicago Press.

———. 2000. "Dancing the Disease: Music and Trance in Tumbuka Healing." In Penelope Gouk, ed., *Musical Healing in Cultural Contexts.* Burlington, Vt., and Aldershot, UK: Ashgate, 67–84.

Fustel De Coulanges, Numa-Denys. 1965[1864]. "The Ancient City." In William A. Lessa and Evon Z. Vogt, eds., *Reader in Comparative Religion: An Anthropological Approach.* New York: Harper and Row, 89–102.

Geertz, Clifford. 1973. *The Interpretation of Cultures: Selected Essays.* New York: Basic Books.

Gelisen, Ilker, Byron J. Good, Mary-Jo DelVecchio Good, A. Guvener, Zafer Ilbars, and Isenbike Togan. 1994. "In the Subjunctive Mode: Epilepsy Narratives in Turkey." *Social Science and Medicine* 38/6: 835–43.

Gerlach, Luther, and Virginia Hine. 1970. *People, Power, and Change.* Indianapolis: Bobbs-Merrill.

Gluckman, Max. 1940. "Analysis of a Social Situation in Modern Zululand." *Bantu Studies* 14: 1–30 (part I), and 147–74 (part II).

Goodman, Felicitas D. 1972. *Speaking in Tongues: A Cross-Cultural Study in Glossolalia.* Chicago: University of Chicago Press.

Green, Jesse. 1979. *Zuni: Selected Writings of Frank Hamilton Cushing.* Lincoln: University of Nebraska Press.

Husserl, Edmund. 1980. *Phenomenology and the Foundations of the Sciences.* Edited by Ted E. Klein and William E. Pohl. Boston: Martinus Nijhoff.

Jackson, Michael. 1989. *Paths toward a Clearing: Radical Empiricism and Ethnographic Inquiry.* Bloomington: Indiana University Press.

Janzen, John M. 1982. *Lemba 1650–1930: A Drum of Affliction in Africa and the New World.* New York: Garland.

———. 1992. *Ngoma: Discourses of Healing in Central and Southern Africa.* Berkeley: University of California Press.

———. 2002. *The Social Fabric of Health: An Introduction to Medical Anthropology.* New York: McGraw-Hill.

Kapferer, Bruce. 1991. *A Celebration of Demons: Exorcism and the Aesthetics of Healing in Sri Lanka.* Washington, D.C.: Berg.

Lewis, Gilbert. 1980. *Day of Shining Red.* New York: Cambridge University Press.

Malinowski, Bronislaw. 1935. *Coral Gardens and Their Magic: The Language of Magic and Gardening.* Bloomington: Indiana University Press.

Mason, Mary. 1924. *The History and Life Work of Elder C. H. Mason and His Co-Laborers.* Memphis, Tenn.: Church of God in Christ.

Mattingly, Cheryl. 1994. "The Concept of Therapeutic 'Emplotment.'" *Social Science and Medicine* 38/6: 811–23.

Merleau-Ponty. 1962. *Phenomenology of Perception.* Trans. Colin Smith. London: Routledge and Kegan Paul.

Morgan, Lewis Henry. 1962 [1851]. *League of the Ho-de-no-sau-nee, or Iroquois.* New York: Corinth Books.

Parham, Charles F. 1925. Editorial. *Apostolic Faith* (Baxter Springs, Kans.). April 3, 9–10.

Patterson, Thomas Carl. 2001. *A Social History of Anthropology in the United States.* New York: Berg.

Polanyi, Michael. 1958. *Personal Knowledge: Toward a Post-Critical Philosophy.* Chicago: University of Chicago.

———. 1967. *The Tacit Dimension.* Garden City, N.Y.: Doubleday.

Reining, Conrad C. 1962. "A Lost Period of Applied Anthropology." *American Anthropologist* 64: 593–600.

Samarin, William. 1972. *Tongues of Men and Angels: The Religious Language of Pentecostalism.* New York: Macmillan.

Sapir, Edward. 1934. "Symbols." In Edwin Seligman and Alvin Johnson, eds., *Encyclopedia of the Social Sciences.* New York: Macmillan, 14:492–95.

Scandrett-Leatherman, Craig. 2005. " 'Can't Nobody Do Me Like Jesus': The Politics of Embodied Aesthetics in Afro-Pentecostal Rituals." Ph.D. diss., University of Kansas at Lawrence.

Schumaker, Lyn. 2000. "The Dancing Nurse: Kalela Drums and the History of Hygiene in Africa." In Penelope Gouk, ed., *Musical Healing in Cultural Contexts.* Burlington, Vt., and Aldershot, UK: Ashgate, 149–70.

Sontag, Susan. 1978. *Illness and its Metaphors.* New York: Farrar, Straus and Giroux.

Stocking, George. 1968. *Race, Culture, Evolution.* New York: Free Press.

———. 1987. *Victorian Anthropology.* New York: Free Press.

———. 1992. *The Ethnographer's Magic and Other Essays in the History of Anthropology.* Madison: University of Wisconsin Press.

Turner, Victor. 1973. "Symbols in African Ritual." *Science* 179: 1100–105.

———. 1977 [1969]. *The Ritual Process: Structure and Anti-Structure.* Ithaca, N.Y.: Cornell University Press.

Turner, Victor, and Edith Turner. 1978. *Image and Pilgrimage in Christian Culture: Anthropological Perspectives.* New York: Columbia University Press.

Tylor, Edward Burnett. 1958 [1871]. *Religion in Primitive Culture.* New York: Harper.

———. 1964 [1865]. *Researches into the Early History of Mankind and the Development of Civilization.* Chicago: University of Chicago Press.

Visser, Margaret. 1991. *The Rituals of Dinner: The Origins, Evolution, Eccentricities, and Meaning of Table Manners.* Toronto: HarperCollins.

Young, David E., and Jean-guy Goulet, eds. 1994. *Being Changed by Cross-Cultural Encounters: The Anthropology of Extraordinary Experience.* Peterborough, Ont.: Broadview Press.

## Recommended Reading

Albrecht, Daniel E. 1999. *Rites in the Spirit: A Ritual Approach to Pentecostal/Charismatic Spirituality.* Sheffield: Sheffield Academic Press.

Alexander, Bobby C. 1989. "Pentecostal Ritual Reconsidered: Anti-Structural Dimensions of Possession." *Journal of Ritual Studies* 3/1: 109–28.

Csordas, Thomas J. 1997. *Language, Charisma, and Creativity: The Ritual Life of a Religious Movement.* Berkeley: University of California Press.

———. 2002. *Body/Meaning/Healing.* New York: Palgrave Macmillan.

Goodman, Felicitas, Jeanette H. Henney, and Esther Pressel. 1974. *Trance, Healing, and Hallucination: Three Field Studies in Religious Experience.* New York: Wiley.

Hiebert, Paul G. 1978 "Missions and Anthropology: A Love/Hate Relationship." *Missiology* 6/2: 165–80.

Lakoff, George, and Mark Johnson. 1999. *Philosophy in the Flesh: The Embodied Mind and Its Challenge to Western Thought.* New York: Basic Books.

MacRobert, Iain. 1988. *The Black Roots and White Racism of Early Pentecostalism in the USA.* New York: St. Martin's Press.

Paris, Arthur E. 1982. *Black Pentecostalism: Southern Religion in an Urban World.* Amherst: University of Massachusetts Press.

Polanyi, Michael. 1969. *Knowing and Being.* Edited by Marjorie Grene. Chicago: University of Chicago Press.

Robbins, Joel. 2004. *Becoming Sinners: Christianity and Moral Torment in a Papua New Guinea Society.* Berkeley: University of California Press.

Smilde, David. 2007. *Reason to Believe: Cultural Agency in Latin American Evangelicalism.* Berkeley: University of California Press.

# 9 Is Integrating Spirit and Sociology Possible? A Postmodern Research Odyssey

*Margaret M. Poloma*

*Pentecostals are people of narrative, and sociologist Margaret Poloma uses her personal story and professional research to provide an account of how she perceives the Holy Spirit at work in integrating experiences of her spiritual life with her work as a social scientist. While social science has been firmly embedded in modernist culture and resistant to the possibility of spiritual influences on behavior, recent post-modern perspectives have provided a framework for seeing God as an agent in social interaction. Poloma illustrates through her odyssey and its research findings how interaction between God and humans is commonplace. Her earlier research is founda-tional for a new interdisciplinary project underway on "godly love"—defined as the "dynamic interaction between divine and human love that enlivens benevolence."*

## Introduction

In recent decades we have passed, like Alice slipping through the looking glass, into a new world. This postmodern world looks and feels in many ways like the modern world that preceded it; we still have the belief systems that gave form to the modern world, and indeed we also have remnants of many of the belief systems of premodern societies. If there is anything we have plenty of, it is belief systems. But we also have something else; a growing suspicion that all belief systems—all ideals about human reality—are social constructions. (Anderson 1990: 3)[1]

I grew up in the 1950s and early 1960s, worshipping in a Catholic church with a Latin ritual that had not changed significantly for centuries, living in a Catholic neighborhood of mixed European heritage (with only two households claiming to be Protestant), and attending a Catholic school where I recall encountering only one non-Catholic student. I graduated from a Catholic college where I was taught (and believed) that the Catholic Church was the only true church of Jesus Christ and that I could always count on it to provide eternal truth. For American European immigrants, the Catholic Church was a patriotic church that believed that God had bestowed a divine destiny on the United States, that this "one nation under God" provided endless opportunities for all, and that the American government would always provide liberty, happiness, and justice for its citizens. This world seemed to change dramatically when I was a graduate student during the last five years of the 1960s, with race riots that screamed for freedom and justice for black Americans, feminist uprisings that unmasked pervasive gender inequality, and an unpopular war that unveiled a side of America that was militaristic and imperialist. I studied the critique of Catholicism offered by supporters of the Second Vatican Council (an event that opened the door to much-needed changes) and the social critiques of a strife-torn secular country whose image had been badly tarnished. *Truth* (at least as I knew it) was in the process of being replaced (as noted in the epigraph) "by a growing suspicion of all belief systems." Like Alice in Wonderland, I found myself peering into a new world of uncertainties and possibilities—one in which God was increasingly insignificant.

Perhaps you find yourself in a similar situation, albeit in a different historical period. You may never have considered how men and women collectively collaborate to create the social world, including their own gods and the religion that attends them. That was exactly the possibility that I began to explore when as a graduate student I started to reflect on the writings of social scientists without the safety net of a Catholic milieu. On the other hand, some of you may be questioning the relationship between the sacred and the secular and recognize the dominant hold that secular thought has on American culture. Maybe you are already aware of changes in the Western culture that cause you to wonder (at least at times) whether your religious faith can withstand the increasing privatization of religion in a secular society where scientific findings have trumped theological tenets. Perhaps you have observed how men and women, especially those in powerful positions, can play significant roles in changing the social world, sometimes for good and sometimes for evil. Maybe you have even gone as far as I did as a graduate student to recognize that the social world—including religion and its gods—is a human creation.

Permit me to invite you on a journey with me as I share how I gave up the unexamined faith of a child to become an agnostic, but how God brought me out of the darkness of non-belief into the light of faith through the power of the Holy Spirit. It is, of course, but one person's story about her struggle to deal with the tension that exists between science and religion, reason and faith, material and nonmaterial realities. It was the study of social science, namely, sociology, that paved the road for my becoming an agnostic in graduate school, and it is paradoxically also sociology that has (I believe) been used by God to draw me into a collaborative relationship with the Holy Spirit. In many ways I have experienced God's creative Spirit leading me and empowering me to do innovative research and writing as a social scientist. I don't always "hear" correctly any more than I fully and consistently understand the message of particular lectures or books of other scholars. But as I reflect on my life and career as a social scientist, there is no doubt in my mind that my life's journey has been bathed by a divine light.

## Embarking on a Journey

My personal research odyssey to integrate faith and scholarship began as a graduate student in the late 1960s during the time that sociology still was firmly in the grip of modernist thought in an extreme form known as *positivism*. Positivists claimed that the only knowledge that is real is that which can be derived from direct observation. They denied the reality of human free will, emotions, and even the mind (as distinct from the biological brain). The positivist's world was limited to material substances that could be directly measured and manipulated rather than a world in which the spiritual or nonmaterial was co-present with directly observable phenomena.

During this same time, however, *postmodernism* was gaining a foothold in philosophy, opening a door that eventually gave way to challenging the stance of a hyper-empirical positivism. The philosophy that challenged modernist theories of knowledge was known as postmodernism, and it soon found its way into the study of literature, history, art, and the social sciences. Postmodernism—whatever else it might be, as Murray Dempster has noted, "is a rejection of the modern mind-set which was forced by the foundational epistemology of the Enlightenment with its emphasis on certain and objective knowledge derived from scientific inquiry and autonomous rationality" (1999: 261). In other words, the certainties of modernity gave way to taking subjective perceptions seriously. By the turn of the twenty-first century modernity's once-believed absolutes were recognized by many social scientists as tentative, incomplete, illusive, and even misleading. Postmodern thought had softened the scientific soil sufficiently for some social scientists to challenge modernist philosophical assumptions that prevented scholars from taking God seriously (at the least perceptions and experiences of God) and to question modernist assumptions about human nature that blinded scholars to the importance of human emotions, including love. As postmodern thought began to invade the rigid boundaries set by a positivistic sociology, it became possible to explore the possibility of a personal relationship with God and its effects.

My personal story traces the role that the Holy Spirit played in guiding me away from an agnostic worldview rooted in modernist thought to that of a pilgrim who has experienced the Spirit leading and guiding her as she did pioneering research on religious experience. This personal narrative is but one story to illustrate how lived religion and scholarship can be integrated. The odyssey is divided into three parts, each providing insight into how the Holy Spirit can affect personal spirituality with the potential to empower innovative and creative scholarship. These parts describe, first, how I embarked on my faith journey and sensed a call to integrate faith and social science; then how I sought to challenge the remnants of positivism in sociology research findings and insights on religious experience; and finally, how I now find myself working with an interdisciplinary team of scholars with the intent of establishing an interdisciplinary study of godly love that takes both God and love seriously.

## From Agnostic Congruence to Faith-Filled Dissonance

By the time I began a graduate program in sociology at a secular university in 1965, I had racked up dozens of A's for religion courses taken throughout my elementary and high school years and for theology courses taken in college. My child-like faith served me well throughout my foundational years of Catholic education. However, the disjuncture between an increasingly cognitive approach to faith and secular approach to knowledge grew into a wide chasm when I began to study the sociology of religion in graduate school. My child-like experiences of God were increasingly strained during late adolescence and were totally ruptured as a young adult.

Although contemporary sociologists are unlikely to prophetically proclaim that their discipline will herald a new social world based on science to displace religion (as did sociology's founder Auguste Comte), they do assert that religion and science are in tension. The masters of sociological thought who crafted social scientific theories of religion during the first couple of decades of the twentieth century were themselves atheists or agnostics. As the century wore on, religious factors were largely ignored by sociologists writing theory and doing research, and those who did profess a religious faith were expected to bracket their religious beliefs when practicing their profession. Most of the best-known sociologists at the most prestigious academic institutions were known to be a-religious if not anti-religious. Although I pursued the study of the sociology of religion as one of my specialties as a graduate student with an agnostic professor, it was primarily to take one last look at a subject that seemed increasingly irrelevant.

I quickly became involved in issues that I regarded as more important than religion at the time. Among the emerging social movements of the 1960s I found a secular trinity in which I put my faith: civil rights, feminism, and the anti–Vietnam War movement. I joined those theologians of the 1960s who proclaimed that "God is dead," existentialist philosophers who claimed that "life is absurd," and sociologists who spoke of religion as a "dying institution."

I can't say that I was consciously seeking anything when God touched my life as a young professor in the mid-1970s and derailed my agnostic world-view. I had adjusted to uncertainty as a fact of life and ridiculed anyone who thought they had found truth and spiritual meaning in the midst of life's absurdities. It was as I was doing contract research for a local Episcopalian church that my worldview was unexpectedly challenged enough to turn to the God I did not believe in with a prayer that I didn't think would be answered. I found myself on one side of an intellectual chasm wondering if there was anything on the other side, knowing of nothing that I could do to see over to the other side. For reasons that can only be described as grace, I quietly and simply prayed an agnostic's prayer in the privacy of my room: "God, if you are there, do something." I had no sooner uttered those words in my mind when I was filled with a sense of the holy—the same sense I had felt (at least at times) when receiving communion during Mass or when interrupting a playful re-cess to make a visit to "Jesus in the blessed sacrament" as an elementary school child. The touch of God's presence was familiar and palpable; I knew I could no longer deny that God existed. I began to weep—partly out of joy and partly out of fear about where this experience would take me.

My training as a sociologist of religion, however, quickly cast a critical beam, taunting me about blindly falling back into the Christianity of my youth. I could not deny sociological tenets about the role that socialization and culture played in shaping human behavior—or the role that humans played in devel-oping religion. Yet after this fresh experience of a sense of the holy, neither could I deny the reality of unpredictable spiritual experience. I became a the-ist, who, while still resistant to my Christian upbringing, did know that God had somehow left a lasting mark on my psyche. I began to attend the New-man Center at the University of Akron, where I found two groups of Catho-lics who had moved away from the traditional Christianity of their youth to forge a new path in a post–Vatican II Catholic Church. There were liber-als who pushed the envelope of change as far as they could, some of whom labeled themselves as post-Christian agnostics; and then there were the more traditional "born again, spirit-filled" Catholics, who seemed to know first-hand about miracles and mystery. The two groups were distant from and sus-pect of each other. Although I first aligned with the liberals, who sang trendy folk songs and otherwise rejected much of the doctrine and ritual of their pre–Vatican II faith, it was the charismatic group that increasingly intrigued me. I recall a graduate student whom I had invited to join me at a service where the charismatic Catholics worshiped joyfully across the room from a diverse group of questioning students and young adults. After this visit she commented, "Don't you feel they [the charismatics] have something we don't have?" I reluctantly had to agree.

Approximately nine months after my conversion to theism, I had another life-changing experience. One very early Easter Sunday morning I awoke unexplainably and could not fall back to sleep. After an hour of tossing and turning, I finally got up to read the four resurrection accounts in the Gospels. Suddenly the lightbulb of faith switched on—I just "knew" deep in my spirit that Jesus was alive! Once again, a profound but unexplainable intuitive and emotional experience broke in to leave a life-lasting mark. I can still recall the look on the celebrating priest's face when I approached him during the liturgical sign of peace at the Easter Sunday service the next morning to say, "I don't believe in the institutional Catholic Church, but I do know that Jesus is risen—He is my Savior and Lord!" It wasn't that this priest did not believe Jesus' resurrection, but it was apparent that he was taken aback by a declaration that was so out of character for me. My newly found faith in Jesus grew quickly to include speaking in tongues and experiences of other "signs and wonders" written about in the book of Acts that found expression within this Catholic charismatic community.

This stage of my odyssey, it is important to emphasize, began with a series of religious experiences rather than any re-embracing of propositional truths that I had memorized from the old Catholic *Baltimore Catechism* or the apologetics of Thomas Aquinas's *Summa Theologica* that I studied in college. Through the faith of the Catholic charismatics, I was introduced to a living God who walked and talked with me. Like the Samaritan woman at the well, these believers had experienced the power of the Holy Spirit and invited me to "come and see" for myself what he was about. While experiences of God breaking into my daily life filled me with joy and gave life a new meaning, they also cut against the secularity and agnosticism found in my discipline and left me in a state of dissonance. I began to question whether it was possible for me to be both a person of faith and a sociologist. If I had to choose between my faith and my vocation as a sociologist to resolve the dissonance, I knew that I would choose the dynamic relationship I had come to experience with God over my career. I started to pray for guidance—for some kind of spiritual roadmap to lead me over the new terrain in which I found myself.

One morning while in prayer, I sensed that if I opened the Bible at random, I would get a word from God that would provide an answer with an appropriate passage. Playing what some might call "Bible roulette," I opened the Bible, and my eyes were immediately drawn to Psalm 32, verse 8: "I will instruct you, I will be your guide, I will show you the way to go." While not knowing exactly how God would fulfill this divine promise or even if I needed to change careers, I sensed peace and a promise. I knew I could count on God to lead me not only in "spiritual" matters but also for career decisions. I soon would find myself in a new stage of my journey—as a Christian sociologist teaching and doing research in a secular university.

## Integrating Modernist Sociology and Non-Modern Christian Experiences

I had used the sociology of religion in graduate school to reason my way to agnosticism, holding the position that there was no way to determine one way or another whether there was a personal God. This stance was foundational to my early understanding of sociology, buttressed by research findings reporting that social scientists were unlikely candidates for deeply held religious faith. While I knew a few professing Christians who were sociologists, they seemed to effectively separate their religious beliefs from their scholarly work. For some unexplained reason, I found the kind of separation they modeled to be less than satisfactory. I began to seek a paradigm that would make room for my non-modern Christian religious experiences—one with the potential to counter a modern sociology that exalted reason and empirical knowledge by *including* human emotions and intuitive ways of knowing. As I struggled with recasting sociology to make room for my personal experiences, I longed for a mentor or mentors with whom to share my journey.

The answer came unexpectedly in part through a colleague in my department who described another sociologist (whom I did not know) as "a former atheist turned 'Bible-thumping' Christian." I knew enough of my colleague's biases to wonder if this sociologist was someone who had, like me, had an intense experience of God that brought him to faith. A few months later I would unexpectedly encounter the late George A. Hillery at the annual conference of the American Sociological Association. I noticed a sign posted on the announcement board inviting anyone who might be interested to a breakfast with Christian sociologists. It was at that gathering that I first met George (then a professor at Virginia Tech in Blacksburg, Virginia), who was the founder of the group calling itself the Christian Sociological Society. I learned of George's dramatic conversion experience about a dozen years earlier that had moved him from agnosticism to evangelical charismatic Christianity. He too believed that God was calling him to integrate his faith with his scholarship while working at a secular university. Although a charismatic Presbyterian, George said he felt God had led him and opened doors for him to study love and community within Catholic monasteries.[2] At the end of this first meeting, George expressed what I was sensing: "I feel as if I am looking into my mirror image." It was George who became both a model and a mentor as I sought to integrate the two seemingly disparate parts of myself: a Spirit-filled Christian and a sociologist.

Even before I encountered the Christian Sociological Society, I recognized that there was more than one way to deal with the tension between religious faith and the modernist paradigm. As noted earlier, I had already observed from a few colleagues who were professed Christians that the most common approach seemed to be compartmentalization. These sociologists believed that sociology and faith were two distinct phenomena that could not be integrated. They contended that just as Americans enjoy a "separation of church and state," so too should the spiritual remain separated from the scientific. For them there was no acceptable way to integrate religious faith and modern scientific thought. One sociologist who was also an evangelical Christian would write, "In fact, a 'Christian' sociology does not exist any more than a 'Christian psychology' or a 'Christian biology.' Sociology, ever since its inception in early nineteenth century France, represents an attempt to apply scientific methodology" (Scanzoni 1972: 124).[3] Others, including the renowned social theorist Peter Berger, would agree. After writing a classic work in the sociology of religion that he admitted read like a "treatise on atheism," two years later Berger would put on a theological hat to modulate his thesis. Rather than modeling the integration of faith and religion, his scholarly work contributed to reinforcing a wall between them (see Berger 1967, 1969).

Others, primarily Christian evangelicals, began to shift the discussion away from whether "Christian sociology" was possible, to how Christian sociology can play a role in the mosaic of a multi-paradigmatic study of human society. They tended to be professors at Christian colleges rather than professor-researchers at secular universities who used modern forms of reasoning to argue the compatibility of faith and sociological thought. With a verbal allegiance to integrating the two approaches to knowledge, their arguments seemed more directed toward other religious educators who questioned how the social sciences could be integrated into a conservative Christian education. While their discussions were of personal interest, they did not have much currency in a secular university.

Building on my interest in sociological theory, I began taking a closer look at the different assumptions that support the differing "schools" of social thought (Poloma 1982). It was widely agreed that there was no single unified body of sociological theory, but rather that sociology is a discipline comprised of varying paradigms resting on often competing and incompatible assumptions: some focus on large-scale structure and institutions, while others focus on microsociological human behavior; some premise the social world as one based on reciprocity and cooperation, others, on the functions of social conflict; some are built on the assumption that there are laws of the social world just as there are laws in the natural sciences, while others contend that social sciences are different in that partially free human beings construct social realities that defy social "laws."[4]

I had been writing an undergraduate text in sociological theory at the time of my conversion. Putting finishing touches on the manuscript provided an opportunity to assess whether the conflicting assumptions provided a way to use Christianity as a source of insight to critique and expand sociological knowledge just as feminist, black, and Marxist sociologists were effectively doing. Although assumptions (by definition) cannot be empirically tested, they underlie all social scientific theories. Paying closer attention to assumptions alerted me to the fact that some approaches to sociology are easier to integrate with religious experience than are others.

I soon began to frame my sociology with a dialectical model in which human behavior is assumed to be both fixed and fluid—a product of recognized social and biological "laws" as well as of nonmaterial "supra-empirical" forces. As Peter Berger (1963)—arguably the best-known social constructionist theorist—noted, there is an ongoing dialectical relationship between objective reality and subjectively perceived realities. In other words, the objective factors reported as a result of scientific investigation both influence and are influenced by subjective perceptions. Central to social constructionist theory is the "Thomas theorem" first noted by an early American sociologist W. I. Thomas: "If people define situations as real, they are real in their consequences" (cited in Coser 1977: 541).

Accepting this dialectical process that occurs between objective and subjective realities provided a theoretical framework for describing the ongoing dance between the "me" that is a trained professional sociologist of religion and the "me" that is a pentecostal (charismatic/Spirit-filled) Christian who continues to experience the power of the Spirit to shape and guide her life. The dialectical dance between experiential faith and professional training has influenced my faith in allowing me to see the Scriptures in a new light as well as in allowing my faith to enlighten my sociology.[5] The creative dance is not simply an exchange that sometimes occurs between Christian doctrine and sociological theories framed within the context of modernism but between the human spirit and the experiences of the divine. For me it has been a creative postmodern dance choreographed by the Holy Spirit, who has led and guided my personal life as well as my sociological career. Once again, I turn to personal narrative to illustrate how God's promise to lead and to guide me, received in a seeming game of Bible roulette, has served to guide my career—one in which "objective" guidelines and theories of social science are modified by researching subjective perceptions of God among Americans.

## Sociology and Pentecostalism in Dialectical Dance

Soon after meeting George Hillery, I was invited to join the steering committee of the Christian Sociological Society (CSS) and to edit its newsletter. While attending a retreat with other CSS leaders several months later, I was troubled by a dream, which I shared with George. The scene was a departmental faculty meeting during which my colleagues were berating my lack of scholarly activity. One of them spoke for the others when he said, "You used to be a good sociologist, but then you became a Christian. Now you aren't doing anything worthwhile. You need to give up on thinking God is going to lead you and start doing some research and writing again." The dream troubled me so much that I woke up with an unusual asthma attack. As I shared my dream and anxiety with George, he listened and then responded: "All that comes to my mind is the biblical story of Martha and Mary. Remember that Mary chose the better part by sitting at Jesus' feet. Continue to wait—and to listen. God will guide you."

Later that same summer George and I were together again—this time at a general reception hosted at the annual meeting of the American Sociological Society. As we were sharing refreshments and conversation, one of George's friends joined us. Irwin Sanders stopped to ask George whether he was interested in writing a book for the new series he was editing on social movements. George declined but added, "She [nodding toward me] can help you out. She can write a book on charismatic Christians as a social movement." I recall freezing inside—fearing that if I returned to the study of the sociology of religion I would fall onto the well-trodden path of agnosticism. I had no intention of using my sociological training to analyze my newly found faith. Sanders seemed visibly less than enthusiastic over the suggestion, but he did politely hand me his business card, adding, "I might be able to use the topic for one of the books once the series is established."

As the weeks passed after returning home from this meeting, I found the idea of writing a book about the charismatic renewal (a neo-pentecostal movement that was then sweeping through the mainline Protestant denominations as well as the Catholic Church) was never far from my mind. I knew I had to take a first step to discern whether this gnawing sense might in fact be a divine nudge. I wrote a short book proposal for *The Charismatic Movement: Is There a New Pentecost?* to trace the neo-pentecostal renewal (of the 1960s and 1970s) in mainline Protestantism and Catholicism to its turn-of-the-twentieth-century Pentecostal roots. In an accompanying letter, I noted that I was not a "value-free" sociologist who could write an ethnography describing some strange and distant subjects; I knew the role that assumptions played in social science. I was someone who had been greatly affected by the movement and wanted the reader to be forewarned of my assumptions. I explained that I believed that "values"—whether acknowledged or not—were always present in the work of social scientists, despite claims of value-neutrality. Since I was involved in the movement I was proposing to study, I needed to address my status as a fully involved participant observer. To my surprise, I received a call from Irwin Sanders the week after I sent my proposal. He said, "I would like to have your book, and I would like it to be the first in the series."

*The Charismatic Movement* marked the beginning of some three decades of researching the work of the Holy Spirit with each project inspired by a "divine nudge," followed by taking some initiative to see if the proposed research was feasible, and then surrendering the outcome with prayer that God's will would be done. God has always provided others—as God had provided George Hillery—to mentor my early career and its discernment process. There are narratives that accompany each major project, including my empirical study of the Assemblies of God,[6] followed by the pioneering research on prayer.[7] In the early 1990s, largely as a result of findings made in studying prayer and its relationship to psychological well-being, I met the late Dr. David Larson, a psychiatrist and scholar who soon afterward would establish a national institute for the study of spirituality and health. Dave became a friend and telephone prayer partner. It was he who introduced me to other scholars in varying scientific disciplines who were also studying religion and health and to the John Templeton Foundation (JTF) with its focus on the integration of religion and science. Both in time would play major roles in my efforts to integrate pentecostal religious experiences and science.

In meeting Dave Larson and his colleagues, I recognized that I was not alone in my struggle to integrate my faith and my vocation as a social scientist while working in a secular milieu. The rigid boundaries erected by modernist thought between secular scholarship and religion were beginning to crumble. There were enough of us for John Schmaltzbauer to write *People of Faith* as he investigated the role of Catholic and evangelical Protestant beliefs in the newsroom and the classroom.[8] As one of his forty research subjects, I was described by Schmaltzbauer (2003: 99) as having "openly acknowledged the connections between her religious identity and as a charismatic evangelical Christian and her sociological exploration of the Pentecostal and charismatic movements" and as going farther than most in "integrating personal faith into her research" (by using religious experiences as a method for studying Pentecostalism). Schmalzbauer then quotes from the interview he conducted with me for his book:

> My role as an insider has not only given me a better understanding of the particular Pentecostal charismatic religious experiences about which I write, but it has also alerted me to the important role experience plays in the social construction of religious reality. Sociologists have acknowledged the experiential dimension of religion but have been remiss in using it in their research. More specifically, it has shown me the importance of distinguishing between spirituality and religiosity long before it became fashionable to write about the distinction. Recognizing the centrality of religious experience for Pentecostal and charismatic Christians is what set me on the path of researching different types of prayer and the relationship that prayer experiences have to health and well-being. (Schmaltzbauer 2003: 102–3)

The 1990s were soon to provide an exciting research venue in the form of unusual revivals and a decade of transition from my tenured position as a professor at a secular university into uncharted waters.

## Changing the Pattern of the Dialectical Dance

Two other significant events through which I was able to build on my experience and knowledge of religious experiences occurred in the mid-1990s. Both were related to my findings on prayer and religious experiences, particularly the prayer form that I labeled as "receptive" or intuitive prayer (that contrasted with one-way conversational or ritual "active" prayer forms). The first involved a career change spurred by an early retirement package that would leave me a free agent to pursue a career outside the secular university. It was not an easy path to choose: I liked my position as a tenured full professor at the University of Akron where I taught both graduate and undergraduate students. I felt it would be hard to find another position that I would find as satisfying. On the other hand, the retirement package was financially very attractive, and I would no longer have to work for a paycheck. I was free to pursue innovative but marginal research interests at my own pace and without regard for appropriate publication outlets. Yet there was also a very real fear that my position as a tenured professor was central to my life and to who I was as a person; I wasn't at all sure I was ready to "retire" at the age of 50! As I prayed about the offer, I had a strong sense that I attribute to the Holy Spirit that if I did not "let go" of what was familiar, I would never know what else God might have for me. I decided to trust and "let go."

The second important event seemed to confirm that I had chosen the right path: a fresh outbreak of pentecostal revivals began just after I made this life-altering decision. Pentecostalism had been a primary research focus for more than twenty years at the time, and the cloud I had described in my writings as the "routinization of charisma" (in which fresh charismatic experiences were being replaced with ritual and doctrine) seemed to have completely engulfed the movement. The dynamic revivals that had birthed classic Pentecostalism and the renewals that refreshed and moved it beyond its original boundaries seemed to be a thing of the past in America by the 1980s. In 1994, however, the "Toronto Blessing" erupted, and a year later the "Pensacola Outpouring" made news in the United States.[9] When I visited Toronto in late 1994 just before my retirement, I personally experienced "revival" like I had only read about before.[10] I began as a pilgrim and then became the sociologist whom John Arnott (founding pastor of the Toronto Airport Christian Fellowship) called the Toronto Blessing's "fruit inspector." I was less interested at this point in continuing my career as a scholar than I was in using sociological lenses to interpret the strange revival for secular audiences. With Arnott's support and encouragement, I used my sociological training to survey and observe the impact the revival was having on the lives of pentecostal believers and on the pentecostal movement. I continued to use my training as a sociologist to do social scientific assessment, but I "went native" and opened myself up to the unusual possibilities of experiencing the presence and power of God that pentecostalism in its charismatic moment has always offered.

The revivals were about more than speaking in tongues, the gift of the Spirit that had become the litmus test of Spirit baptism for many pentecostals. The strange somatic manifestations (uncontrolled laughter, falling in a seeming trance, animal sounds, and bodily contortions of shaking, jerking, quivering, etc.) were known in earlier revivals, including the Azusa Street revival (1906–1909) that birthed historic Pentecostalism. These manifestations were given a sacramental-like interpretation—they were the outward sign of an inner work of God's offering forgiveness and healing. I found myself appearing on national television and public radio, called by reporters for consult, and involved in Internet discussions of revivals and Pentecostalism, forums that were different from writing articles for academic journals and books for academic presses. The dialectical dance continued, but personal and subjective charismatic experiences assumed a partnership more equal to objective sociological research findings at this stage of the odyssey. Old distinctions between objectivity and subjectivity were melting together in postmodern perspectives that acknowledged how master narratives are made up of a cacophony of voices. These voices, although sometimes dissonant, should not be silenced by the dominant scientific voice that sought to limit "reality" to empirical knowledge, systematized through the lenses of modern rationality. Some scholars, even "hard scientists," were beginning to admit that there may be ways of knowing that were eluding modern science. I was able to frame the pilgrims to the Toronto revival as "Main Street Mystics" and to begin a sociological exploration of the power that I hypothesized was generated by intense experiences of God.

## The New Millennium, Postmodernism, and Researching Godly Love

In *Main Street Mystics*, I offered "thick description" through participant observation and detailed narratives of a wide variety of paranormal experiences (believed to be from God) that were commonly found in the varying streams of the North American revivals of the 1990s. The ethnographic and survey findings suggested that something happened to many Toronto pilgrims—changes in their personal lives that affected others. Pilgrims experienced a deeper sense of being loved by God and an increased love for God that flowed over into human relations, including the healing of broken relationships and demonstration of a greater love toward others. In many cases these reported personal experiences had a notable social impact in establishing new ministries and breathing life into old ones.[11]

Survey research on the Toronto Blessing and other projects conducted over the years that focused on religious experiences, healing, prayer, and pentecostal/charismatics seemed to be pointing to the feasibility of using the techniques of social science to explore the relationship between divine and human love. These findings included the positive effect of experiencing the gifts of the Spirit on evangelism and church growth (Poloma 1989), the role of prayer experiences for understanding differences in subjective perceptions of well-being (Poloma and Pendleton 1991), the positive impact of revival experiences on outreach and service (Poloma 2003), the role of the charismata in health and wholeness (Poloma 2003), and the significance of the charismata in accounting for differences in altruism scores (Poloma and Hood 2008). With the normal cautionary caveat about causation in mind, these relationships between godly love and the noted outcome variables have passed statistical tests of significance. The social scientific findings suggest that the human experience/perception of encountering divine grace may have a decided impact on human behavior.

The decades of research on the effects of religious experiences, particularly common pentecostal experiences (including speaking in tongues, healing, and prophecy) provided a foundation for writing a proposal and securing funding from the John Templeton Foundation for an interdisciplinary team of twelve social scientists, philosophers, and theologians to further explore such findings.[12] We call the phenomenon under study "godly love," a heuristic label for the Great Commandment: loving God above all and one's neighbor as oneself. Godly love is defined in the Flame of Love project as the "dynamic interaction between divine and human love that enlivens benevolence" (see Lee and Poloma 2009). Although this project singles out pentecostals (using a broad definition that includes a wide range of Spirit-directed Christians), we recognize that Christians are not alone in experiencing godly love. In time we plan to extend the study to other religious groups and to compare the findings with those we are collecting from Christians who have experienced the power of the Holy Spirit. As someone who has long struggled against sociology's theoretical and methodological atheism that has failed to take reports of God's activity in human behavior seriously, coming together with other like-minded scholars to explore godly love has been a most welcome step in my ongoing journey.

## Godly Love, Social Science, and Postmodernity

Many would contend that the modern world has been obsessed with a quest for certainty. Postmodernity, as we see in the epigraph to this chapter, has grown wary of modernity's rigid and divisive belief systems. It has challenged the core modernist assumption that there is a unique truth assessable through human reason that will one day be common to all. The rise of skepticism and doubt about a decisive triumph of (Enlightenment) rational knowledge (including the scientific perspective) has bolstered a postmodern worldview in which, as Walter Truett Anderson notes, "reality isn't what it used to be."

As a Christian sociologist, I contend that postmodern thought (at least in moderate dress) need not to be feared. It has produced good soil in which to plant the seeds of creative scientific research and theory and to explore non-material phenomena that are a part of daily life. It permits social scientists to consider not only the dominant materialistic and empirical phenomena that are more readily measured but also spiritual and emotional factors that were ignored by modern social science for much of the twentieth century. The Flame of Love project may be one such example as it studies godly love, a construct that includes human perceptions of divine-human interaction and their relationship to love. The project strives to integrate the wisdom of tradition and the experience of faith with the methods and tools of social scientific research.

Rather than slipping into Alice's Wonderland, it is possible to function as a social scientist and to remain receptive to the presence and power of the Spirit of God and God's kingdom—a kingdom of love that is already among us and is paradoxically still to come. Postmodernism reminds us that truth is not something that can be possessed, but faith dictates that is a treasure to be pursued. Coming into truth, however, is not an event but a journey. Integrating science and Spirit, similarly, is not a task that is accomplished once and for all, but rather it is a process that unfolds as divine grace is poured out and finds human response.

## Notes

1. For an informative and delightful discussion of the postmodern world and our place in it, see Anderson 1990.
2. Hillery's research (1992) on freedom, love, and community included both qualitative ethnography and quantitative survey techniques, taking him twenty years to complete. Although he conducted other research and wrote on other aspects of community, his work on *The Monastery* most intrigued me and provided a model for my own research.
3. While many evangelical Christians would agree with this position that compartmentalizes secular scholarship from faith, others would respond with a more focused sociological approach rooted in evangelicalism that would critique the narrow modernist perspective (Swatos 1989, 1998).
4. For an assessment of contemporary modern social thought in light of such assumptions about human nature and the social order, see Poloma 1979.

5.　In this article I am focusing primarily on how my faith journey influenced my sociology, but social lenses can also have an impact on religious thought (as illustrated by my experience in graduate school). Sociologists teaching in Christian universities provide countless examples of how sociological lenses can be used for a better understanding of the Scriptures. An excellent example can be found in the writings of sociologist and evangelist Tony Campolo (2006, 2008).

6.　See the "Methodological Appendix" found in Poloma 1989: 245–54, for a brief account.

7.　Although the research on prayer seemed to move my work outside the pentecostal focus, it was actually my earlier research that provided the insight needed to pioneer in this arena. After I finished my book on the Assemblies of God, it appeared that my major thesis about the "routinization of charisma" had actually taken hold of American pentecostalism. I was in a quandary about how to proceed on a new project when I had the opportunity to use a departmental research project to launch an area-wide survey on religious experience (Poloma and Pendleton 1991). This local project then paved the way for a national survey with pollster George H. Gallup Jr. (see Poloma and Gallup 1991).

8.　Schmaltzbauer 2003, esp. 99–103 and 174–76.

9.　See Poloma 1998 for a comparison and contrast of the two leading revival epicenters.

10.　See Ann Taves 1999 for an excellent account and interpretation of what she refers to as *fits, trances and vision* (the title of her book) in American religious revivals. For a discussion of the physical manifestations at the Toronto revival, see Poloma 2003.

11.　One of the best-known accounts, although certainly not the only one, is that of Heidi and Rolland Baker's work in Mozambique through Iris Ministries (www.irismin.org). See also Poloma 2003.

12.　Together with Stephen Post, a theologian who introduced the late Pitirim Sorokin's work on love ([1957] 2002) to a new generation of scholars, and Matthew Lee, a junior scholar who shares our vision for studying the interface of human and divine love, we are directing a three-year interdisciplinary study titled "The Flame of Love: Scientific Research on the Experience and Expression of Godly Love in the Pentecostal Tradition."

# References

Anderson, Walter Truett. 1990. *Reality Isn't What It Used to Be.* San Francisco: Harper and Row.

Berger, Peter. 1963. *Invitation to Sociology: A Humanistic Perspective.* Garden City, N.Y.: Doubleday.

———. 1967. *The Sacred Canopy. Elements of a Sociological Theory of Religion.* Garden City, N.Y.: Doubleday.

———. 1969. *A Rumor of Angels. Modern Society and the Rediscovery of the Supernatural.* Garden City, N.Y.: Doubleday.

Campolo, Tony. 2006. *Letters to a Young Evangelical.* New York: Basic Books.

———. 2008. *Red Letter Christians: A Citizen's Guide to Faith and Politics.* Ventura, Calif.: Regal.

Coser, Lewis A. 1977. *Masters of Sociological Thought.* New York: Harcourt, Brace and Jovanovich.

Dempster, Murray W. 1999. "Issues Facing Pentecostalism in a Postmodern World." In M. W. Dempster, B. D. Klaus, and D. Petersen, eds., *The Globalization of Pentecostalism: A Religion Made to Travel.* Oxford: Regnum Books, International, 262–67.

Hillery, George A., Jr. 1992. *The Monastery. A Study in Freedom, Love and Community.* Westport, Conn.: Praeger.

Lee, Matthew T., and Margaret M. Poloma. 2009. *The Sociological Study of the Great Commandment in Pentecostalism: The Practice of Godly Love as Benevolent Service.* Lewiston, N.Y.: Edwin Mellen Press.

Poloma, Margaret M. 1979. *Contemporary Sociological Theory.* New York: Macmillan.

———. 1982. "Toward a Christian Sociological Perspective: Religious Values, Theory and Methodology." *Sociological Analysis* 43: 95–108.

———. 1989. *The Assemblies of God at the Crossroads: Charisma and Institutional Dilemmas.* Knoxville: University of Tennessee Press.

———. 1998. "The Spirit Movement in North America at the Millennium: From Azusa Street to Toronto, Pensacola and Beyond." *Journal of Pentecostal Theology* 12: 83–107.

———. 2003. *Main Street Mystics: The Toronto Blessing & Reviving Pentecostalism.* Walnut Creek, Calif.: Alta Mira Press.

Poloma, Margaret M., and George H. Gallup Jr. 1991. *Varieties of Prayer: A Survey Report.* Philadelphia: Trinity Press International.

Poloma, Margaret M., and Ralph W. Hood Jr. 2008. *Blood and Fire: Godly Love in a Pentecostal Emerging Church.* New York: New York University Press.

Poloma, Margaret M., and Brian F. Pendleton. 1991. *Exploring Neglected Dimensions of Religion in Quality of Life Research.* Lewiston, N.Y.: Edwin Mellen Press.

Scanzoni, John. 1972. "Sociology." In R. W. Smith, ed., *Christ and the Modern Mind.* Downers Grove, Ill.: InterVarsity Press, 123–33.

Schmaltzbauer, John. 2003. *People of Faith: Religious Conviction in American Journalism and Higher Education.* Ithaca, N.Y.: Cornell University Press.

Sorokin, Pitirim A. [1954] 2002. *The Ways and Power of Love: Types, Factors, and Techniques of Moral Transformation.* Edited with an introduction by Stephen Post. Philadelphia: Templeton Foundation Press.

Swatos, William H. 1989. "Religious Sociology and the Sociology of Religion in America at the Turn of the Twentieth Century." *Sociological Analysis* 50: 363–75.

———. 1998. "Christian Sociology." In William H. Swatos Jr. et al., eds., *Encyclopedia of Religion and Society.* Walnut Creek, Calif.: Alta Mira Press, 86–87.

Taves, Ann. 1999. *Fits, Trances, and Visions: Experiencing Religion and Explaining Experience from Wesley to James.* Princeton, N.J.: Princeton University Press.

## Recommended Reading

Berger, Peter L. 1992. *A Far Glory: The Quest for Faith in an Age of Credulity.* New York: Anchor Books.

Ellul, Jacques. 1964. *The Technological Society.* New York: Vintage Books.

Gellner, Ernest. 1992. *Postmodernism, Reason and Religion.* New York and London: Routledge.

McLaren, Brian D. 2004. *A Generous Orthodoxy.* Grand Rapids, Mich.: Zondervan.

Miller, Donald E. 1997. *Reinventing American Protestantism: Christianity in the New Millennium.* Berkeley: University of California Press.

Rieff, Philip. 2007. *Charisma: The Gift of Grace and How It Has Been Taken Away from Us.* New York: Pantheon Books.

Smith, Christian. 2003. *Moral, Believing Animals, Human Personhood and Culture.* New York: Oxford University Press.

Smith, James K. A. 2006. *Who's Afraid of Postmodernism? Taking Derrida, Lyotard, and Foucault to Church.* Grand Rapids, Mich.: Baker Academic.

Young, Wm. Paul. 2007. *The Shack.* Los Angeles: Windblown Media.

# 10 Is There Room for the Spirit in a World Dominated by Technology? Pentecostals and the Technological World

*Dennis W. Cheek*

*Technology is the most pervasive attribute of the modern world. Its influences on human beings and life on Earth are unprecedented, with impacts that are rarely considered by Christians, including pentecostals/charismatics. Our Christian duty as creation stewards requires that we more clearly and carefully come to understand, appreciate, critique, and influence modern technology. Such engagement will require the best intellectual and spiritual resources of the Christian church since technology in all its diverse forms is the greatest global threat to organized religion. This essay highlights some key issues, provides some critical questions, and outlines the beginning of an appropriate Christian response to technology.*

## Today's Youth Culture

Mark, Maria, Miguel, and Monica are sophomores at a Christian college in the central United States. Mark and Monica are pastoral studies majors, Maria is in psychology, and Miguel plans on being an elementary school teacher. All have standard college e-mail and Internet access as well as accounts on Facebook. Three of the four also have accounts on MySpace, Ziddio, and Flickr, and several have private e-mail accounts on various free services. PlayStation, iPods, Xbox, and cell phones provide immediate contact with music, friends both near and far, and 3-D immersive gaming environments. Mark and Miguel have recently opened accounts in Second Life and increasingly gravitate toward this immersive world where their avatars that bear no resemblance to them can engage in fantasy play with varied humanlike and nonhuman avatars operated by other in-world residents. Mark also sometimes plays World of Warcraft (WoW). They all pay their bills electronically, possess generous credit card limits due to a special student-preferred program for cards they obtained their freshman year, and take some of their courses and tests online using Blackboard.

The four friends have their own Christian worship team and frequently use synthesizers and carefully remixed sounds to create cutting-edge music to accompany self-created lyrics as well as drawing upon copyrighted songs available through Christian Copyright Licensing International (CCLI)—although they never pay the required fees that CCLI was designed to collect. Considering themselves monetarily poor undergraduates, they manage to stay current with fashion trends in clothing, hair, and accessories—at least those that are permitted at this more conservative college. Two of the four have tattoos but keep them out of sight as much as possible because many on campus, especially administrators and teachers, frown on such body adornment. Three of the four have cars on campus, although keeping up with the fuel costs is starting to be a real drag and freewheeling excursions have been curtailed in light of the rising prices. Cars are used for the obligatory Thursday night pizza run when they hang out together and for travel to various churches for ministry or internships required for their programs.

These four college sophomores are more typical than atypical of contemporary youth in the United States, other industrialized nations, and a growing number of counterparts in the developing world. They live, breathe, and move in a world made possible by technologies of various kinds in a manner so ubiquitous and seamless that they scarcely pause to consider the human-designed world they inhabit. When employing an iPod, launching a browser, changing into a new outfit, sitting in a warm classroom, participating in chapel, or engaging in a myriad other daily activities, they rarely consider how their world might look or feel different, the underlying design assumptions that led to the devices they use, or the costs and benefits of the various technologies they access and employ so easily and readily. Nor have they ever asked themselves what a Christian view of their contemporary technologies or uses for those technologies might be—except in those obvious cases where the commission of a "sin" is clearly involved. And certainly no one, in any of their experiences in churches or classes at a Christian university, has ever posed this question to them: How should a Christian approach the design, appropriation, and use of technologies to satisfy human needs and human wants? This chapter will explore this question in a cursory manner and help the reader begin to think more adeptly and seriously about this issue. We will gain a sense of the range and impact of modern technology within society; explore some ways in which Christians have appropriated technology in their work, lives, and the life of the church; articulate some principles concerning technology; and think through selected theological concepts and biblical principles that might inform our uses of technology.

## The World of Technology

Since the dawn of time, human beings have taken raw materials from their environment and combined, reshaped, transformed, and repurposed them to serve human needs and address human wants. The making and use of technology, therefore, is one of the essential characteristics of what makes human beings human, although rudimentary tool use, language, and learning are not unique to humans (Oller and Griebel 2004; Pennisi 2006; Thornton and McAuliffe 2006). Yet clearly no species on Earth exhibits the enormous range of technologies that human beings invent, deploy, and utilize on a recurring basis, and only humans have the capacity to think deeply about technologies and the varied aspects of design, application, and ethics.

The concept of technology is not foreign to the Bible; in its canonical form, it is replete with references to ancient technologies of many types. God is sometimes presented in the Old Testament in a manner that we would today call a *systems engineer*. He creates (designs) a universe and world and places within it creatures, including human beings. Technologies within the Old Testament include altars (Genesis 8:20), boundary markers (Job 24:2), fortifications (2 Samuel 20:15), golden calves (2 Chronicles 11:15), language (Genesis 2:19–20), and systems such as education (Daniel 1:17) and the temple sacrifices. In addition to passing references to literally hundreds of technological artifacts and systems, the Old Testament employs technological language or artifacts metaphorically to draw out moral lessons. For example, Jeremiah 6:27–30 uses various images from the metallurgist's craft to drive home the point that the Lord will weigh his people, check the fidelity of their character, and judge them. The New Testament continues this theme of technologies by noting in passing people's occupations, the use of boats, roads, houses, synagogues, commercial instruments, and so forth. Jesus frequently employs technological objects or systems to make spiritual points: working with a winepress (Luke 6:38); having a proper foundation or cornerstone for a building (Luke 6:48, 20:17–18); and an acropolis as a challenge to Christian witness (Matthew 5:14). The sacrificial death of Jesus is presented as an act that was designed (in modern parlance, "engineered") and sanctioned by God as

Table 10.1. A Sampling of Technological Devices Deployed Globally (Niemann 2008)

| Technology | Number of Estimated Devices Worldwide |
|---|---|
| Data Servers | 27 million |
| Personal Computers | 1.2 billion |
| Cell Phones | 3.3 billion |
| MP3 Players | 220 million |
| Digital Cameras | 120 million |
| Webcams | 100 million |
| Personal Data Assistants (PDAs) | 85 million |
| DVRs | 44.6 million |

a means to present a spotless "Lamb" who takes upon himself the sins of the world (see Cheek 2007: 32–62).

Within the modern world, technology is so pervasive, so expected, and so routine that human beings scarcely stop to think about its power, presence, meaning, and impact except in the most rudimentary manner or when it fails to "work." Just consider the sets of numbers about the global scale of a range of modern technologies represented in table 10.1.

It is estimated that there are about 5.2 billion text messages sent per day and 250 billion unique images sent electronically per year (Niemann 2008). The amount of data that is generated, transmitted, received, and stored in today's world challenges the imagination. A terabyte is a unit of data equivalent to a computer hard drive that holds 260,000 songs. Twenty terabytes are the amount of data in the form of photographs uploaded to Facebook every month. All of the digital weather data compiled by the National Climatic Data Center since its inception equals 460 terabytes, while all the videos on YouTube equals 530 terabytes. A petabyte equals 1,000 terabytes and this is the amount of data that is processed every 72 minutes by Google's servers (Anderson 2008).

Most people think of technology as being "applied science." While this concept is not completely false in the modern milieu, technology predates the rise of science by millennia. A useful saying that both captures the differences and is helpful for other reasons is that "science is to theology as religion is to technology." Science and theology are heavily theory-laden endeavors that attempt to make human sense of the natural world and of God, respectively. Each arena employs empirical data that is analyzed for patterns that lead to predictions, testing, and refinement of ideas that provide explanations for complexities that initially seemly impervious to human understanding (see table 10.2).

Table 10.2. Similarities among Science, Theology, Technology, and Religion

| Arena of Human Activity | Purpose | Arena of Human Activity | Purpose |
|---|---|---|---|
| Science | Discover how the natural world works, using empirical observations, mental constructs, prediction, and testing of hypotheses to derive theories that have great explanatory power | Theology | Understand and explain the nature of God as fully as possible, including the relationship of God to the cosmos and to human lives and societies in the past, present, and future |
| Technology | The application of knowledge, tools, skills, and systems to solve practical problems, extend capabilities, and expand opportunities to meet or invoke human needs | Religion | The application of practices, rituals, objects, and written materials to transcend the human condition and encounter the divine |

Technology and religion are siblings in that both arenas of human endeavor take "stuff" within the world and shape and refashion it to meet or invoke human needs—technology focused on human comforts and desires; religion focused on the worship and transcendent encounter with God or the divine.

Albert Borgmann, a distinguished philosopher of technology, has taken up the question of modern technology to explore how, and in what manner, it is alike and different from ancient technologies (Borgmann 1984). He argues that in earlier times it was easy to trace the paths of raw materials to a finished product and account for the appearance of the technological artifact and relate it back to nature. Similarly, ancient technological systems could be easily disassembled in terms of their components and be understood as to how they came to be. In modern times, more and more devices are opaque to the user, and the convoluted process of design, manufacture, shipping, acquisition, and use is much more complex and nonreducible. Many modern devices in our homes, workplaces, and wider community are black boxes whose overall function is clear but whose operation and creation are impossible to discern. These "devices," to use Borgmann's term, because of their very opaqueness and ubiquity, become commodities in the modern world. They operate within a "device paradigm" where consumerism, and the acquisitiveness inherent within it, commodify human beings and their interactions with reality on a continuing basis. We shape our technologies in an evolving and accelerating pattern, and our technologies, in turn, shape us. No longer tethered to a concrete reality that consists of a single geographic location on planet Earth, we systematically roam the Earth or even near space in the flesh or vicariously. We use technological systems to remake the world in our image even as they also remake us into something different than what we once were or appeared to be.

There is little question that many modern technologies have been of incalculable benefits to the human race and, to a lesser degree, to other creatures on our planet. This includes the Green Revolution, which made food abundant (even if not still readily available and obtainable in many places in the world due to human avarice and cruelty); the elimination of many deadly plagues and the eradication of many diseases; the construction of buildings and other structures that insulate us from the power of the weather and that moderate the effects of climate; communication devices that enable us to stay in touch with other human beings of interest to us across long distances; and a myriad other advantages to the modern world that make few human beings wish to return to some former "golden age." Conversely, many modern technologies have also wrought havoc in the form of widespread habitat destruction, monoculture plants that are highly susceptible to a pandemic, weapons of warfare that can literally destroy the entire planet, and the intensive concentration of human beings in geologically or meteorologically unstable areas where massive destruction of life within the span of a few minutes or hours is possible. Technologies frequently impose significant burdens on portions of human or nonhuman populations while benefiting other segments of those same populations.

The dual-edged nature of technologies is rarely considered in church settings or within Christian circles. Christian churches have adopted and adapted to modern technologies with little consideration of how those same technologies now come to control the parameters within which "God speaks," "God moves," and human worshippers have their very being. Powerpoint presentations, pretaped music accompaniment, synthesizers, video clips, global distribution of sermon materials and Bible study materials "McDonaldize" the faithful through print, radio, and television; and various other technological accoutrements encountered in churches both large and small commodify the experience of God's people as they gather weekly to participate in a technologically saturated worship experience that might leave a dispassionate observer to wonder who or what is the real focus of the encounter (Focus Group Discussion 2007; Hipps 2009; Twitchell 2007). Is there a transcendental dimension to the proceedings, or are people simply living, moving, and experiencing a technologically rich environment and mistaking it for divine presence? And if there is indeed divine presence, is the technology subtly shaping the encounter in particular directions and with particular effects?

A current example only possible in the modern technological world is the phenomenon of the global influence of Saddleback Community Church in southern California and its senior pastor, Rick Warren (Sheler 2006: chap. 4). Warren has pioneered a series of programs at this Southern Baptist congregation, refined them in light of local experience, and then exported them en masse to the entire globe. Millions of Christians, from highly diverse cultural, ethnic, and religious settings and traditions, have been exposed to the *Purpose Driven Life*, the *Purpose Driven Church*, and numerous other programs that blend Christian learning, experience, and viewpoints. These programs are adopted with little or no consideration of the implicit assumptions of their creator, the cultural and ethnic assumptions embedded within them, or the doctrinal or theological views that inform their orientation and advocacy of response. What does it mean to be a *local* congregation in the midst of a technological milieu where programs, viewpoints, and meanings from afar have such tremendous impact? Do megachurches exert influences that are inappropriate or incommensurate with local, regional, or national needs? Are technologies of social control within the Christian community replacing transcendental encounters with God? These are difficult questions to answer in a definitive manner, but the very ubiquity of modern technologies within church settings and the manner in which they operate to alter the environment should give us pause and stimulate deeper reflection (Hipps 2009).

Pentecostals and charismatics have been especially eager to adopt the latest technologies to both promulgate the gospel and to utilize it for regular worship and teaching of the faithful. Pentecostals were dominant in the front wave of the use of radio with F. F. Bosworth, Richard and Adele Carmichael, Aimee Semple McPherson, and Robert Craig being early examples. Later examples from the 1940s include A. A. Allen, R. W. Schambach, Gordon Lindsay, Oral Roberts, C. M. Ward, and Kathryn Kuhlman. Oral Roberts urged listeners "to touch their radios as a 'point of contact' and then to 'release [their] faith'" (Warner 2002: 1015). Similarly, television was rapidly embraced by pentecostal preachers as the newest and best means to reach the lost world. Oral Roberts was a particularly successful pioneer with his broadcasting of tent crusades in 1954, ultimately morphing this foray into a variety program that quickly became the top religious program on the still relatively new medium. The largest television followings throughout subsequent decades tended to be those of charismatic and pentecostal figures, with the notable exception of Billy Graham crusades. The Trinity Broadcast Network co-founded by Paul Crouch and Jim Bakker, the Christian Broadcast Network of Pat Robertson, and Bakker's later Praise the Lord Network stand out as exemplars of this phenomena. One can add to the list the worldwide television broadcasts of Jimmy Swaggart, Kathryn Kuhlman, Rex Humbard, Kenneth Copeland, Jack Hayford, Marilyn Hickey, James Robison, Benny Hinn, Rod Parsley, and Morris Cerullo (Hedges 2002). Pentecostals and charismatics have been equally quick to adopt the latest forms of technologies, whether it is in church architectural styles, electronic music, stage lighting, blogs, wikis, Web sites, automatic phone messaging transmission systems for invites and "personal" prayers for the sick and needy, listserves, or a multitude of other tools, techniques, or systems. Already some churches have established a presence in 3-D virtual worlds like Second Life. The religious implications of these virtual worlds has not escaped scholarly scrutiny as they increasingly serve religious functions for some of their participants by the very nature of how they are organized and the way things "happen" in-world. Many of these secular platforms may reflect implicit religious symbolism and "sacramental" acts that convey transcendental meanings to participants (Bainbridge and Bainbridge 2007).

Commodification of the religious world by technology did not begin with the modern century; medieval cathedrals or ancient Jewish synagogues with their associated technologies and rituals also shaped human experience and encounters with the divine (Scott 2003; VanderKam 2001; White 1994). "Church shopping" has become so common because the religious experience and religious life itself has become a commodity just like any other commodity in the modern world that can be bought, sold, or traded (Budde and Brimlow 2002; Cimino and Lattin 1998; Hangen 2002; Schultze 1991, 2004; Twitchell 2007). Some would simply see this phenomenon as an indicator of the psyche of modern people. We could also understand it as an inevitable consequence of the many ways in which technological artifacts and systems, including churches, have become "devices" that can be bought, sold, exchanged, and accumulated (Borgmann 1984) and the attendant and pervasive consumerism that follows in its wake.

Even within the wider secular world only selected aspects of technologies are routinely examined and often by narrowly framed inquiries that only focus on environmental impacts or economic cost-benefit analysis (Pool 1997). The commodification power of modern technologies is rarely contemplated except by a devoted group of experts who largely publish papers and books on the topic that are read by few outside of their specialized academic circles. So let us now consider selected aspects of the way modern technology is commodifying the human person (Bess 2008).

> Mark has lately been mastering the art of taking video clips of commercial films and other online materials shot by amateurs and repurposing the footage by inserting new materials drawn from other sources, digitally altering images, and inserting other graphics and audio into the clips. Last week he took some amateur footage from several different sources to make selected Hollywood personalities seem to speak out in favor of particular Christian positions. That same week, he took a professor's lecture on campus and repurposed it to highlight some points at which he strongly disagreed with the views presented, including modifying the audio of the professor's lecture remarks to create entirely new sentences and altering other sentences through excision and

insertion—some designed to make the professor appear foolish. Mark considers this to be "all in good fun," and several of his friends as well as a growing list of admirers on his MySpace and YouTube accounts register their appreciation of his labors.

Maria has struggled for many years with her self-image, especially as related to her body. Next week, she is eagerly anticipating going to a plastic surgeon to obtain a consultation about image enhancement procedures that she has watched many times on television shows. She prays earnestly that the Lord will make it possible for her to obtain a tummy tuck, some liposuction on her thighs, minor breast enhancement, and some nose, chin, and cheek alterations. She loves that she lives in a world where one no longer has to accept that somehow one's body is unalterable and just to be accepted as "given." She thinks the liposuction will do the work that thousands of hours in a gym would require, and she has already roughly calculated that the procedure would really "pay for itself" when you consider the amount of gym fees and time it would take to achieve similar results.

Some weeks ago the college issued a special e-mail bulletin and had a special chapel speaker about the dangers of pornography. Miguel downplayed in his own mind the severity of several issues the speaker raised for him personally as he rarely surfs the web for pornography and only occasionally watches films with significant amounts of nudity. Miguel dismisses the notion that activities in which his avatar in Second Life (SL) is engaging have anything to do with the real-world struggles of pornography that many men, Christian or otherwise, experience. Last week he bought some biological enhancements for his avatar and engaged in his first virtual sex experience with another avatar that he considered to be really hot. While engaging in the encounter, complete with simulated sounds supplied by the two parties, he traded e-mails of a simulated sexual nature with the owner of the other avatar. He found the entire experience quite amusing. He'll never meet the owner of the other avatar face to face, and she (if it was a "she") will never meet him. Besides, it's not like he was having sex—it was his avatar—which bears no remote resemblance to himself and exhibits within the world of SL an entirely different persona than the real Miguel.

Monica has always struggled with school and found retaining information very difficult. Recently it was mentioned in her psychology class that some new forms of drugs are being developed that may hold promise for those with various cognitive disabilities. A quick perusal of the Internet yielded a number of sites that now make Monica hopeful that perhaps by the time she is in graduate school there will be one or more drugs widely available that will enhance her memory retention capabilities and make it possible for her to excel as a student. She can then be the "A" student she has always wanted to be, and it should ensure that her path to a doctorate is clear and virtually certain.

## Commodifying the Human Person

As more and more technologies fill our modern world, reality as it truly is in the form of nature itself becomes ever more remote. Draw a circle of one hundred miles radius from almost any location where many people live and you can hardly touch anything in the environment that is truly natural. Even wooded areas, lakes, streams, and hills have been shaped and reshaped by our human ancestors. Parks allow us to experience nature in the controlled manner and design decisions of the landscape architect. The grass underfoot is uniform and carefully clipped and managed on a continuing basis. The artificially constructed environment that surrounds us insulates us from the "wildness" and allows us to plan for events and things despite what "Mother Nature" might have in mind. The retreat from reality has succeeded in a manner that would amaze our ancestors, and in its place we have created a world of motion, excitement, and entertainment. What is nature, even in "managed" national parks like Yellowstone and Yosemite or the "active" volcanoes of Hawaii, as compared to the nature films we can call up on our TV sets through digital cable at any time (Borgmann 1999)? Editors compress within an hour of footage what would take a year or more to see in nature, and even then we might miss those rare events that the camera lens has now captured so precisely and reduced to the level of a commodity to be bought, sold, and viewed whenever the inclination strikes. On the other hand, we must agree that sometimes viewing nature in this manner is decidedly safer than viewing nature "in the raw" and that seeing natural processes telescoped in time does aid learning about such processes. All technologies embody tradeoffs that convey certain benefits and impose certain burdens/restrictions.

Right in the center of the modern technological world stands the human being. Just as nature itself has become more remote to modern human beings due to humanity's deliberate reshaping of the natural world, so the human being is under relentless modification by technologies of all types. Many things that people used to pray to God about are now resolved through the wonders of modern technology. Technology is the great modern savior, providing seemingly unlimited benefits and further reducing the uncertainties of life. "Give us this day our daily bread"—a supplication that used to be intoned with great purpose and meaning where there were no guarantees of bread on the table due to the vagaries of nature—is now replaced by weekly trips to the grocery store or, for the really busy, by online purchases delivered to your door with a range of choices that would astound our ancestors. Human ailments that used to afflict large numbers of people are now addressed by injections and a dizzying array of medications. The therapeutic society causes people to rely on technological fixes to human problems that can result in diminished desire to ever "work things out" using our minds and spirits and drawing upon or building our moral fiber and character traits. Every problem comes to have a technological answer, disempowering human beings from solving their own problems directly and relying upon extrinsic devices and processes to achieve desired results. Recent years have witnessed the publication of books advocating a future where robots may become friends and even sexual partners to human beings. The First International Conference on Human-Robot Personal Relationships at the University of Maastricht in the Netherlands contemplated matters such as what it might mean to be "loved" by a robot (Norton 2008). God has tended to recede from many humans' conscious thoughts due, at least in some measure, to the way technologies have replaced religion as a means to face and deal with varied problems associated with the human condition.

We have finally reached the stage in the process of technological evolution where even the human body itself can be altered seemingly at will. Artificial organs, artificial limbs, enhancements, reductions, alterations, and cosmetic beautifications can be ordered up as needed from an ever-expanding list of options and possibilities. No longer is the will of God expressed or perceived as a fixed set of physical traits explained by genetics. Now human beings are true co-creators of themselves. Even genders can be changed and changed back again through the use of surgeries and hormone treatments. While these procedures are complicated and are presently restricted by various ethical, technical, and medical considerations, the very fact that they can occur has clearly taken us farther down a path of human capability to alter what appeared in the past to simply be "God-given" traits and characteristics.

The near term holds the prospect that parents can select the sex, eye color, hair color, and physique of their future child. In the not-too-distant future, it is predicted that parents can have doctors prescribe various cognitive and personality-altering drugs to advantage their children in the world they inhabit (Sahakian and Morein-Zamir 2007; cf. Horn et al. 2008). The prestigious British science magazine *Nature* conducted a poll in 2008 that focused on three drugs: methylphenidate (i.e., Ritalin, which is used to treat ADHD but is also used by many college students illegally as a "study aid"); modafinil (i.e., Provigil for the treatment of sleep disorders but also used by some to deal with general fatigue or to counteract jet lag); and beta blockers (used for cardiac arrhythmia but employed by some to counteract anxiety attacks). In an online poll 1,400 respondents from 60 nations were asked questions about their use of these substances. One in five reported that they used one or more of these drugs for non-medical reasons (Maher 2008). This is one of many indications that people in general are not opposed to the idea of using drugs to enhance human functioning.

Some scientists are envisioning a future bio-incubator world where laboratory-fresh models are generated for human organ replacements before the organs fail (Bavley 2008). At least fifteen businesses currently offer personal genetic test kits that provide various types of personalized genetic information and the likelihood of various genetic problems for prices ranging from $100 to $350,000. Some are heralding these kits as the first step in an inevitable and widely anticipated path toward completely personalized medicine through pharmacogenetics (Katsanis, Javitt, and Hudson 2008; Singer 2008). The first successful creation of an electrode implantation in a monkey's brain that enables it to control a robotic arm and feed itself has now occurred (Barry 2008). This should make it possible in the future for amputees to control robotic arms that will restore and in some cases, perhaps even improve upon, "natural" human limbs. Human beings are indeed being commodified by their technologies with ever-increasing intensity.

## Some Questions

How are Christians to respond to these many developments within our technological societies? Is there a distinctly Christian (or pentecostal/charismatic) approach to technology that can guide us when confronting the amazing cornucopia of technological innovations? Can the commodification of modern life be controlled, and if so, by whom and guided by what principles? Does virtual reality "count" and "matter" in the same way that non-virtual reality does? How do ethics apply to these artificial worlds, and are the same approaches advocated in the past adequate for the situational demands of the present and the future? How have pentecostal or evangelical theologians thought about these matters, and can their insights fruitfully guide us? What is the responsibility of a pastor, youth leader, or other Christian leader to explore these matters with fellow Christians? What might Christians contribute to public arenas and discourse where the use and control of technologies is contemplated?

## Technology among Theologians and Christians

The twentieth century witnessed the greatest acceleration of technology in human history. It also was a century in which theologians tried to create systematic theologies that would speak more directly to the human condition and human concerns that transcend biblical and doctrinal issues. Hundreds of "contemporary theologies" have been produced as well as topically focused books on contemporary societal issues from a Christian perspective. The century also witnessed the articulation and growth of the practical theology movement. Despite these efforts, it remains largely true that technology and its sibling, modern science, have been largely ignored within most theological writing, including that of evangelicals and even more so of pentecostals and charismatics. Extensive discussions of technology can only be found in papal encyclicals, Catholic social theory, and a few Protestant theologians such as Donald Bloesch and Jacques Ellul (who was not, strictly speaking, a theologian). A random selection of twenty-one systematic theologies produced in the latter half of the twentieth century across ecumenical lines and including evangelicals and charismatics/pentecostals, were examined as to the attention they gave to technology. *Technology* as a word or concept appeared on average only once every 566 pages in the over 32,000 pages of text that make up these theologies (Cheek 2007). This is a rather startling absence, considering that technologies in all their varied forms are the pervasive presence in the modern world. The past few decades have witnessed specialty books targeted to particular technological issues, especially those related to human genetics, human fertility, and other biomedical and bioethics topics directly involved with the human qua person (Cheek 2007: 63–118). Yet these various treatments are generally lacking in any kind of an overarching framework that provides a comprehensive orientation to inform personal decision making about technologies in the daily lives of contemporary Christians. This large lacuna in Christian theology needs to be taken up as a vital challenge by theologians present and future if we are going to better inform Christian practice and have any hope of guiding further technological developments.

Fortunately, a number of Christians active in technological fields have risen to the challenge and provided some provisional guidance for interested Christians. Taken collectively, their writings provide some principles that can be helpful for modern Christians as they wrestle with the hegemony of technology. It must be admitted that these principles are theologically naïve at times and often misappropriate or misinterpret biblical passages in support of one or more principles being enunciated. A notable exception to this observation is the work of Celia Deane-Drummond (2006), who holds doctorates in both biology and theology and centers her work on bioethical topics and concerns. There is a vital need for more theologians to acquire expertise about technology in the modern world and to bring their theological acumen to bear more fully on these issues. A survey of modern literature demonstrates that theologians are doing far more to engage with modern science than with modern technology, yet the latter is arguably far more powerful in its impact in the wider world and in the life of the church than scientific research.

Albert Borgmann, in his entire corpus, addresses many dimensions of the technology challenge. He recognizes that technology, in its diverse manifestations and ubiquity, presents the most serious threat to the continuance and vitality of religions of all types within the modern world. The commodification of life by technology does not stop at the door of the believer or the church where believers regularly gather. Much like the presence of the Lord that was observed in Jonah's day, wherever we attempt to flee from technology, it is there. It is impossible, therefore, to find a safe and secure refuge where technology does not intrude or assert itself. At the same time, Borgmann believes that we can actively resist the domination of technology by purposefully focusing on what he terms "focal things" and "focal practices." A "focal thing" is something that we appreciate and hold dear, in part because we can see with the mind's eye, embodied in the thing, the various constituent parts that come together to make it what it is. This is the antithesis of the "black box" devices of the modern world that were discussed earlier in this chapter. Thus, a fireplace in the modern home, where a family gathers in the evening to enjoy one another's company and where we can make a firm connection between the wood or heat-generating source of the fire and the world from which it was taken, is a focal thing. The purposeful employment of one or more focal things in a ritualized manner becomes, for Borgmann, a "focal practice." So the sharing of a home-cooked meal together around a table with the conviviality of good conversation and appreciation of one another's humanity is a focal practice (Borgmann 1984).

Borgmann argues that every time we invoke the use of a focal thing or engage in a focal practice we are balancing the technological world with the importance of the cultural world and the informational world. It is vital to strike a balance among these various worlds that we inhabit so as to inhibit the unnatural but very likely tendency of the technological world to dominate and drown out completely the other two worlds that are vital to human being and human becoming (Borgmann 1999). He also advocates that entire communities engage in active celebrations that bring us together as humans and celebrate focal things and focal practices. Borgmann finds rich Christian meaning in these public acts and believes that Christians should be at the forefront of movements such as the slow food movement, which requires a commitment to locally grown products, the careful and slow preparation of them, and the enjoyment of them in the form of communal meals where time is held in abeyance and where conversation and human bonding can occur unhurried and uninhibited by the pace of modern technological world.

Christian engineers such as Jack Swearengen (2007), Ken Funk (2007), and others have provided us with the following set of common principles that can be abstracted from their thought (Cheek 2007: 268–73):

1. Culturally appropriate technology should seek the common good and treat one's neighbor as oneself.
2. Technology must promote justice with particular reference to the marginal and the poor.
3. Technological creativity should encourage stewardship of the environment, openness toward the future and the ideas of others, and joy on the part of the users of the technology.

4. Respect for limits, human finitude, and the diversity and plenitude of creation must be paramount when considering technology.
5. Trust and care that balances technical, organizational, and cultural aspects of technology with genuine human need and larger societal contexts should be evidenced.
6. Communication concerning technology should be open, respectful, accurate, and timely to allow others affected by technology to respond.

Taking these six principles and applying them to the various situations that our four Christian college students present to us should enable us to start working out how generalized principles like those enunciated here can inform decision making about concrete technological situations and decisions. Marked success at such endeavors will require Christians to learn more about some technical aspects of particular technologies as well as to think anew and afresh about how to appropriate technologies in a manner that maximizes their enormous potentials and minimizes their considerable negative consequences. These tradeoffs are inherent in the very nature of technology and require astute, patient, thoughtful, prayerful, and Spirit-inspired actions to successfully navigate life and living in a technological world.

I do not believe that there is any particular difference between how pentecostals/charismatics, as distinguished from other Christians, should reflect, react, or respond to technology in the modern world. Nor do I currently see how pentecostal/charismatic theologians will offer something overwhelmingly distinct from their Christian peers. Yet given that pentecostals and charismatics have been on the forefront of new technology appropriation for ministry purposes, it is important for theologians within this tradition to wrestle with the deep theological and ethical challenges that technologies pose and to figure out ways to subvert its dangerous tendencies to cause God and Christianity to ever recede in modern consciousness.

## References

Anderson, Chris, ed. 2008. "The Peta Age." *Wired* (July): 106–21.

Bainbridge, William Sims, and Wilma Alice Bainbridge. 2007. "Electronic Game Research Methodologies: Studying Religious Implications." *Review of Religious Research* 49/1: 35–53.

Barry, Patrick. 2008. "Monkeys Move Arm with Mind." *Sciences News* 173/19: 9.

Bavley, Alan. 2008. "Modern Prometheus." *Illumination* 11/2: 36–41.

Bess, Michael D. 2008. "Icarus 2.0: A Historian's Perspective on Human Biological Enhancement." *Technology and Culture* 49/1: 114–26.

Borgmann, Albert. 1984. *Technology and the Character of Contemporary Life: A Philosophical Inquiry.* Chicago: University of Chicago Press.

———. 1999. *Holding on to Reality: The Nature of Information at the Turn of the Millennium.* Chicago: University of Chicago Press.

Budde, Michael, and Robert Brimlow. 2002. *Christianity Incorporated: How Big Business Is Buying the Church*. Grand Rapids, Mich.: Brazos Press.

Cheek, Dennis William. 2007. "Theology and Technology." Unpublished manuscript. A revision of "Theology and Technology: An Exploration of Their Relationship with Special Reference to the Works of Albert Borgmann and Intelligent Transportation Systems." Ph.D. thesis, Department of Theology, University of Durham, 2006.

Cimino, Richard, and Don Lattin. 1998. *Shopping for Faith: American Religion in the New Millennium*. San Francisco: Jossey-Bass.

Deane-Drummond, Celia. 2006. *Genetics and Christian Ethics*. New York: Cambridge University Press.

Focus Group Discussion. 2007. "The Use of Computer Software and the Internet by Local Church Congregations." *Review of Religious Research* 49/1: 54–68.

Funk, Ken. 2007. "Thinking Critically and Christianly about Technology." *Perspectives on Science and Christian Faith* 59/3: 201–11.

Hangen, Tona J. 2002. *Redeeming the Dial: Radio, Religion, and Popular Culture in America*. Chapel Hill: University of North Carolina Press.

Hedges, D. J. 2002. "Television." In Stanley M. Burgess and Eduard M. Van Der Maas, eds., *The New International Dictionary of Pentecostal and Charismatic Movements,* rev. and expanded ed. Grand Rapids, Mich.: Zondervan, 1118–20.

Hipps, Shane. 2009. *Flickering Pixels: How Technology Shapes Your Faith*. Grand Rapids, Mich.: Zondervan.

Horn, Sir Gabriel, et al. 2008. *Brain Science, Addiction and Drugs*. London: Academy of Medical Sciences.

Katsanis, S. H., G. Javitt, and K. Hudson. 2008. "A Case Study of Personalized Medicine." *Science* 320: 53–54.

Maher, Brendan. 2008. "Poll Results: Look Who's Doping." *Nature* 452: 677–75.

Niemann, Christoph. 2008. "The Planetary Computer." *Wired* (July): 53–55.

Norton, Ingrid. 2008. "How to Turn on a Robot." *Chronicle of Higher Education* 54/42: A7.

Oller, D. Kimbrough, and Ulrike Griebel, eds. 2004. *Evolution of Communication Systems: A Comparative Approach*. Cambridge, Mass.: MIT Press.

Pennisi, Elizabeth. 2006. "Social Animals Prove Their Smarts." *Science* 312: 1734–38.

Pool, Robert. 1997. *Beyond Engineering: How Society Shapes Technology*. New York: Oxford University Press.

Sahakian, Barbara, and Sharon Morein-Zamir. 2007. "Professor's Little Helper." *Nature* 450/20: 1157–59.

Sheler, Jeffery L. 2006. *Believers: A Journey into Evangelical America*. New York: Viking.

Schultze, Quentin J. 1991. *Televangelism and American Culture: The Business of Popular Religion*. Grand Rapids, Mich.: Baker Book House.

———. 2004. *High-tech Worship? Using Presentational Technologies Wisely*. Grand Rapids, Mich.: Baker Books.

Scott, Robert A. 2003. *The Gothic Enterprise: A Guide to Understanding the Medieval Cathedral*. Berkeley: University of California Press.

Singer, Emily. 2008. "Buyer's Guide to Personal Genomics." *Technology Review* 111/4: 18.

Swearengen, Jack Clayton. 2007. *Beyond Paradise: Technology and the Kingdom of God*. Eugene, Ore.: Wipf and Stock.

Thornton, Alex, and Katherine McAuliffe. 2006."Teaching in Wild Meerkats." *Science* 313/5784: 227–29.

Twitchell, James B. 2007. *Shopping for God: How Christianity Went from in Your Heart to in Your Face.* New York: Simon & Schuster.

VanderKam, James C. 2001. *An Introduction to Early Judaism.* Grand Rapids, Mich.: Wm. B. Eerdmans.

Warner, W. E. 2002. "Radio." In Stanley M. Burgess and Eduard M. Van Der Maas, eds., *The New International Dictionary of Pentecostal and Charismatic Movements*, rev. and expanded ed. Grand Rapids, Mich.: Zondervan, 1015–16.

White, Susan J. 1994. *Christian Worship and Technological Change.* Nashville, Tenn.: Abingdon Press.

## Recommended Reading

Borgmann, Albert. 2003. *Power Failure: Christianity in the Culture of Technology.* Grand Rapids, Mich.: Brazos Press.

Deane-Drummond, Celia, and Peter Manley Scott, eds. 2006. *Future Perfect? God, Medicine and Human Identity.* New York: T & T Clark.

Jardine, Murray. 2004. *The Making and Unmaking of Technological Society.* Grand Rapids, Mich.: Brazos Press.

Schultze, Quentin J. 2002. *Habits of the High-Tech Heart: Living Virtuously in the Information Age.* Grand Rapids, Mich.: Baker Academic.

Simmons, Paul D., 2008. *Faith and Health: Religion, Science, and Public Policy.* Macon, Ga.: Mercer University Press.

Waters, Brent. 2006. *From Human to Posthuman: Christian Theology and Technology in a Postmodern World.* Burlington, Vt.: Ashgate.

# Contributors

STEVE BADGER (Ph.D., Chemistry, University of Southern Mississippi) is Professor of Chemistry at Evangel University in Springfield, Missouri. He has taught biology and chemistry courses at public and private Pentecostal colleges for more than twenty-five years and has done chemical research with the USDA and EPA. He is an ordained minister, has served as senior pastor and associate pastor, and has had over a dozen articles published in various Assemblies of God periodicals. Badger and Mike Tenneson have been collaborating for years.

DONALD F. CALBREATH (Ph.D., Physiological Chemistry, Ohio State University) is Emeritus Associate Professor of Chemistry at Whitworth University in Spokane, Washington, with a background in biochemistry and the neurosciences. Prior to coming to Whitworth, he was Director of Clinical Chemistry at a large community hospital in Durham, North Carolina, that was a teaching hospital for Duke Medical School. He also taught in the Duke physician's assistant program. Dr. Calbreath has published in the fields of biochemistry and behavior and in the bioethics of stem cell research.

DENNIS W. CHEEK (Ph.D., Curriculum and Instruction/Science Education, Pennsylvania State University; Ph.D., Theology, University of Durham) is a Senior Fellow at the Ewing Marion Kauffman Foundation and a Professor in the midcareer doctoral program in educational leadership, Graduate School of Education, University of Pennsylvania. Cheek is an ordained minister of the General Council of the Assemblies of God and has served as senior administrator in two state education departments, as a college trustee, and as a consultant to corporations, government agencies, and nonprofit organizations. He has authored, edited, or contributed to more than 800 publications and multimedia products.

MARGARET M. POLOMA (Ph.D., Sociology, Case Western Reserve University) is Emerita Professor of Sociology at the University of Akron. She has written extensively about religious experience in contemporary American society with a particular focus on Pentecostal and Charismatic Christians. Her major works include pioneering studies of prayer and divine healing and book-length monographs on the Assemblies of God and the Pentecostal/charismatic revivals of the 1990s. She is presently Research Professor at the

University of Akron and a principal investigator for a three-year longitudinal study (2008–2011) funded by the John Templeton Foundation titled "The Flame of Love: Scientific Research on the Experience and Expression of Godly Love in the Pentecostal Tradition."

CRAIG SCANDRETT-LEATHERMAN (Ph.D., Anthropology, University of Kansas) is Adjunct Instructor at Washington University in St. Louis. Craig has been an urban studies director and Free Methodist pastor in Chicago. He has written articles and reviews for *Missiology: An International Review, Pneuma: The Journal of the Society for Pentecostal Studies,* and *Zygon: Journal of Religion and Science,* and is now working on a book, tentatively titled *African Roots and Political Dance: Cultural History and Political Aesthetics of Afro-Pentecostal (COGIC) Ritual Arts.*

JAMES K. A. SMITH (Ph.D., Philosophy, Villanova University) is Professor of Philosophy at Calvin College. He specializes in contemporary French philosophy, philosophical theology, and philosophy of the social sciences. Some of his books include *The Fall of Interpretation: Philosophical Foundations for a Creational Hermeneutic; Speech and Theology: Language and the Logic of Incarnation; Introducing Radical Orthodoxy: Mapping a Post-Secular Theology; Who's Afraid of Postmodernism? Taking Derrida, Lyotard, and Foucault to Church; and Desiring the Kingdom: Worship, Worldview, and Cultural Formation.* His work has also appeared in *Christianity Today, Christian Century, First Things,* and *Books & Culture,* and he has been featured on NPR's program *Speaking of Faith.*

MIKE TENNESON (Ph.D., Science Education, University of Missouri–Columbia) is Professor of Biology at Evangel University. An ordained Assemblies of God minister, he has taught college biology for more than twenty-five years and has done field research on birds, frogs, porcupines, lizards, and snails. His current research interests include measuring attitudes and beliefs about origins and using the debate to teach critical thinking. Tenneson and Steve Badger have been collaborating for years.

WOLFGANG VONDEY (Ph.D., Systematic Theology and Ethics, Marquette University) is Associate Professor of Systematic Theology at Regent University School of Divinity. A German-born, ecumenical scholar and teacher credentialed with the Church of God (Cleveland, Tennessee), he has authored works of constructive theology in the area of the church, the Holy Spirit, Pentecostalism, and science, the most recent being *People of Bread: Rediscovering Ecclesiology* and *Beyond Pentecostalism: The Crisis of Global Christianity and the Renewal of the Theological Agenda.*

FREDERICK L. WARE (Ph.D., Religion, Vanderbilt University) is Associate Professor of Theology at Howard University School of Divinity. An ordained minister in the Church of God in Christ, he is active in ecumenical affairs, including being a participant in the World Council of Churches and Pentecostals Consultation. He is author of *Methodologies of Black Theology.* His interpretive essays on Pentecostalism include "The Church of God in Christ and the Azusa Street Revival" in *The Azusa Street Revival and Its Legacy* and "Spiritual Egalitarianism, Ecclesial Pragmatism, and the Status of Women in Ordained Ministry" in *Women in Pentecostal-Charismatic Leadership.*

TELFORD WORK (Ph.D., Theology and Ethics, Duke University) is Associate Professor of Theology at Westmont College. He is author of *Ain't Too Proud to Beg: Living through the Lord's Prayer; Deuteronomy* (Brazos Theological Commentary on the Bible) (forthcoming); and *Living and Active: Scripture in the Economy of Salvation.* He is also a contributor and signatory of *In One Body through the Cross: The Princeton Proposal for Christian Unity.* He maintains a Web site at http://telfordwork.net. He embraced Pentecostalism through his involvement at Christian Assembly Foursquare Church in Los Angeles.

AMOS YONG (Ph.D., Religious Studies and Theology, Boston University) is J. Rodman Williams Professor of Theology at Regent University School of Divinity. An Assemblies of God PK (pastor's kid) and MK (missionary kid) and a credentialed minister with the movement, he has authored or edited ten books on theology of religions, theological method, theology of disability, pentecostal theology, political theology, and theology and science, the most recent being *In the Days of Caesar: Pentecostalism and Political Theology* and *The Spirit of Creation: Modern Science and the God-World Relation in Pentecostal-Charismatic Perspective.*

# Index

abiogenesis, 111
Adler, Mortimer J., 103
aesthetics, 164–170
agnosticism, 41, 47, 175, 177–180, 183
alchemy, 84
altered state of consciousness, 121, 165
altruism, 187
American Psychiatric Association, 142–143
American Sociological Society, 180, 183
angel, 25, 40
anthropic principle, 62
anthropology, 5, 17, 29, 168; cultural,
    156–157
anthropomorphism, 80
antidepressant, 134, 138, 140–142, 145–146
anti-intellectualism, 2, 20, 22, 28
apocalypse, 21, 29
apocalyptic, 15, 21–22, 24, 31n6
apophatism, 81
applied science, 195
Aquinas, Thomas, 52–53, 65n6, 179
Aristotle, 52–53, 62, 63, 64n5, 65n6
Assemblies of God, 3, 95, 103, 105–107,
    112n10, 137–138, 184, 189
ateleology, 96, 99, 100, 111n2
atheism, 77, 82, 93, 181; methodological, 187
Augustine, 18, 46–47, 110–111
Ayala, Francisco J., 8n9

Behe, Michael, 96, 100
Berger, Peter, 181–182
Berkeley, George, 65n7
biochemistry, 98, 100, 134, 144–146
bioethics, 204
biology, 17, 35, 38, 44, 46, 181; evolutionary,
    29–31; molecular, 98
Boas, Franz, 169
Borgmann, Albert, 196, 199, 201, 204–205
Bowler, Peter J., 98–99
brain, 18, 59, 134, 139, 140, 148, 176, 203
Brandom, Robert, 38
Bruner, Frederick D., 127

Calvin, John, 65n9
causality, 52–54, 60–62, 63, 65n6
charisms, charismatic gifts. See gifts of the
    Spirit
charismatic spirituality, 4, 37, 44, 47n4, 81,
    121, 185–186
charismatic tradition, 1, 4, 7n1, 20–21, 25, 27–
    29, 129, 180, 183
Christian Sociological Society, 180–182
Church of God, 105, 107, 112, 127
Church of God in Christ, 127–128, 156–157,
    169–170
Church of God of Prophecy, 107, 112
Clayton, Philip, 4, 60, 108
cognitive sciences. See neuroscience
cognitive-behavioral therapy, 142, 145, 148
Collins, Francis, 95–96, 112n12
Comaroff, Jean, 169nn5–6
common descent, 96–99, 103, 111n2
compartmentalization, 17–18, 155, 181, 188n3
complementarity, 79, 87–88
Comte, Auguste, 177
consciousness, 57, 122–125, 129, 162
consumerism, 196, 199
cosmological argument, 85–86
cosmology, 16–18, 20, 22, 52–54, 56, 62–63,
    83, 85, 99, 160; mechanistic, 19, 63, 82
Council of Christian Colleges and Universi-
    ties, 111
counseling, 134–135, 137–138, 142–143, 145–148
Craig, William Lane, 85
creation, 61, 77, 82, 85–88, 206; doctrine/
    theology of, 22–23, 30, 47; new, 25–26
Creation Research Society, 94, 106–107
creationism, 6, 16, 19, 92, 101, 103–105, 107;
    old earth, 17, 94–95, 98, 103, 109; young
    earth, 6, 93–95, 98, 103, 107
creeds, 20, 30, 35
Csordas, Thomas J., 165–166, 169
Cushing, Frank Hamilton, 157–159, 161,
    166, 169
Cuvier, Georges, 99

D'Aquili, Eugene G., 121, 129n1
Darwin, Charles, 8n10, 93, 98, 99, 100, 102
Darwinism, 8n10, 17, 30, 93, 96, 98–100, 102–103, 123; neo-Darwinism, 15, 28, 31n9
Dawkins, Richard, 2, 30n4, 96
Dayton, Donald, 25, 29
Deane-Drummond, Celia, 204
deism, 25, 45–47, 54–56, 63, 77, 82, 93
Dembski, William, 100
demonology, 23, 36, 29, 41, 134, 137
Dempster, Murray, 2, 176
Dennett, Daniel, 15–19, 24–25, 30, 40, 122–124, 128, 129n1
depression, 39, 43, 59, 133–134
Descartes, René, 36, 54, 65n12
devil, 29, 51, 137. *See also* Satan
Discovery Institute, 100
divine action, 5, 25, 30, 46
divine foreknowledge, 65n13
divine transcendence, 58, 121
DNA, 17, 100, 101
Dobbins, Richard, 134–135, 144
Dobzhansky, Theodosius, 109, 112n19
Durkheim, Émile, 161–162, 166, 169nn4,5
Dyer, Anne E., 20, 25, 27

ecstatic experience, 127, 170n9
education, higher, 4, 6, 136
Einstein, Albert, 19, 56, 75, 78–88, 89n1
Eldredge, Niles, 99
Ellul, Jacques, 204
emergence, 60, 108
emotion, 96, 120, 135, 137, 146–147, 161–166, 169, 176, 179–180, 188
Enlightenment, 36, 147, 176, 188
environment, 38, 57, 99, 125, 128, 139, 140, 143, 146, 193–194, 197–199, 201, 205
epidemiology, 26, 29
epistemology, 75, 86, 127, 155, 161, 169, 176
eschatology, 21, 25, 28, 50, 60, 63; eschatological verification, 66n24
ether, 81–83
Eucharist, 26, 28, 178
Evangelicalism, 6–7, 8nn3,8,9,11, 28, 108, 111n2, 134, 136, 137, 144, 169n2, 180, 181, 184, 188, 203–204
evil, problem of, 53, 55
evolution, 6, 8, 15–16, 19, 24–28, 31, 48n6, 57, 92–116; biological, 29, 30n1, 31n5, 92–116; Darwin's theory of, 54; macroevolution, 92, 94–98, 100–101, 104, 106, 108–110; microevolution, 92, 97, 98, 100–101, 108–110
evolutionary creationism, 95, 103, 106–107
evolutionary psychology, 29

Falk, Darrel R., 8n9, 31n5
Farrar, Austin, 65n8
feminism, 175, 178, 182
finely tuned universe, 100
flood, 94, 98, 103–104, 108, 170
Fodor, Jerry, 42
forgiveness, 20, 30, 145, 147–148, 186
fossils, 97–99, 101, 103–104
Foursquare Church, 25, 106–107, 112nn10,13
Freddoso, Alfred J., 65nn7,9
freedom, 55, 148, 175, 188n2
Freud, Sigmund, 135
fundamentalism, 16–17, 20, 27, 30, 102, 108

Gaia theory, 100
Gap theory, 103–104, 107, 112n11
Genesis, 6–7, 8n8, 17, 25, 31n6, 95, 98, 102–106, 110, 112, 194
genetics, 97, 99, 202–204
geology, 17, 54, 93–94, 99, 103–104, 197
Giberson, Karl, 8n9, 16, 18, 31n8
gifts of the Spirit, 20, 51, 60, 61, 86, 187
glossolalia, 6, 7n1, 27, 58–61, 66n19, 119–122, 126, 136, 163, 165, 169n6, 170n9, 179, 187. *See also* Spirit baptism
God, 8, 54, 80, 82, 92, 96, 98, 104, 107
godly love, 174, 177, 186–188, 189n12
God-of-the-gaps, 101
Goetz, Stewart, 40–41, 43
Goodman, Felicitas D., 59, 165
Gould, Stephen Jay, 18, 99, 130n3
Green revolution, 197
guilt, 103, 135, 139, 143–148

Harris, Sam, 2
Haught, John F., 8n10
healing, 2, 27–29, 34–35, 39, 44–45, 51, 61, 66, 102, 125–126, 134–138, 146–148, 162–163, 166, 169, 186–187; spiritual, 145, 184
Hebblethwaite, Brian, 65n8
Heidegger, Martin, 122
hermeneutics, 6, 63, 104
Hewlett, Martinez, 8n9
historiography, 29
Hitchens, Christopher, 30n4
Hocken, Peter, 25

holiness, 29, 102, 156
Holy Spirit. *See* Spirit of God
*homoiousios,* 80
Horton, Harold, 26–27
Hume, David, 36, 39, 44
Hunter, Cornelius G., 42
Husserl, Edmund, 122–124, 170
Hutton, James, 99

image of God, 102, 109
incarnation, 61, 86
inerrancy, 6, 102
Institute of Creation Research, 94, 106
Institute of Scientific Creationism, 107
intelligent design, 19, 47, 97, 100–116
interventionism, 27, 36, 43, 45–46, 51, 53–58, 64, 89, 108, 148

Jackson, Michael, 169nn5–6
Jesus Christ, 16–17, 19–23, 26–27, 29–30, 31n6, 35, 39, 77, 80, 126, 164, 170n9, 175, 179, 183, 194; resurrection of, 19, 24–25, 47n4; Son of God, 22, 66n24
John Templeton Foundation, 184, 187
Johnson, Mark, 127
justice, 27, 175, 205

Kay, William K., 20, 25, 27
Kenny, Anthony, 64n5
*kenosis,* 85
Kepler, Johannes, 54
Kildahl, John P., 66n19
Koenig, Harold G., 135, 139, 143, 147

Lakoff, George, 127
Lamarck, Jean-Baptiste, 99
Lamoureux, Denis O., 8n8, 95
laws, 34, 41, 43–48, 101, 130, 181, 182
laws of nature, 36, 39–40, 47, 54–56, 63, 77, 79, 83, 181; regularity theory of, 36, 39–48
Lewis, C. S., 46
Livingstone, David N., 8n10
Lovekin, A. Adams, 60
Luther, Martin, 65n9
Lyell, Charles, 99

Macchia, Frank D., 25, 61, 64n2
Malinowski, Bronislaw, 169
Malony, H. Newton, 60
Malthus, Thomas, 99
Marxism, 182

Mason, Charles Harrison, 118, 125–129, 169–170
materialism, 6, 40, 42, 96, 117–118, 124, 128, 129n1, 136
Mayr, Ernst, 98
McGrath, Alister E., 8n9, 9n12
medicine, 2, 16, 26–27, 35, 38, 50–51, 110, 147, 203
Mendel, Gregor, 99
mental health, 134–135, 137, 139, 143, 148n2
Merleau-Ponty, Maurice, 122, 170n10
metaphor, 45, 58, 64n2, 119, 123, 127–128, 130n3, 163, 169n6, 194
metaphysics, 16, 37, 41–42, 44–45, 47–48, 62–63, 79, 101, 127
Miller, Kenneth, 95–96, 101
miracle, 23, 28–29, 34–37, 39, 44, 47, 51, 61, 66n23, 125, 178
modernism, 21, 102, 168, 174, 176–177, 184, 188
monotheism, 104
Morgan, Lewis Henry, 157–158, 166
Morris, Henry, 94, 103
Murphy, Nancy, 30
mystical experience, 19, 127

narrative, 5–7, 16, 20, 25, 29, 31nn6,11, 50, 56, 58, 60, 63, 94–95, 104–105, 128–129, 163, 169n6, 174, 177, 182, 184, 186
natural selection, 16, 54, 96–99
naturalism, 2, 4, 6, 27, 34–49, 96, 98, 123, 136; metaphysical, 41–42, 48; methodological, 41, 44–45, 47n4, 136
Nelson, Paul, 94
Nesteruk, Alexei, 8n3
neuroscience, 5, 42, 47, 59, 118–119, 122–124, 128–129, 177; neurobiology, 59; neuro-chemistry, 133–134, 139, 197; neuro-imaging, 117, 119–121, 124, 128–129; neurotheology, 119, 121
Newberg, Andrew B., 119–122, 124, 128, 129n1
Newton, Isaac, 36, 54, 56, 65, 75, 78–85, 88, 89nn1–2
Noë, Alva, 119, 121–122, 124, 128, 129n2
Numbers, Ronald L., 8n2, 48n8, 102–103, 107

Occam's razor, 54, 65
ontology, 34, 45–46, 80
open theism, 55–56, 65n13
Oral Roberts University, 1, 2, 108
Orthodox tradition, 8n3, 20

paleontology, 54, 99
Paley, William, 100
panentheism, 77
Pannenberg, Wolfhart, 66n24
pantheism, 77, 81–82
participant observation, 155, 157–159, 161, 163–166, 169, 170n8, 183, 186
Pentecostal spirituality, 2–6, 50, 59, 81. *See also* charismatic spirituality
personal knowledge. *See* tacit knowledge
pharmacology, 141, 145
phenomenology, 117, 128, 166, 170; of consciousness, 122–125
philosophy of nature, 79, 82
physics, 5, 17–19, 34–38, 47, 52, 54, 60, 75–91, 100, 110, 160; Newtonian, 19, 56, 82, 84
placebo effect, 142, 146
Plantinga, Alvin, 41, 47n2
Platonism, 52, 64n3
pluralism, 20, 129
Polanyi, Michael, 155, 157, 159–161, 165–166
Polkinghorne, John C., 23, 31n7, 57, 66n15, 84
Poloma, Margaret M., 26, 175–188, 189n5,7,12
positivism, 167, 176–177
postmodernism, 2, 4, 50–62, 167, 169, 174–191
pragmatism, 19–20
prayer, 23, 27, 44, 54, 59, 64, 127, 134–135, 137–138, 148, 163, 178–179, 184–185, 187, 189n7, 199, 206
process theology, 55, 63, 65n13
prophecy, 23, 86, 187
Protestantism, 20–21, 65n9, 102, 175, 183–184, 204
psychiatry, 133–134, 138, 145, 148
psychology, 7, 17, 29, 38, 42, 59, 60, 77, 135–138, 181, 192, 200
psychopathology, 133–136, 139, 143–144
psychotheraphy, 134, 142–143
punctuated equilibrium, 99

quantum mechanics, 18, 23, 56–57, 75, 85

radio, 94, 104, 111, 120, 186, 197–198
reductionism, 3, 6, 40, 43, 59, 118, 128
relationality, 85–86, 137, 161–162, 165–166
relativism, 17, 20
relativity: general theory of, 79–80; special theory of, 83
resurrection, 19, 22, 25, 30, 39, 47, 61, 111, 179
revelation, 21–23, 76, 112n12
Reynolds, John Mark, 94, 111n1

Ricoeur, Paul, 122
ritual, 161–163, 166, 169; Afropentecostal, 163–167
Roberts, Oral, 1, 2, 27, 108, 198
robotics, 202–203
Roman Catholicism, 3, 20, 175, 177–179, 183
Ross, Hugh, 94, 100, 106
routinization of charisma, 185, 189
Ruse, Michael, 101, 109
Russell, Robert John, 62

Samarin, William, 59, 165
Sartre, Jean-Paul, 122
Satan, 26, 127. *See also* devil
scientism, 2, 43, 96
Scopes trial, 102
Searle, John, 42, 129n1
secular humanism, 17, 105, 137–138
self-transcendence, 117, 119, 124–128
shamanism, 1, 44
Shermer, Michael, 15–16, 19, 24–25, 30n1
signs and wonders, 1, 7, 19, 21–22, 26–27, 29, 34, 37, 39, 43, 47, 51, 61, 169, 179, 201
sin, 29–30, 87, 102, 134, 144, 147, 193, 195
skepticism, 15, 20, 188
Smith, James K. A., 31n10, 77
social construction, 174, 182, 184
social Darwinism, 18, 167
sociobiology, 100
sociology, 16–17, 38, 59–60; modernist, 180–182
Sorokin, Pitirim, 189n12
soteriology, 46, 53
soul, 17, 40, 51, 126, 147, 164, 167
space, 54, 56, 79, 82
speciation, 98, 108, 111
Spirit Baptism, 7n1, 26, 86, 118–121, 125–127, 134–136, 186; initial evidence of, 7n1, 121
Spirit of God, 23, 37, 39, 42, 46, 63, 80, 88, 110, 157, 168, 188; absence of, 86–87; activity of, 25, 28, 51, 82, 133–152, 163, 182; in creation/nature, 45–47, 87–88; dynamic presence of, 45–47
spiritual gifts. *See* gifts of the Spirit
spiritualism, 27–29
stress, 95, 139, 143–148
structuralism, 98, 100–101, 119, 161, 167
supernaturalism, 5, 29, 36, 40–41, 45, 87, 136; metaphysical, 41, 44, 45
supervenience, 30, 66n20
syncretism, 20

tacit knowledge, 159–161, 165–166, 168
Taliaferro, Charles, 40–41, 43
Taves, Ann, 189n10
teleology, 25, 29, 30, 50, 53, 58, 60–63, 66n23, 96, 99, 100, 108, 111n3. *See also* ateleology
television, 2, 186, 197–198, 200
Tertullian, 16
testimony, 19, 30, 64, 118–119, 125, 129, 163–164, 166, 169–170
thermodynamics, 78
Thompson, Evan, 119, 121–122, 124, 128, 129n2
time, 79, 82
Toronto Blessing, 185–187
Torrance, Thomas F., 86
trance, 165, 186, 189n10
transcendence, 4, 58, 82, 121. *See also* self-transcendence
Trinity, 20, 28, 42, 63, 80–81, 83, 85
Turner, Victor, 155, 157–158, 161–163, 167, 169
Tylor, Edward Burnett, 157, 166

uniformitarianism, 54, 94, 98, 111
Unitarianism, 83

United Pentecostal Church, 107
universe, 5, 40–41, 56, 75–91

values, 100, 117, 129, 183
Van Til, Howard, 95, 108
Vondey, Wolfgang, 8, 56

Wallace, Alfred Russell, 99
Waltke, Bruce K., 8n8, 104, 112n12
Welker, Michael, 4, 26
Wells, Jonathan, 97
Whitcomb, John, 94, 103
Whitehead, Alfred North, 55, 63
Wilson, E. O., 4, 24–25, 30n2
wisdom, 15, 21–24, 27–28, 35, 86, 158, 188
worship, 25, 51, 64, 104, 119, 124, 155–156, 163–168, 175, 179, 193, 196–198
Worthington, E. L., Jr., 147
Wright, N. T., 19

Yong, Amos, 27, 46, 82, 85, 101, 108, 136

Zuni, 158, 166